What people are saying about

For many of us, our heroes are untouchable, their accomplishments unattainable for us mere mortals. In *Anything But Ordinary*, we meet a humble hero who not only inspires us but allows us to hope, "Maybe I could too!" Jesse Morales embodied hope for the rest of us.

—Connie Cavanaugh
speaker and author of *Following God One Yes at a Time*

I devoured this incredible true story in one sitting. It kept leading me to pray, "God, help me live my faith in such a way that my nine-month-old daughter will grow up to be inspired the way Stephanie was by her father." Jesse's story will draw tears from even the driest eyes and will compel you to follow Jesus with a renewed passion.

—Mike Blackaby
pastor of Canvas Church and author of *Experiencing God, Teen Edition*

I opened the book at about nine at night and I couldn't put it down. I was deeply touched by this story and the beautiful way Stephanie honoured her parents and her dad's legacy. This book will have a powerful impact on many people!

I met Jesse when he came to work with Outreach Canada. He was no ordinary guy and certainly didn't live an ordinary life. Instead his life was consumed by his love for Jesus and his desire to share Jesus with everyone he encountered.

Outreach Canada remembers Jesse every year by awarding one of our staff the Jesse Morales Award. We present it in recognition of someone who has made a significant difference in the Kingdom of God. The award carries Jesse's picture and this powerful message: "If you were to live with the perspective that today could be your last day on earth, what would you do to make a difference in the King of God?" This is how Jesse lived an extraordinary life!

—Dr. Craig C. Kraft
Executive Director, Outreach Canada

Does God really transform lives? Families? Friendships? Absolutely! The past several years I've had the privilege of cheering from life's bleachers as "Jesse's girls" carry on his enduring legacy of living and sharing the gospel—the good news of Jesus. This gripping story will undoubtedly encourage, challenge, and inspire you as it has me. May it motivate us to entrust our very ordinary lives into the hands of an extraordinary God!

—Dr. Susan Booth
professor of Evangelism and Missions at
the Canadian Baptist Theological Seminary & College,
and author of *Longing for Home*

I picked up Stephanie's book and couldn't put it down. It's raw and real. The telling of her dad's story is a beautiful reminder that when God gets hold of someone, He can turn what might seem like an ordinary life into something extraordinary for His kingdom. Jesse was that man—an ordinary man with an extraordinary life of love and service to others. Stephanie's writing will remind you that God loves faith and can use anyone willing to trust Him. This life is not pain-free, and from Jesse we learn that even in our struggles we can experience joy. This is a life worth learning from. Thank you, Stephanie, for this heartfelt memoir of your dad.

—Lorie Hartshorn
co-host of *700 Club Canada*, Bible teacher, and author

Although I never had the privilege of meeting pastor Jesse Morales, I have spent nearly a decade witnessing the godly legacy he left for his family and our city. This wonderfully honest telling of his story has given me fresh encouragement as a fellow pastor to pursue on earth only those things that will matter in eternity!

—Dan Sweaza
pastor of Connect Church and church-planting coach

For those who have never heard or don't believe their "ordinary" lives can be used for a greater purpose, this heartfelt true story will inspire people in all stages and from all walks of life to see themselves in a new light. They will see that their lives don't need to be perfect in order to have an impact. They too can be anything but ordinary!

—Jennie Thompson
Executive Assistant, RockyView School Division

I've known the Morales family for many years and hold them in high esteem. Stephanie's father Jesse was one of the most effective and winsome evangelists I have ever met. In *Anything But Ordinary*, Beaulieu shares far more than an insider's look into the Morales household; she transparently and thoughtfully writes of her father's "inspiring faith cultivated in the soil of impossible struggle." Once you read this book, the only reasonable response is to praise our Lord Jesus Christ for his faithfulness, provision, and emboldening power to do all that He asks of us. I highly recommend.

—Jeff Christopherson
author of *Once You See, Kingdom First* and *Kingdom Matrix*
National Ministry Leader, Canadian National Baptist Convention
Executive Director, Church Planting Canada
Co-founder and Missiologist, Church Multiplication Institute

The Scriptures tell us that you recognize a tree by its fruit and a disciple of Jesus by the love that is displayed in their lives. The life and legacy of Jesse Morales was all about bearing fruit and sharing the love of Jesus to all who had the privilege of meeting him or had the opportunity to be influenced during a season of their lives.

In 1995, I had the joy of meeting Jesse and his beautiful family for the first time. I had no idea how God would use his friendship and his life to challenge my thinking and sharpen my heart for God and for the people in and around my life. Being with Jesse was far from ordinary,;it was always an adventure of being in God's presence and witnessing His power in a fresh way.

Jesse's daughter Stephanie does an incredible job of bringing us into a relationship with her dad, helping us all to see how ministry is full of highs and lows, and how every season of our lives is an opportunity for God to use us and how our lives can be lived far from ordinary by being who God created us to be. If you are looking for an opportunity to see and experience God move in a fresh and exciting way, begin reading this book today.

—Brian Harrell
Middle Tennessee Multi-Area Director
Fellowship of Christian Athletes

This remarkable true story forces you to ask two questions. What would my children think of me when I pass? Am I leaving a legacy that will lead my children to faith or fear? Being a father of two young girls, I find myself relating to Jesse and being inspired and challenged to be the man, father, husband, and spiritual leader God has created me to be. Pick this book up now and find out for yourself how all it takes is a little bit of faith to do the extraordinary.

—John Hasegawa
husband, father, and teacher

# anything but
# ORDINARY

# *anything but* ORDINARY

## Finding Faith That Works When Life Doesn't

### STEPHANIE MORALES-BEAULIEU

# ANYTHING BUT ORDINARY
Copyright © 2023 by Stephanie Morales-Beaulieu

Printed in Canada

Print ISBN: 978-1-4866-2321-1
eBook ISBN: 978-1-4866-2322-8

Word Alive Press
119 De Baets Street, Winnipeg, MB R2J 3R9
www.wordalivepress.ca

Cataloguing in Publication may be obtained through Library and Archives Canada

# CONTENTS

## PART I: THE START OF SOMETHING NEW

## PART II: THE JOURNEY

# PART III: THE SLIPPERY SLOPE

# PART IV: THREE LIFE-CHANGING LETTERS

# FOREWORD

One of my favourite passages of Scripture is Hebrews 11. It is the Bible's Hall of Fame and includes stories of some of the Bible's greatest, such as Abraham, Sarah, Moses, and David. Every time I read it, I am inspired that the same God who guided and empowered them is the God who now guides me.

God's work has certainly been advanced by spiritual giants like Abraham, Moses, and David. Many of our favourite Bible stories involve these spiritual heroes who enjoyed great triumphs over opposition and adversity. The majority of the chapter highlights the heroes of the faith.

But there is one verse that always makes me pause. I've often pondered the opening words of Hebrews 11:36: *"Still others..."* (NKJV) These other men and women go unnamed. Their identities are lost to us in history, but we are confident that God knows and cherishes every single one of them. They, too, served God faithfully, but they never conducted their lives on a large stage before a vast audience. No one felt inspired to record their deeds or acts of faith. Moreover, these saints didn't always experience the same levels of success as Moses or David. Some endured great suffering and death.

Nonetheless, they were faithful.

In many ways, we identify much more closely with this group than with the former. Most of us would readily identify with the ordinary people who have faced adversity over the years. Yet it's largely because of these that God's kingdom has advanced so dramatically. Jesus chose twelve disciples to be with Him. But the Gospels are clear that there were many others, including the seventy who were sent, women such as Mary Magdalene, as well as friends like Mary, Martha, and Lazarus. It is clear that God's kingdom includes, and prizes, people of all kinds, whether or not their names ever become widely known.

When I think of Jesse Morales, I am reminded of Hebrews 11:36. You have perhaps never heard of him, but I had the privilege of walking with him for several years. I first met him when I began serving as the interim pastor at Towers Baptist Church in Richmond, British Columbia. I was the Director of Missions for the Capilano Baptist Association and was asked to be the interim pastor while they searched for their next minister. Jesse and his wife Kathy were relatively new believers at that time.

I was immediately struck by several things about Jesse. One was his humility. He was an auto mechanic by trade. He wasn't the type of person who sought the limelight or was comfortable behind a microphone. Nonetheless, he was a person of great influence.

I soon noticed that Jesse and Kathy naturally ministered to others. Jesse used his workplace as a platform to boldly yet unoffensively share his faith. He and Kathy were gifted at leading people to Christ. They loved God with all their hearts and wanted everyone to know their Jesus. Jesse and Kathy constantly ministered to neighbours and colleagues.

I also noticed his faithfulness. You could count on him, and so he and Kathy quickly became key members of the church.

Jesse's joy and sense of humour also stood out. People were drawn to him. His smile was contagious.

I was so impressed with what God was doing in Jesse's life that I offered to meet with him regularly to disciple him. He readily agreed. Those were special times as we studied God's word together and I had the privilege of investing in the life of one of God's finest servants.

I have spent my lifetime watching to see where God is working. I didn't have to watch Jesse for long before I recognized that God had a unique purpose for him. He was someone who embodied the truth that if you are faithful in a little, God will give you more. I wasn't surprised when several years later Jesse sensed

God leading him to move to Cochrane, Alberta to attend the Canadian Baptist Theological Seminary and College. Jesse didn't see himself as a great scholar; he simply sought to be faithful. He worked hard at his studies.

He and Kathy began to minister in their new jobs and neighbourhood. They continued to bring people to Christ. Ultimately, they started a church and Jesse served as a pastor for many years. It was obvious that God was at work everywhere they went.

Jesse's life was cut tragically short. We certainly wondered why God would allow such a choice servant to die of such a terrible disease. We assume there was much more God could have done through His faithful servant. But as Hebrews tells us, God has unique callings for each of us. Some will minister on large public platforms for many years. Others will serve in relative obscurity for a briefer time and then quietly depart to their reward.

No matter what our assignment, it is our undeserved honour to serve God in any capacity. Oh, that each of us would serve the Lord in the time allotted to us as faithfully as did Jesse Morales! Jesse did not have long to serve God, but he used his time well.

Jesse left a spiritual legacy behind him. Perhaps his greatest tribute is his family. His wife and children loved him and deeply respected him. His four children grew up to serve the Lord as their parents had modelled before them.

I am so pleased to see Jesse's daughter Stephanie writing this book. I know he would have been so proud of how each of his children and grandchildren are following his Jesus.

I am rarely able to write forewords these days. However, I wanted to compose one for this book. God has blessed me in so many ways. One of the richest blessings I have experienced has been the wonderful saints I have been privileged to meet over the course of my life. I have met great preachers, famous authors, government and military leaders, and sports legends, but truly it has been people like Jesse Morales who have blessed me most. They serve out of the spotlight. They joyfully minister in obscure settings. They faithfully witness to those who would never step foot inside a church. They consistently model for their children what joyfully serving the Lord looks like.

And when they depart this earth, they leave it a far better place for having steadfastly fulfilled their divine calling.

My prayer is that as you read these pages you will be inspired to live your life to the full, just as Jesse did. I pray you will learn how to see where God is at work around you and join him.

May you be encouraged to live your life in such a manner that your family and friends are inspired to follow Jesus in the same way you do. What this world desperately needs is legions of people like Jesse, who will go out in the world and be salt and light the way Jesus commanded us to be.

Read this book carefully and prayerfully. Great truth and inspiration can be found in its pages. I hope that as you walk alongside the life of Jesse Morales in print, you will be motivated to live your life wholly devoted to God. It was truly my honour to call Jesse Morales my friend. I am confident that you, too, will be encouraged by his life.

—Henry Blackaby

Founder, Blackaby Ministries International (www.blackaby.org)

Author, *Experiencing God*

*August 24, 2009*

# INTRODUCTION

*Remember, dear brothers and sisters, that few of you were wise in the world's
eyes or powerful or wealthy when God called you. Instead, God chose things the
world considers foolish in order to shame those who think they are wise. And he
chose things that are powerless to shame those who are powerful. God chose things
despised by the world, things counted as nothing at all, and used them to bring to
nothing what the world considers important.*

—1 Corinthians 1:26–28, NLT

Time passed in slow motion as we made our way down the aisle in the funeral
processional with our extended family. As I glanced around the room through
tear-filled eyes, I saw that the huge auditorium was filled to the brim on that
August Monday in 2009.

For the next two hours, we celebrated the life of my dad, Jesse Morales.
Almost exactly one week earlier, he had gone home to be with his Lord Jesus
Christ after a fifteen-month battle with ALS.

He was eulogized by his youngest of four daughters, brother, sister, sister-
in-law, and friend. Another friend brought a message from a passage of the Bible
my dad had chosen before his passing. Tears flowed as we watched a slideshow of
his sixty-one years roll across the screen to a soundtrack perfectly matched to his
vibrant life.

Another of my dad's friends shared about how to have a relationship with
God and another friend performed one of his songs, *Rich Man*, which had grown
to be one of my dad's favourites.

If anyone had been able to hold their tears until that point, the lyrics of the
next song, *I Want to Be*, written by my older sister, opened the floodgates. There

wasn't a dry eye in the room as pictures of my dad and his four daughters danced across the screen and tugged at our hearts.

Most people, myself included, left feeling inspired to live the kind of life the two-hour celebration evidenced. But would we? Would we only feel moved? Or would we actually be changed?

Over the years, I've observed something that I've since concluded is a bit problematic: the longer my dad has been gone, the more perfect his memory becomes.

Why is this a problem, you may ask?

Perfection leaves us impressed, but not inspired. We intuitively understand that no human is perfect, but that doesn't stop us from forgetting that our heroes are, in fact, human.

You could easily learn about the things my dad was known for through stories. He always thought he was so hilarious, often slapping his knee wildly while throwing his head back in easy laughter when he told a joke, even if only he thought it was funny. He was never the slightest bit bothered that he was the only one laughing, which made it even funnier. He had this sly smile that rendered him innocent even if guilty. His easygoing nature made it impossible for him to rub anyone the wrong way.

My dad loved people, especially his family, along with basketball, the Bible, and old muscle cars. He was particular about getting dishes perfectly clean and always inspected the dishes back when he first taught us to wash by hand; he mercilessly sent the dishes back to the start of the assembly line if they weren't clean enough. He also loved babies and had a gentle and fun way with children. He could diagnose an engine simply by listening to it and never encountered a vehicle problem his masterful mechanic hands couldn't fix.

My dad spoke with a strong Filipino accent despite having learned to speak English from a young age while living in the Philippines. It never occurred to me that my dad spoke with an accent, though—not until my teen years when my friends told me they had trouble understanding him.

He also had this effortless and inoffensive way of talking about Jesus with absolutely anyone who would listen. It seemed to happen most commonly at the coffee shop, which was often jokingly referred to as his office.

These stories of my dad that make their way into everyday conversation are highlights. They're stories of people coming to know Jesus Christ, not my dad experiencing pain. They're stories of provision, not desperate prayer. They're stories of happy endings, not messy middles. They're stories of God's perfect timing, not the weariness felt by being worn down from waiting. They're stories of how he courageously battled ALS until his last breath, not of the heart-wrenching moments when he just wanted to die.

These stories are all true. No other story can disqualify them.

But that doesn't mean they tell the whole story. There are many stories that never find their way into everyday conversation.

The messier stuff didn't find its way into any eulogy. The middle of the stories, when life was heavy and difficult long before there were signs of things working out, was not on the slideshow. And the seemingly mundane—the day-to-day stuff of everyday life that required faithfulness with no applause—wasn't in the message that day when we celebrated his life.

We remember his laughter but rarely speak of his tears. We celebrate his strengths, easily forgetting his weaknesses. When we talk about his faithfulness, we forget the darkness of depression and all the discouraging days. We talk about his effectiveness but forget that he struggled with punctuality and priorities.

The difficulties of the trials are easily lost in the shadow of the triumphs.

When you only know or remember a person through their highlights, they automatically become heroes. Since most of us don't ascribe heroism to ourselves, we simply deem the heroics impressive, excusing ourselves from the party. There is too great a distance between the strength of our heroes and the struggle of us humans. We're off the hook for living the same kind of faithful life.

But if we recognize that inspiring faith is often cultivated in the soil of impossible struggle, our perspective shifts.

Perhaps we could acknowledge that our heroes are simply human, closing the gap between us and them. And since they're just like us, they don't belong on a pedestal. We belong together, both standing on the level ground at the foot of the cross, where all the ordinary folk have the opportunity to live lives of faith.

The perceived gap between humans and their heroes is not the space we think it is.

Truthfully, no earthly measure would have deemed my dad's life impressive. He wasn't overly educated, wealthy, well-known, or powerful. He didn't drive a new car, own nice things, have a fancy house, or travel the world. In almost all ways, my dad was ordinary, just like you and me, but his bold faith, steadfast love, and unwavering hope was anything but.

You will get to know my dad over the pages of this book, but my hope is that you will come to experience the faithfulness of God.

When life isn't working, I hope you will catch glimpses of the God who always is.

Every obstacle has a unique opportunity to live by faith. And I pray you'll be moved to follow Jesus more deeply into the story He has written for your life.

Your life doesn't need to be perfect in order to have an impact. My dad is proof of that. You simply need a little bit of faith, and then for that faith to grow some feet so it can work.

Come and see for yourself the birthplace of the bold faith, steadfast love, and unwavering hope that laid the foundations for my own when life wasn't working.

Ready?

*May 5, 2008*

# PROLOGUE

*The fundamental fact of existence is that this trust in God, this faith, is the firm foundation under everything that makes life worth living. It's our handle on what we can't see. The act of faith is what distinguished our ancestors, set them above the crowd.*

—Hebrews 11;1, MSG

*What should I make for dinner?* I thought to myself as I opened the fridge, then the freezer.

My uninspired culinary thoughts were interrupted by the phone ringing.

"Hello?"

"Stehh—ph. Is Mike home?"

It was my dad, Jesse. His strong, gentle voice was instantly recognizable and guaranteed to improve your day just by hearing it. And after thirty-plus years in Canada, his Filipino accent still gave him away.

My dad had walked me down the aisle the previous summer before officiating our wedding. His voice had cracked with emotion, causing him to swallow hard and take a deep breath before composing himself enough to continue. His emotion had taken me by surprise, causing a lump to form in my own throat during his long pause. If his emotions had found their way out, no doubt mine would've too, along with everyone else in the building.

That moment of hesitation had seemed like minutes, but he had quickly been able to shift gears from a father about to give away his daughter to a pastor preparing two individuals to become one. He even playfully scolded Mike and me during the sermon for being too busy smiling and giggling at each other to listen closely.

I kind of listened to that sermon. He used a lot of basketball analogies.

After returning from our honeymoon, we moved a few hours south of our families so I could attend university in a different city. Mike worked nearby, too.

In this new season, we didn't see my dad as often as we used to. The last time my dad had called, he had started the conversation like he always did: "Stehh-ph… it's your coach."

He always called himself my coach!

We then made small talk for a few minutes before I asked why he had called.

"I just want to see how you're doing," he had explained.

I'd smiled at the heart-warming gesture.

As a young child, I had spent lots of time in the garage with my dad as his little apprentice. I'd loved his orange hand cleaner and always found something in the garage to dirty my hands with, anything to warrant the use of the citrus and industrial-smelling scrub.

As a teen, I had gone through a phase of being mad at my dad for never having time for me. That was no longer the case.

Now, with no drive to school or basketball games at which to cheer me on, he simply called to connect. We were ushering in a new season in our relationship, one where he wasn't just my dad and I wasn't just his daughter. He wasn't just going to be my coach, but my friend.

I was looking forward to it. He worked part-time as a corporate chaplain and one of his companies was going to extend his hours to the office in the city where we now lived. This would allow him to spend a couple of nights with us each month when he was in town.

But this didn't sound like that kind of call.

"Is Mike home?" he inquired calmly.

"Yes, he's in the shower. Why?"

"Are you sitting down?"

Whatever this was, it didn't sound good. But how bad could it be? I took a seat at our kitchen table, feeling my heartrate quicken.

"I am now," I told him.

"I hab bad news," he continued, his voice still strong, calm, and even. "The doctor said I hab A–L–S." He emphasized each letter. "It's fatal. I hab three to five years to live."

My mind spun. I didn't know what ALS was, but I didn't need to for grief to swoop in. I knew what fatal meant—and I definitely knew how to count. Three to five years weren't nearly enough for my dad, coach, and friend. He was only sixty years old!

My dad might be gone less than five years from now?

I had no words after my dad told me the hourglass had been flipped on his life. Time was now slipping through my fingers at a much more rapid pace.

Mike came into the room to see what the commotion was all about. Tears came like a storm. Everything went blurry, like I was trying to see underwater.

I walked to the living room and dropped to my knees. With tears soaking the floor underneath me, I said to God, "Thank You."

The words surprised me, as though someone else had deposited them in me for this exact moment. Thank you? I had just received news of my dad's death sentence. Those words didn't feel appropriate.

Months before this phone call, my dad had been experiencing a loss of strength in one of his fingers. In our minds, it was simply a matter of time before the doctor diagnosed the problem and prescribed some medicine to make him healthy again.

We expected a fix, not a fatal illness.

Nothing had warned me of the news I received that day, but in hindsight I realized that something had prepared me for it—something that had happened back in 1986.

Or rather, it was someone my dad met.

In 1986, for the first time, he became willing to admit that his life wasn't working.

The faith that grew in him, the same faith that laid the foundation for my own, prepared me for the day when my world began to crumble. Because even in the face of death, there was the promise of life.

*Part One*

# THE START OF SOMETHING NEW

# 1

*February 4, 1986*

# ONE TUESDAY EVENING

*Now faith is the reality of what is hoped for, the proof[b] of what is not seen.*
—Hebrews 11:1, CSB

"By the way, I'm going to do it," Jesse said casually to his wife. His tone was the same he would've used to announce a decision to clean the car or mow the grass.

"Do what?" Kathy asked without looking up.

"I'm going to become a Christian."

Kathy slowly looked up in disbelief, trying to not let her jaw hang open. Had the words she'd never thought to hear just come out of her husband's mouth?

Jesse had made the statement so matter-of-factly that she wasn't sure she had heard correctly. She had to clarify.

"Like right now?" Kathy asked, trying to pick her jaw up off the floor.

"No, not now. And not with you. You'll cry and get too emotional." His voice was calm and without a trace of cruelty. "I almost became a Christian last Sunday. I put one foot forward during the invitation time at church, but then I hesitated and changed my mind. But I'm going to go and talk to your pastor tomorrow."

Kathy couldn't argue with facts. She *was* emotional, and Jesse was no stranger to this after five years of marriage.

Keeping her expression even, she got up and quietly walked to the bathroom, closing the door behind her. In the privacy of the bathroom, with complete abandon, she silently cheered and danced, overwhelmed with gratitude. God had been at work in Jesse's life, even when she had seen no evidence of it.

Taking a few deep breaths to regain her composure, Kathy then calmly exited the bathroom like it was any other night. She didn't want her enthusiasm to make him change his mind.

———◆———

The next morning, Kathy wrote the phone number for the pastor's office on the bottom of his brown paper lunch bag in the biggest, boldest numbers she could manage. She didn't want to chance him forgetting to follow through on this life-changing decision.

As Jesse headed for the door, she handed him his lunch and kissed him goodbye.

"Don't forget to become a Christian today!" she said with a smile.

She watched her husband leave for work, her heart exploding with gratitude and joy.

Only a year and a half earlier, Kathy's life had completely changed from the inside-out. Because of what happened on an August day in 1984, she was no longer the same person she once had been, and it was all because of her newfound faith in Jesus. Although she had grown up going to church, she had never trusted Jesus Christ alone for salvation.

And if today worked out the way it was supposed to, by the time Jesse walked back through that door after work, he too would be changed from the inside-out.

Today was the day.

# 2

*August 1984*

# ONE AUGUST DAY

*From the ends of the earth I call to you, I call as my heart grows faint; lead me to the rock that is higher than I.*

—Psalm 61:2

The twins had just gone down for a nap, giving Kathy the rare opportunity to pause and ponder.

Her life was exactly as she had hoped it would be. She had a good husband, healthy and happy baby girls, two cars, and a beautiful home.

So why did she feel so unhappy?

The weight of her past sat heavily on her shoulders. The emptiness she felt deep inside nagged at her.

Her eyes searched the room for answers and landed on the dusty Bible on her bookshelf. She never touched it. But today her mind drifted back to the summer of 1975, nine years earlier, the night she had reluctantly gone to a Christian rock concert with her cousin Diane.

Kathy had spent many summers at her uncle's farm sharing a room with Diane. They'd always gotten along just fine, but on this particular visit Diane had been acting strangely. She read the Bible every night before going to bed, sometimes even aloud.

During the day Kathy dodged her Christian friends, but at night, sharing the same room as Diane, there was no escaping it. Even the pillow Kathy put over her head couldn't drown out her cousin's voice.

Diane's idea of a good time was getting together with her friends for Bible study and playing guitar and singing songs about God and Jesus. At sixteen, Kathy preferred the party life. Diane and her friends were so weird.

But eventually Kathy found herself attracted to their weirdness. They had joy and peace. Kathy did not.

A few weeks later, Diane invited her to the concert.

"No thanks," Kathy had said. A rock concert, sure. Christian? Nope.

Diane didn't give up so easily. She persisted in inviting Kathy again and again, telling her that her Bible study group was praying for her.

Praying for her? The only prayer Kathy knew of was the rote grace said before dinner on special occasions—that, and the refrain said at bedtime: "Now I lay me down to sleep. I pray the Lord my soul to keep." It was new and strange for someone to be praying—for her specifically.

Kathy soon became intrigued by the concert poster Diane brought home. The band members had long hair like every other 70s rock band, and they were dressed in the same style as Kathy and her friends—jeans and Joe Cocker T-shirts. Kathy hadn't expected a Christian rock band to look so much like her friends!

Her interest piqued, she decided to go. What did she have to lose?

Right away, Kathy knew this rock concert was different. There was no smell of marijuana drifting through the line as they waited. Once inside, when people bumped into her they apologized rather than barking "Watch it." No one was puking their guts out in the bathroom from drinking too much.

Surprisingly, Kathy liked this new kind of rock concert experience. There was something different in the air that she couldn't quite put her finger on. The people mulling around seemed more like Diane and her friends. And there seemed to be more to the music. Kathy felt moved when the lead guitar player took a few minutes to share his story. It didn't take her long to realize that he had something she didn't.

Though she had been in church most Sundays as a girl, this was the very first time Kathy had heard about having a personal relationship with Jesus Christ. Wasn't everyone who lived in Canada a Christian? Kathy always thought going to church with her family made her a Christian.

But on this particular night, it seemed like being a Christian was about much more than memorized prayers and church attendance.

As the concert came to a close, an invitation was given for anyone who wanted to begin a personal relationship with Jesus Christ. Kathy wasn't sure. Was this offer for her? Her current strategy to get to heaven—do more good than bad and hope the scales tipped in her favour—seemed like a bad gamble.

Instead Kathy leapt out of her seat and walked towards the stage, eager to receive what was being offered. In a sea of teenagers, Kathy repeated the lead guitar player's prayer to repent of her sins and receive forgiveness through Jesus. In a single miraculous moment, the peace and joy Kathy had been so drawn to in Diane and her friends came to reside inside of her.

Kathy's family was about to move to the Philippines for her father's new job in fisheries with the United Nations Development Programme. Since the move was only two weeks away, Diane and her house church friends encouraged her to be baptized immediately to make her new faith public.

At the local pool, she was declared to be buried with Christ and dunked under the water. Then, declared to be raised to new life in Jesus, she was pulled up and out. Kathy didn't really understand what it all meant but she was excited nonetheless.

Diane and her friends sent Kathy off to the Philippines with a Bible, a devotion book, a pack of Jesus stickers, and instructions to find a church when she arrived.

Upon arriving in the Philippines, Kathy looked through the Yellow Pages and found the phone number and address of Union Church of Manila, started by Americans. She showed up to the Friday night youth group eager to learn more about her new faith with her brand-new Bible in hand.

The local high school hottie immediately caught her eye, and evidently she had caught his.

"Check out the new chick," he said. Kathy's ears perked up. "She has a Bible."

What did he mean? What was that in his tone? Was she a fool for having brought her Bible? Why didn't anyone else have one? Weren't you supposed to bring Bibles to church?

This didn't feel like the kind of attention Kathy wanted. She felt a twinge of panic, mixed with embarrassment as she looked around and noticed that she was the only one holding a Bible.

Flustered, she made a mental note to leave the Bible at home next time.

She went back to that youth group one more time Bible-free, and the next week she stayed home. It felt easier to watch Christians from a distance than try to figure out how to be one.

Kathy sighed as the memory of gaining her so-called faith nine years earlier faded away.

The rock concert, the Bible, and her first attempts at church felt like missed opportunities. Her chance with God seemed to have gone. The nagging question remained: why did she feel so unhappy? Yet as she stared at the Bible, she couldn't ignore the flicker of hope in her heart.

*Maybe this book has some answers,* she thought. *It's worth a shot.*

Surprisingly, the twins were still sleeping and Jesse wouldn't be home for a few more hours. Kathy had nothing to lose.

Having tried everything else, Kathy pulled the Bible from the bookshelf and dusted it off. She flipped it open to the middle, not having any clue where to start looking for answers to her emptiness.

Her eyes fell on Psalm 61:1–2: *"Hear my cry, O God; listen to my prayer. From the ends of the earth I call to you, I call as my heart grows faint; lead me to the rock that is higher than I."*

She slammed the Bible shut, her heart racing, and tossed it on the floor like a hot potato. That was spooky! How did this book know so much about her?

The spooky book was no longer in her hands, but the words she had just read still echoed in her mind. Was it possible God had heard the silent cry of her heart? Kathy felt about as far away from God as the ends of the earth. And her heart felt faint. And she had definitely not been living her life on any kind of rock.

She could usually maintain a bit of distance from the guilt and shame that had accumulated steadily over her twenty-six years. But not at this moment. At this moment, it poured over her mind and heart like a flash flood. She felt the tears surface but had no strength to fight as her body surrendered to uncontrollable sobs.

"Look at my life," she cried to herself, unsure if anyone was listening. "Look what I've done."

The string of poor choices she had made in the Philippines replayed in her mind in slow motion. She would've given anything to go back and rewrite the story that had been written for her at the age of seventeen. If people only knew the truth about her disastrous past, they would withdraw their love. Her fear of being found out served as constant background noise.

She would've never struck up a conversation with that handsome Italian soccer coach at the pool by their apartment complex when her family first arrived in the Philippines. She would've listened to her father's warnings to steer clear of the man rather than feel flattered by the tantalizing attention he gave her. She would have never taken him up on his invitation to look at pictures in his house.

She was convinced that what had happened that day, despite her protests, was somehow her fault. The handsome Italian soccer coach had raped her, leaving her to feel dirty and ashamed.

She shuddered at the memory she wished she could erase. Ever since that day, heavy guilt and shame had been her constant companions. She felt powerless to rid herself of them.

But sitting in her living room nine years later, she no longer felt alone. Hope flickered in her heart again as another memory flashed into her mind, almost as if someone was wanting her to remember something important.

What had her cousin Diane told her all those years ago? That God loved her unconditionally? Was it still possible in light of all that she had done and all that had been done to her? She felt so unworthy.

Unconditional love sounded good. Maybe too good to be true? It was so different from what she had concluded in her childhood, that she could merely do more good than bad and hope that the scales tipped in her favour.

But who was she kidding? If she had to earn this unconditional love by doing enough good, she knew she could never tip the scales. She was sure of it.

She hoped it was true that God still loved her. The alternative—being better and doing more—was exhausting.

Especially considering the fact that her rap sheet didn't end there. Her string of poor choices hadn't ended in the Philippines. After the Italian soccer coach had sworn her to secrecy, Kathy's high school graduation hadn't been able to come fast enough.

Afterward she put the Philippines behind her and headed back to Canada for a fresh start. By the time she'd begun her first year studies at the University of British Columbia she had decided that her life would be easier if she did her own thing and left God out of it. But no matter how hard she ran from God, she couldn't seem to get away.

At UBC, He caught up with her in the halls of the sixth floor.

Kathy had seen ads on the dorm bulletin board inviting students to a Bible study and praise time. She didn't dare go. She'd once heard one of the guys in the dorms say, "Don't bother inviting the girls on the sixth floor. They're all

Christians." Kathy's partying ways were surely incompatible with what she imagined the sixth floor girls were like. She wasn't like them. She didn't belong there.

Yet she found herself drawn to the sixth floor.

She rode up the elevator and quietly followed the sound of singing until she found herself standing outside the dorm door of those Bible study girls. Though she didn't know the words or melodies, the sound moved her to quiet tears.

Unsure of what to make of her feelings, she quickly dried her tears and returned to her room. She didn't belong on the sixth floor.

On weekends, she headed to the beer gardens to drown her feelings. But even there she couldn't hide. The campus missionary, who only had a handful of conversations with her, spotted her drunk and staggering one night. Why had he had to be there, on that day of all the days? She couldn't avoid him or his pointed questions.

"Kathy, what are you doing with your life?" he asked her bluntly, yet without judgment and somehow full of compassion.

Clearly she wasn't doing anything with her life; she was hiding from it.

Instead of answering, she laughed it off, careful not to make eye contact. She couldn't risk him looking into the window of her soul and seeing the truth: she was unworthy of love.

Life continued on its downward trajectory for the entirety of her freshman year—more drinking, more drugs, and more parties. Her parents were still living overseas, far away from her failures. What they didn't know couldn't hurt them, right?

Her major in partying proved to be incompatible with actual studying. Her parents didn't need to know she dropped out of university a few months into her second year. At best, they would be furious. Post-secondary education was among their top priorities—so much so that her mother, a schoolteacher, had only agreed to marry her father, a fisherman, if he went back to finish high school.

Though Kathy had successfully hidden all her other failures from them, her decision to drop out probably couldn't stay hidden forever.

For a month, she managed to keep this a secret from anyone who might get word back to her parents.

Kathy quickly discovered that you had to actually attend UBC to live in their dorms. She was now in the market for a new place to live, and she would need a job to pay for it. She found a job selling magazine subscriptions that provided shared hotel rooms for employees on the road.

At first, dropping out of school felt like freedom. Her new travelling job was adventurous, and she enjoyed not telling anyone about it.

But then, like everything else, it too disappointed her.

Kathy had never felt as alone as she did a month later when she called her Auntie Margie, Diane's mom, from a payphone in Winnipeg and asked if she could come back to spend Christmas with their family. She rode the train, alone, from Winnipeg to Richmond.

It was Auntie Margie who then convinced her to quit the job and instead find work in B.C. And when all her friends returned to UBC for the winter semester in 1978, she could only think of one friend that wasn't.

Jesse.

———

She had first spotted Jesse with a group of his friends while eating at Denny's one year earlier. Because of her time in the Philippines, she'd found herself noticing Filipino people everywhere she went and was able to easily strike up a conversation once they knew she had lived there.

That night, she and Jesse had made small talk and gone their separate ways, but she had never been able to forget that smile.

As fate would have it, Kathy had run into him a couple of months later while wandering through a department store. Jesse invited her out to a club with his friends who had just returned from working in the navy. Eagerly, she had gone back to the dorm to collect her friends for a night on the town.

But none were as eager as she was.

"Are you kidding?" her friends had wondered. "We aren't going out with a bunch of strange men to a club."

She managed to convince two reluctant people to go with her, so at least she wouldn't be going alone. She'd put herself in far too many dangerous situations in the past.

She spent that night evading Jesse's friends' passes at her. Apparently those who had been at sea for six months were only interested in one thing, but she was only interested in getting to know one guy.

Jesse just sat at his table—quiet, cool, and confidently sipping his rum and coke. His contagious laughter kept finding its way to her ears.

As it turned out, Jesse had a girlfriend, but Kathy didn't give up easily. His girlfriend eventually broke up with him, and with Kathy's wide open schedule, which no longer included university, they began spending more time together in the fall of 1978.

This new love gave Kathy hope and temporary relief from the emptiness deep inside her.

But the happiness soon faded and hope was drowned out by the darkness of a certain fateful day in 1979. Of all the poor choices Kathy had made in her life, this was the one she wished with everything in her that she could take back… the one she was certain she would pay for every day for the rest of her life.

While on a road trip with friends, Kathy suddenly realized that the thought of eating her favourite foods made her want to vomit.

"I bet you're pregnant," said her friend and coworker from the music store where she'd found work.

Kathy panicked at the possibility. What would her parents say? They had been so disappointed that she'd dropped out of school.

Fear shouted that she had a problem that needed fixing. The mistake, she told herself, needed to be covered up rather than faced.

Kathy's coworker offered to help her find someone who could "take care of it." Impulsiveness drowned out the voice of reason—not to mention Jesse's offer to marry her, his promise that everything would be okay, and his assurance that they were in it together.

What her coworker didn't know was the high price she would pay. By the time she rose out of the fog and came to her senses, realizing what she had done, it was too late.

She had an abortion and her baby was gone. The problem remained. Guilt, shame, and the deepest regret she had ever known weighed heavily on her.

Kathy already loved to party, but afterward she took it to a whole new level. Jesse often raised an eyebrow, asking her if it was a little early in the day to be drinking, but Kathy didn't care. It helped numb the pain.

———

A year later, in the spring of 1980, Jesse proposed—sort of. He was never a man of many words or one for romantic gestures.

"So I guess we should tell your parents?" he said with a nervous laugh and sly smile. He tossed an engagement ring towards her as they sat in the car, of all places.

It wasn't exactly the proposal of her dreams, but perhaps getting married would be the fresh start she longed for. Maybe her unbearably heavy companions—guilt and shame—would finally leave.

October 25, 1980 marked the start of their lives together as husband and wife, but it didn't take long to figure out that it wasn't the solution to her problems. Marriage couldn't fix what was broken inside her.

If anything, it made life harder.

In addition to the usual challenges involved in merging two lives, they were merging two cultures, Filipino and Canadian. Everything was a conflict—what to eat, how to spend money, and how to enjoy themselves socially, just to name a few. Jesse wanted to eat rice every night while she was more of a potato girl. When she cooked spaghetti for dinner, he insisted that spaghetti was a snack, not dinner. How was she supposed to know? There was no book on all the unwritten and unspoken rules of his culture. It was like walking around in the dark; she only discovered the rules when she bumped into them.

Kathy, along with most of their friends, wasn't sure their marriage would make it through the first year.

Beyond the clash of cultures, they also had some big conflicts. Their passionate and quick-tempered natures triggered each other, often at the same time.

One night, with nowhere else to go in their tiny apartment, Jesse walked out in the middle of a fight.

*I'll show him,* Kathy thought, furious that he had left without saying a word. *I'll be gone when he gets back.*

She packed her overnight bag and took the elevator down to their apartment parkade.

But that was as far as she got.

When she turned the key in the car's ignition to make her getaway, nothing happened. The car wouldn't start.

As if this night could get any worse.

When she went to try again, she heard something move in the backseat. Before she could even scream, Jesse's face appeared in the rearview mirror.

"Ahhhh!" he shouted, triumphantly raising his hand. "I knew you would try to leave, so I took out the spark plugs!"

Kathy was furious—but only for a moment. Their crazy antics soon had them both laughing. Hurt and anger could make even the most rational people do crazy things, and they were no exception.

They soon moved out of their tiny Vancouver apartment into a bigger house on Williams Road in Richmond. But more space didn't seem to solve their problems, either.

Jesse's garage provided him space to blow off steam but didn't offer a solution to it. If he wanted to leave, at least he had somewhere to go that wasn't far. He would throw things around in there.

Marriage didn't solve their problems. Maybe a baby would make things better?

Kathy was thrilled when she found out about the new life growing inside her. Perhaps she could make up for the life that had been lost.

But that hope too was soon destroyed. She miscarried. The baby was gone and Kathy was certain it was all her fault. God was surely punishing her. She didn't fight it; she deserved it.

———————

As the traffic light turned from yellow to red, Kathy glanced out the car window and noticed how beautiful the sky looked. Spring had brought signs of new life everywhere she looked. She was pregnant again but filled with fear of another miscarriage.

For the first time in many years, her thoughts wandered to God. She had been running from him ever since she messed up her chance.

A quiet, gentle, and strong voice interrupted her thoughts: "Kathy, I love you. Twins!"

She looked around confused. Was that God? There was no way He could still love her after all she had done. She was certain of that.

She carried on to the ultrasound and an hour later the doctor announced, "Twins! Did you have any idea?"

Kathy shook her head but then remembered the voice at the red light. She supposed she had known but wasn't about to give the doctor any reason to think she was crazy.

She wasn't going to have one baby, but two. Two babies gone—an abortion and a miscarriage—and two babies on the way.

It sure felt like hope to Kathy.

Angela and Christina, her very own Christmas angels, were born on Jesse's birthday: December 25, 1982. Jesse was so happy and proud, grinning ear to ear when she passed him his soft, cuddly birthday present in one arm and his Christmas present in the other.

---

Now, almost two years later, with the Bible on the floor, Kathy was resigned to the fact that she had no solution to the baggage she carried.

"I'll give the spooky book one more try," she reasoned as she wiped her tears.

She flipped again to the middle, this time landing on a different page:

*Create in me a pure heart, O God, and renew a steadfast spirit within me. Do not cast me from your presence or take your Holy Spirit from me. Restore to me the joy of your salvation and grant me a willing spirit, to sustain me.*
                                                            —Psalm 51:10–12

Was a pure heart even possible after all she had done? Would God restore her joy? It once again sounded too good to be true, but before she could talk herself out of it the floodgates reopened, but this time with tears of joy. These felt like healing tears, like the kind that had overtaken her at that rock concert and in the sixth floor hallway of the UBC dorm.

This time, she didn't fight them. She welcomed them.

It felt as if God was washing away the guilt, shame, and regret that had stained her heart, just like the verse said. Joy overwhelmed her and peace seemed to fill the deep void within her.

Kathy couldn't explain it but knew she was different on the inside. She was forgiven—for *everything*.

She had to tell someone.

---

Jesse was barely through the back door after arriving home from work that evening when Kathy ran up to him. She had been waiting hours to tell him all that had happened to her. The excitement of her newfound forgiveness was bursting out of her like water released from a dam.

"God is real!" she practically shouted. "I got *zapped* today!"

Jesse stared at her, clearly confused as he tried to figure out what was happening. "Are you okay?" he asked slowly, concern on his face.

Kathy laughed. He wasn't getting it. She barely understood what had happened herself.

"I'm better than okay! I'm *so* okay! I'm the best I've ever been!"

He paused, the concern on his face turning to alarm. He chose his next words carefully. "Did you take anything?"

"No, of course not," she replied, his words unable to dampen her ecstasy. "It's Jesus!"

Jesse's face relaxed but remained sceptical. Kathy could tell that he didn't understand or share her enthusiasm. She herself could barely put it into words.

But nothing could dampen her excitement. She was forgiven. She had never felt so free.

# 3

*Fall 1984*

# THAT'S WHAT IT'S CALLED

*Jesus replied, "I tell you the truth, unless you are born again, you cannot see the Kingdom of God."*

—John 3:3, NLT

Kathy hadn't been able to put down her Bible since that August day. She filled up their tiny wading pool and let the twins play with the two front legs of her lawnchair in the water so she wouldn't forget to supervise. They would splash. She would read.

She couldn't get enough of this spooky book that seemed to know so much about her. She couldn't explain why, but she was getting more comfortable with things she couldn't explain.

Looking back, Kathy was able to recognize all the flickers of hope throughout her life; they had been God's pursuit of her despite her years of running. She smiled. Her heart had always craved His love. She still didn't know why He would come after her, but she was grateful.

Now that she'd been zapped, it seemed logical for Kathy to go to church.

She returned to the church of her upbringing the very next Sunday, but it didn't seem like whatever had zapped her was there. She told people about the experience she'd had with God in her living room and they didn't understand; they only looked at her strangely.

Week after week, she found fewer similarities between what she read in the Bible and what she experienced at this particular church.

Months later, she made an appointment with the pastor to find some much-needed clarity. She was new at this Bible-reading thing and had just finished the New Testament. But in her reading, she hadn't come across the ordinance she had witnessed the previous Sunday. Had she missed it? The pastor had been at this longer than her. Surely he could explain the discrepancy.

He smiled kindly and then told her, much to her surprise, that he understood if she wanted to go to another church.

But where would she go? She could still barely explain what had happened to her that day in the living room. No one she knew seemed to be able to help her understand.

While wandering through downtown Richmond one fall day, uncertain of what to do next or where to go, her eyes landed on a poster. Hanging in the window of a Christian bookstore was an advertisement for prayer groups that would be meeting in preparation for an upcoming crusade. The ad included a picture of that preacher, Billy Graham, she had seen on TV.

*He's always holding a Bible,* she thought. *Maybe he's had the same experience I did. Whatever kind of Christian I am, maybe he is too.*

She jotted down the phone number listed on the bottom of the poster. It was settled. She would call this prayer group. They were connected to the TV preacher with the Bible who was coming to Vancouver in October. Maybe these people would know what had happened to her.

Kathy called the number, talked to the woman hosting the group, and committed to attend.

When she told the group her story at the first meeting, an older woman chimed in right away: "Dear, you've been born again!"

The zapping finally had a name. Kathy had been spiritually born again.

Eager to stick closely with these women who understood her, Kathy volunteered her services and was given the task of calling every woman on their list before each meeting.

She connected especially with a woman named Jaylyne, who always ended their conversations by saying "See you at the next meeting." But then something would inevitably come up.

Despite never meeting Jaylyne face to face, there was something about her that Kathy was drawn to.

As the October crusade neared, Kathy headed to Willingdon Mennonite Church in Burnaby along with women from all over the greater Vancouver area. They were going to pray for the crusade and celebrate the work God had been doing.

On their last phone conversation, Kathy asked Jaylyne if she planned to attend the rally. Also, Kathy wanted to know what she looked like.

"I'm 5'1" with brown hair."

"Okay," Kathy said, up for the challenge. "I'll find you."

"There will be thousands of women there…"

"I'll find you."

God had done far more impossible things in her short time of knowing Him.

On the day of the rally, Kathy entered the church along with the busloads of other women. She sat down just in time to overhear a woman in front of her exclaim, "I can't believe Towers has an entire row!"

Kathy tapped her on the shoulder. "Excuse me? Did you say Towers, as in Towers Baptist Church?"

The woman nodded.

"Do you know Jaylyne Hogue?" Kathy inquired.

The woman next to her, with short brown hair, turned around slowly, the realization dawning on her like a slow sunrise. "I'm Jaylyne."

"I'm Kathy!" she exclaimed. "Told you I'd find you!"

Amazement washed over Jaylene's face and a coffee date was put on the calendar.

Kathy had made her first born again friend.

# 4

*October 1984*

# THE NOT-QUITE CRUSADE

*In their case, the god of this age has blinded the minds of the unbelievers to keep them
from seeing the light of the gospel of the glory of Christ, who is the image of God.*
—2 Corinthians 4:4, CSB

K athy's excitement about her newfound faith had grown every day for the
past two months. Naturally, she wanted Jesse to experience the same forgiveness and freedom she had.

He had his share of pain from the past that burdened him. Why wouldn't
he want to be made new, especially after all he'd been through? Though he was
a good guy by everyone's standards, and had been loosely religious in his grow-
ing-up years, he didn't know Jesus personally.

But Jesse wasn't interested and showed no signs of changing his mind. In
fact, he had only ever inquired once about her newfound faith.

"I just have one question," Jesse said. "How long is this Jesus thing going
to last?"

It was a fair question. He had, after all, married the party girl. All Kathy's
other highs had been temporary.

"I have no idea," Kathy answered. "But every morning when I wake up, He
is still here!"

Despite Jesse's lack of enthusiasm, Kathy convinced him to attend one night
of the eight-night crusade in October 1984.

She carefully chose the night when a football player would be giving his testimony. Jesse's love for football was only second to basketball. She was certain that if he could just hear about Jesus from a fellow sports guy, he would be made new like she had been.

They found their seats in the newly built BC Place and she waited in anticipation. After a powerful message, Billy Graham began the invitation. Kathy moved to the edge of her seat. This would for sure be Jesse's moment of crossing the starting line into a new relationship with Jesus, and the peace and joy with God that she now knew.

"I believe the time for everyone to be born and die is in God's hands," Billy began in his strong yet gentle southern accent. "If it's my time to die, I'm prah-par-ed." His accent made it sound like three syllables. "I don't know what the future holds... but I know Who holds the future."

Kathy quickly surveyed the stadium. People were already weeping. She was careful not to steal a glance at Jesse, which might distract him.

Billy went on. "I was asked by a person today, 'Are you absolutely sure that you're going to heaven?' I said, 'I'm absolutely sure. But not because of anything I have done... I've sinned... I'm going to heaven because of what Christ did on that cross... and the fact that God raised him from the dead... What about you? Is there a doubt in your heart that if you died at this moment you'd go to heaven? Now is an accepted time! Today is the day of salvation! Come while you can!'"[1]

When the music started, people flooded the aisles. The words of the invitation song flooded the speakers:

Just as I am, without one plea,
but that Thy blood was shed for me.
And that Thou bid'st me come to Thee
O Lamb of God, I come! I come.[2]

This was it. Surely this would be Jesse's moment of finally having peace with God.

---

1  The words of this invitation are taken from one of Billy Graham's crusades. See: "Just as I Am—Michael Neale (Intro by Billy Graham)," *YouTube*. Date of access: July 13, 2022 (https://www.youtube.com/watch?v=82nP4HIT68A&ab_channel=heavenlysoundsful).

2  Charlotte Elliot, "Just as I Am, Without One Plea," 1838.

Kathy turned to ask if he wanted her to accompany him to the front to receive Jesus as his personal Lord and Saviour or if he preferred to walk the aisle alone.

In that eight-day crusade, 100,000 people made decisions to receive Jesus Christ.[3]

Jesse was not one of them. Not only did he not bound out of his seat, eager to join the flood of people filling the aisle, he was sound asleep. Head back. Arms crossed. Snoring. In the middle of the stadium.

Kathy was furious. How could he sleep at a time like this? There wasn't a more powerful preacher in the world than Billy Graham. Jesse could sleep through anything.

The next morning, the realization hit: *I can't save him.*

The reply from God was swift, quiet, and reassuring: *"You can't save him. But I can."*

The voice was becoming more familiar. Though discouragement still echoed in her heart, the promise was enough to give her hope and bolster her faith.

She could not save Jesse, but apparently God could. And if God could save her husband, Kathy would pray, trusting God to keep His promise.

---

3    Lloyd Mackey, "Remembering Billy Graham, and His Vancouver Crusade," *Church for Vancouver*. February 21, 2018 (https://churchforvancouver.ca/remembering-billy-graham-and-his-van-couver-crusade/).

# 5

*Winter 1985*

# LESS CHURCH

*I can do all this through him who gives me strength.*

—Philippians 4:13

O ver coffee with her new and only born again friend, Jaylyne, Kathy learned
that the woman's husband Ron was the pastor of Towers Baptist Church.
Ron both preached the sermon and led the worship every Sunday.

After learning that Kathy was a pianist, Ron invited her to be the accompa-
nying pianist at the Christmas service, giving him a break from double duty.

As it turned out, Towers was right down the street from their home. By
the spring, Kathy began attending regularly and jumped at every opportunity
to be more involved. For the Tuesday morning prayer group, Kathy was there.
Wednesday evening prayer meeting; she was there. Bible study; she was there.

Anytime anything was happening at the church, Kathy was there.

Church life was growing on her. She felt understood by her new spiritual
family, and they were all praying for Jesse.

But Kathy's new life wasn't growing on him. As she sat alone in church, she
felt the discouragement in her heart gaining ground. She desperately wanted what
all the other couples at church seemed to have: a shared faith in Jesus Christ.

Sure, Jesse was a good man—sincere, reliable, honest, kind, and hard-work-
ing. When he was home, he was a hands-on dad giving the girls baths, rocking
them to sleep, and caring for them when they were sick. He played and wrestled

with them no matter how tired he was after work... as long as they gave him his daily ten-minute power nap.

But he often still chose to go out with the guys instead of coming home. Their cultures were still bumping up against each other. They still fought often, triggering each other's insecurities and sending Kathy into a spiral of doubt and discouragement.

Though she no longer lived their old lifestyle, Jesse still did. Why did he continue on this path despite her best efforts to love and pray for him? She could feel resentment silently grow in the space between them.

At the crusade, God had said that He could save Jesse, but Kathy figured it couldn't hurt to help. In addition to praying persistently, she left her Bible memory verses in visible places like the bathroom mirror, hoping he might notice. She added them to his lunch bag some days. And not wanting to miss any opportunity, she left tracts—small pamphlets with the gospel message and how to have a relationship with Jesus—conveniently around the house.

It wasn't working. Jesse wasn't interested. Worse, he seemed put off by her attempts.

Apparently, Pastor Ron had noticed all the time she spent alone at church, because one day he confronted her bluntly but compassionately.

"You're at church too much," he said. "Make Sunday worship a priority. Everything else is optional. Your home is your ministry. Go love your husband."

The loving correction was hard to hear. Kathy had been at church often, meaning that Jesse was home with the girls on his own, tripping over tracts and Bible verses.

So she tried. One night she cooked a nice dinner—not her go-to spaghetti meal, but his favourite traditional Filipino food. It truly was an act of love because her fingers felt raw from all the chopping. There was so much chopping in every recipe!

When it was finally ready, she set the table.

She waited. And waited. No call. No Jesse.

When dinnertime had passed and bedtime arrived, she put the twins to bed and then waited some more. With each passing minute, she felt her anger mounting.

*How could he? What kind of husband doesn't bother calling? And why tonight of all nights is he out drinking with his buddies instead of coming home to his family?*

Despite her newfound faith, their marriage felt like it was getting worse.

"I think I'm done," she told herself.

Her thoughts were interrupted by the sound of a car pulling up to the back alley. That could only mean one thing.

*Great,* she thought. *Not only did he not call or come home for dinner, he was too drunk to drive home. Now I'll have to pack the twins up early tomorrow morning to drive him downtown to pick up his car.*

He didn't do it every night, but this also wasn't the first time.

Sometimes the guys hung out in the parking garage after work near the car dealership where Jesse was a mechanic. Someone would bring out the beer and they'd all have a few. Some of the guys would head home in time for dinner while others would drink all hours of the night until security kicked them out.

Or they'd head to the pub. Tonight must have been one of those nights.

From the end of her rope, with every last ounce of desire to love him completely drained from her heart, Kathy cried out, "God, I can't love him."

*"You can't, but I can."*

There it was again. Her end, God's beginning.

The gentle and strong response filled her with peace. The realization settled into her heart. She couldn't save Jesse. She couldn't even love Jesse. At the end of her rope, she had expected to feel hopeless, but she didn't. The familiar flicker of hope blazed in the darkness of doubt and discouragement.

God was holding out another promise for her to grab hold of. But did she believe God? Could she grab hold of something she couldn't see? Was that how faith worked?

There was no sign of any change in Jesse, no proof she could point to as evidence that change was coming, and no indication that his heart was softening towards God. He hadn't so much as asked about her newfound faith since wanting to know how long this Jesus thing was going to last.

As Jesse began to stumble up the steps, her heartbeat quickened. She was still so mad. A war waged in her heart between how she felt and believing that God would do what He said He could do. Anxiety coursed through her veins as she heard his keys fumbling in the lock.

The patio door slid open and they made eye contact. Despite his drunken state, he was clearly still ready for the wrath of Kathy, the well-deserved verbal assault on his thoughtless behaviour.

She opened her mouth, but what came out shocked them both: "Hi honey. Are you hungry?"

It was almost enough to sober him up. Almost. Where was the barrage? Where were the accusations? Where were the reminders that he didn't measure up?

He stared, dumbfounded, and she stared back, equally surprised and confused. She was uncertain what had compelled her to say those words.

Finally, his words returned to him. "Uh, no, I'm fine. I just want to go to sleep."

She helped him into bed and said "I love you," hardly able to believe how God had intervened and literally spoken different words through her than the ones that had been ready to spew out.

As she stood in the hallway after closing the bedroom door, she thought, *That was amazing. How did I not scream at him? How did 'I love you' come out of my mouth?*

Mornings after nights like this were usually heavy with silent resentment. But the next morning was different too.

"Sorry about last night," Jesse mumbled when he came into the kitchen.

Once again, Kathy was shocked. Not once had Jesse ever apologized for coming home late, getting drunk, and not calling. Could it be that God was doing what He had said He would? She was almost afraid to hope, but God's intervention and Jesse's apology was enough to give her something to hang onto. If God could act this quickly, Kathy concluded that she should've given up sooner.

Her end always seemed to be God's beginning.

# 6

*Summer 1985*

# TRADING WAYS

*That is why, for Christ's sake, I delight in weaknesses, in insults, in hardships, in persecutions, in difficulties. For when I am weak, then I am strong.*

—2 Corinthians 12:10

Kathy took a break from unpacking their moving boxes and rested a hand on her growing belly. She was grateful. In the middle of their messy marriage, God was still growing their family. As life grew inside her physically, she was also growing spiritually. Their new white house with green shutters on Berry Road had ample room for the new baby due to arrive in the fall.

She was far from perfect but learning how to let God love Jesse through her. This was such a relief. If it had depended on her own strength and ability to love, their marriage might have been over a long time ago.

But God was doing it just as He promised. She continued to wrestle with what she believed God might do, and how quickly He might do it. Some days she was full of faith, remembering that God could save Jesse, especially when she was with her church family. Other days, doubt and discouragement came at her like a storm, threatening to destroy her trust in God. On those days, she was sure that change would never come, that Jesse would never change. Those were the days when she was most tempted to give in to her old ways and go at him with accusatory words.

Thankfully, God continued to meet her on the pages of the Bible. So often, the words breathed life into her. This verse stopped her in her tracks:

*Wives, in the same way submit yourselves to your own husbands so that, if any of them do not believe the word, they may be won over without words by the behavior of their wives...*

Jesse definitely didn't believe this, yet he would be won over? Without words? This promise seemed unlikely at best, and impossible at worst.

She stared at the verse again, and this time it seemed to stare back at her. God was revealing how every failed attempt to win Jesse over with words had actually pushed him further away. She had wondered why her new faith wasn't attractive to Jesse, but now it was becoming awfully clear.

Her new faith hadn't yet changed her old way of relating to her husband.

With the exception of the night in the kitchen when God had intervened, she still didn't love Jesse with the unconditional love she had received from God. Instead she always took the liberty of telling Jesse about all the things she thought needed changing. Jesse only ever seemed to interpret this as meaning that he was a failure. That was never what she'd meant, but it didn't matter. When was the last time she had thanked Jesse for all the hard work he put in every day to provide for their family? When was the last time she had thanked God for having someone with whom to share the load of life?

She had been so desperate for change that she'd lost sight of everything that was right and good. No wonder Jesse kept his distance.

Kathy just wanted what was best for Jesse, and she was convinced it was for him to trust Jesus. But clearly her way wasn't working.

She read the verse again. There it was again—an invitation to put aside her independent efforts and trust. God seemed to be beckoning her to believe it would work.

She closed the book and stood to her feet. *Okay, God. We'll do it Your way. But I'm going to need Your help.*

# 7

*November 1985*

# THE PRAYER WARRIOR

*...pray continually... for this is God's will for you in Christ Jesus.*
                                                    —1 Thessalonians 5:17

K athy breathed a sigh of relief as she dropped the almost three-year-old twins off with the childcare workers. Now all she had to do was find a quiet corner to nurse the baby in.

Desperate for a break and some adult conversation, Kathy had found a moms group at a local Pentecostal church with childcare. Plus, she took every opportunity to gather with other women who shared her faith.

Her church family saw her as being so full of faith. This was true, but it felt easier to believe while in the presence of other believers.

At home, it was a different story. She desperately needed the joy the Lord to be her strength—and it was. Home was a spiritually lonely place where discouragement and doubt always came knocking. So she didn't miss an opportunity for fellowship here or at Towers.

Her only Sunday morning absence since she'd started attending the previous December came on the morning of October 20. She had needed to call Pastor Ron to tell him that instead of coming to church, she was going to have a baby!

Kathy was discreetly nursing the baby in a quiet corner when she noticed a woman with bangs and a pixie cut fast approaching.

"Good for you!" said the woman in a thick German accent. "Moses knew he was a Hebrew by the time his mother was done nursing him."

Kathy was caught off-guard by the woman's boldness in this otherwise discreet moment. She was vaguely familiar with the story of Moses but uncertain what the woman was getting at.

Unsure of how to respond, Kathy simply smiled, feeling a bit awkward, then nodded and thanked her.

Later in the lobby, she noticed the woman approaching her again.

*Oh boy,* Kathy thought. *She looks like a woman on a mission.*

"This baby," the woman prophesied, pointing to me, "will grow up to live for the Lord."

Clearly she needed no permission to speak her mind!

That particular morning, Kathy felt full of doubt, not faith. Was it possible that her daughters might grow up to live for the Lord when their dad did not?

"But her dad isn't even saved," Kathy hesitated.

The bold woman's confidence wasn't the slightest bit dampened by Kathy's objection. She pulled out a worn index card and explained that every morning she walked the perimeter of Minoru Park and prayed for the people on her list who didn't have a personal relationship with Jesus Christ. All the names that had been crossed out were the people who had taken a step of faith and to trust Jesus as their Lord and Saviour.

Kathy felt a small surge of faith rise up in her discouraged heart. Many names on the list were crossed out.

"What is your husband's name?" the confident woman asked.

"Jesse." She figured it wouldn't hurt to have one more person praying, especially a woman with this much conviction.

The woman jotted his name down on her card and looked at her with certainty. "Your husband *will* get saved."

Maybe God was going to do exactly what He had promised.

But when?

# 8

# SURPRISE

*He will bring you a message through which you and all your household will be saved.*

—Acts 11:14

Kathy stared at Jesse quizzically. It was Sunday morning and he was getting dressed; he appeared to be putting on clothes that could be worn to church. It had been a few weeks since the confident woman had assured her Jesse would be saved. Was he planning to come with her? It seemed impossible.

Jesse mumbled something about how it would just be easier if he came with her rather than having to circle back to pick him up before attending the lunch they'd been invited to. Every once in a while, the whole church gathered for lunch in small groups in different homes, giving members of the church the opportunity to get to know one another in a smaller setting.

He'd never come to church with her before. Was God working in his heart?

———

Jesse began to attend church sporadically, and then in the new year a little more regularly. She could never tell from her stolen glances in his direction during the service what he was thinking. Was he interested? At least he wasn't asleep!

Pastor Ron shared the good news at the end of every sermon, no matter what the message had been. He kept it simple: "Admit you're a sinner and confess that you need Jesus to save you. Believe that He will forgive your sins and come to live in your heart and lead your life."

Week after week, other people responded to the invitation to new life with Jesus. They walked down the aisle, prayed with the pastor, and were welcomed as new members in the family of faith.

But week after week, Jesse stayed in his seat.

# 9

*February 4, 1986*

# ONE TUESDAY MORNING

*See, I am doing a new thing! Now it springs up; do you not perceive it? I am making a way in the wilderness and streams in the wasteland.*

—Isaiah 43:19

"I've noticed Jesse has been at church a little more," said one of the women in her Tuesday prayer group. "Is he getting close to trusting in Jesus?"

The floodgates opened and Kathy burst out crying.

"There's no change at all," she said between sobs. "He's coming to church, but only to look after the kids so I can play the piano."

Discouragement settled over her and her tears flowed as the group opened the Bible and read Psalm 126 before going to prayer.

*The Lord has done great things for us, and we are filled with joy. Restore our fortunes, Lord, like streams in the Negev. Those who sow with tears will reap with songs of joy. Those who go out weeping, carrying seed to sow, will return with songs of joy, carrying sheaves with them.*

—Psalm 126:3–6

Suddenly, she felt a quickening in her spirit. Was Kathy sowing with tears? A picture flashed through her mind. She saw herself weeping for a second and then rejoicing as Jesse, as a sheave, was carried with her.

Was God speaking to her? Kathy opened her eyes and pushed the thought aside. What a silly idea. Jesse had given no indication that he was anywhere close to wanting to begin a personal relationship with Jesus.

But much to her surprise, as Jesse rolled up his sleeves to fill the sink to wash dishes that very night, he said, "By the way, I'm going to do it."

"Do what?" Kathy asked without looking up, running through the possibilities in her mind. Wash the car? Or mow the grass?

"I'm going to become a Christian."

After all they'd been through—the fights, the tears, the almost-calling-it-quits, the prayers, and the faith of others when she'd struggled to believe—much to her surprise Jesse was finally going to say yes to Jesus?

Redemption was on the horizon.

Maybe he did look a little like a sheave after all.

# 10

*Wednesday, February 5, 1986*

# I HAVE DECIDED

*"Come, follow me," Jesus said, "and I will send you out to fish for people."*
—Matthew 4:19

Jesse glanced down at the lunch bag on the passenger seat as he drove to work. No way would he forget to call the pastor with those bold numbers shouting up at him. Not that he would've anyway. He'd been thinking about this for months even though he hadn't said anything to his wife.

At first, he hadn't been sure how long her high was going to last. Jesse had thought she was crazy when she'd said she had been zapped by God. What did that even mean? He hadn't known what to think of any of it and just assumed it was a phase that would pass.

But then it didn't.

After Kathy had joined the crusade prayer group, she had switched from describing her living room experience from being zapped to being born again. Jesse had no idea what she meant by either. All he knew was that his wife was really into Jesus.

Jesse had questions, but who could answer them?

Then one day his coworker Richard mentioned that he went to church. Richard was a friendly guy who worked on the used car lot side of the dealership. Jesse saw Richard when he came down to the basement to borrow a tool every now and then.

Jesse figured it couldn't hurt to ask. "Richard, my wife says she's born again. Is that a cult?"

He couldn't think of another explanation for what was happening to his wife. The change in her had been so abrupt! His vivid memories of how she used to be only added to his confusion.

Richard pulled out a small and worn New Testament from his coveralls and replied with his own question. "You're Catholic, right, Jesse? So you believe in the Bible?"

Jesse nodded. Most people from the Philippines were at the very least culturally Catholic. He had been baptized as a baby. But his family hadn't gone to church together and they never had a Bible in their house. Religion had no personal meaning to Jesse.

Richard flipped open his small pocket Bible to a story which mentioned the term "born again." He explained that Jesus was talking to a religious leader named Nicodemus and told him that a person had to be born again to enter the kingdom of God.

Jesse still couldn't explain what had happened to his wife, but at least she wasn't in a cult.

Before they'd gotten married, they had always partied together with friends. Kathy had been the life of every party, often needing Jesse to cut her off and help her walk when she began staggering. Once the twins came, Kathy slowed down, but after this born again phase had started her partying had come to an abrupt halt. His old wife was gone and his new one was all spiritual. She was all about Jesus.

That's when things had really started to unravel.

Jesse wasn't the one who had changed. Kathy was. And he reasoned that he didn't have to change just because she had. He was the same as he had always been—watching the game, playing basketball in the Filipino league, and going out and drinking with his buddies. He had the right to have fun, didn't he? He worked hard, after all. What he did was typical of men back home in the Philippines.

Jesse loved his growing family. He also liked the feeling of freedom.

But he couldn't do anything right at home. After a while it just felt like there was no point in trying. Why keep trying at something you constantly felt like a failure at? No matter what he did or didn't do, it never made Kathy happy. They didn't seem to have anything in common anymore and couldn't agree on much. They fought often, even when he wasn't sure what they were fighting about.

His mostly gentle and patient nature was near its breaking point. The real problem was that when they fought, the feelings of failure took him right back to his childhood. Jesse had never been able to make sense of the way his father Zachary had treated him.

---

Out of eleven children, Jesse was the seventh born to the Morales family in Dau, Mabalacat. Every sibling knew without question that he'd received the harshest treatment by their father but no one knew exactly why.

Sure, times had been tough. Jesse was born two years after World War II ended. The Morales family and their community were still living in the aftermath. The family was impoverished, merely surviving the wartorn conditions in which their country had been left. It wasn't uncommon on a scarce day for the older siblings to be sent looking for food instead of going to school.

Everyone who was old enough to earn money contributed. Some of Jesse's older sisters worked as seamstresses. One worked as a beautician. His older brother worked nights as a waiter.

Once he was old enough, Jesse also began earning his way by delivering newspapers at the nearby military base. To maximize his efforts and profits, Jesse collected, refolded, and resold the papers discarded by the officers once they finished reading them.

But the tough times still didn't explain why Jesse was the most frequent recipient of his father's mistreatment.

Jesse loved his family, but he often preferred hanging out with friends. Home life was hard. Friends were fun. Plus, he made friends effortlessly with his quietly charismatic personality and easy laughter.

As he got older, he continued his galivanting ways, often sneaking out the window at night to hang out with his friends, despite his mother's warnings, and skipping school to go to the movies.

Boxing in the streets quickly earned him street cred. He didn't pick fights, but he also didn't back down from them, especially if he was standing up for someone. His heart was always soft and protective towards those he loved.

Despite his tough guy persona, he never fought back at home. The beatings from his father for coming home in the middle of the night weren't enough to deter Jesse from continuing his late night fun.

During Jesse's young adult years, things began to look up for the Morales family. His father, though uneducated, took it upon himself to learn English and automotive mechanics. He worked for a few years on the military base as a mechanic before opening his own business, Super Auto Repair Shop. The proximity to the base, combined with his people skills and work ethic, ensured that the shop had a steady stream of well-paying American customers. But things didn't look up for Jesse.

In their community, Zachary was well-respected and well-liked. He taught several young men in the community how to fix cars, providing them the opportunity for a better life. He lived generously towards those in need.

But with his own family, he couldn't control his temper. Especially with Jesse.

Jesse could still hear his father yelling at him, enraged at his son for not doing the work right in the automotive shop. It was humiliating. He could still see the tools his father threw in his direction. He could still feel the impact of the solid metal wrench colliding with his forehead, and the screwdriver. He could still feel the tears he'd tried to fight as he stared helplessly at the floor.

Why would someone treat their own son like that? He couldn't understand it. Not only had mistakes not been allowed, but no matter what he did, it was never good enough.

Only one time, through tears, did Jesse ever talk back. And even then, it wasn't to retaliate but to understand. He looked at his father and cried out, "Why are you doing this?"

Realization washed over Zachary's face and he simply walked away without explanation.

Jesse wouldn't soon forget the humiliation, pain, and, most of all, feelings of inadequacy.

Though the success of the shop made life easier for the family, it made life harder for Jesse. He got so tired of how his father treated him that he asked his brother Bert for money so he could run away. But he couldn't even seem to get that right. Jesse only made it a few hours away from home before resigning himself to the realization that he was hungry, had no more money to buy food, and had no place to go. He went home even more defeated, feeling like there was no way out.

Jesse's last sliver of hope for getting out was his sister Cleo, who had immigrated to Canada. But this hope was soon dashed when she returned to the Philippines in 1972. She hadn't liked the winter there.

For days he felt depressed, staying at the shop and speaking to no one. Now he had no way out. To make matters worse, martial law was declared in the Philippines, which meant no one was allowed out in the streets after 9:00 p.m.

Finally, in March 1973, Cleo returned to Canada, determined to help get Jesse there. Twice his immigration papers were denied, since Cleo didn't make enough money to support him. But thankfully she persisted, working three jobs until she could prove she could support her brother when he came.

Finally, on the third attempt, his immigration papers were approved and Jesse found himself on Canadian soil in March 1974, age twenty-six, ready to begin a brand-new life.

———

His life in Richmond bore almost no resemblance to his life back in the Philippines, except for his work as a mechanic. Every once in a while, he was still reminded of the wounds that had immigrated with him.

Most people never got near these wounds, though, so they didn't affect his daily interactions with people. He was himself—easygoing, hardworking, quiet, and friendly.

But not in his marriage. This became obvious when Kathy's words got close to his wounds. This was the most important relationship in his life, the one with the highest stakes. Anytime their conflict made him feel inadequate, Jesse's anger got the better of him. Neither of them knew what to do about it. Jesse would escape to the garage and take it out on his tools. At least he didn't throw them at anyone, only at things.

At the height of their conflict, Jesse concluded that he couldn't be the kind of man Kathy wanted or needed. Maybe she would be better off with someone else, someone who was more like the person she had become.

He wanted to leave. He'd never thought he would be that guy, but it felt like the only way. He only told one person—his coworker, Rey, who was like an older brother. With their Filipino culture, they shared an instant respect, bond, and trust.

But Rey would have none of Jesse's proposed solution and instead gave him words of wisdom.

"Your wife is not the problem, and your family is not the problem," Rey said. "You are the problem."

His friend pointed right at him, his tone no-nonsense, the way you'd expect an older brother figure to talk.

"You're the one living like a single man when you're a married man with a family," Rey continued. "You drink too much. You spend too much money. You're away from your family too much watching basketball with the guys at the pub. You will break up your family. I won't allow it."

At the time, Jesse thought he had told the wrong guy, but in hindsight maybe he had told exactly the right one. Rey had looked him in the eye and told him the truth, point blank. Rey's words had made him look in the last place he wanted to look: the mirror.

Some time later, after a night at the bar, Jesse's friend dropped him off in the alley behind their house. He hoped Kathy had gone to bed, to avoid the confrontation, but the light was still on. Jesse knew what he was in for.

He fumbled with his keys, opened the door, and there she was. He braced himself.

"Hi honey. Are you hungry?" she asked him.

Jesse almost fell over, the shock almost enough to sober him up. Had Kathy just called him honey, with an impossibly kind tone? And offered him food? Usually she would threaten to change the locks, yelling at him for his thoughtless and irresponsible behaviour.

Jesse didn't say anything for a long time. Where was the fight? Who was this woman? He mumbled something about just wanting to go to sleep. He remained in silent shock the entire time Kathy helped him get settled in bed.

The morning after, he felt something unfamiliar. Not having needed to defend himself the previous night had left only quiet, empty, uncomfortable space to think about what he was doing. When she was furious and he felt like a failure, it was easy to justify his behaviour. He could just blame her, since he was simply acting consistently with the way her words made him feel.

But now, with no fight on his hands, instead of feeling angry and defensive, he felt guilt and remorse.

What was he doing? He loved his wife and his three little girls, even though he wasn't good at verbalizing it.

"Sorry about last night," he mumbled to her in the kitchen.

Though there was a much longer list of things he was sorry for, it was a starting point. He couldn't figure out why she had suddenly been nice to him.

He wanted to make things right but didn't know how. However, after Kathy told him about an upcoming lunch invitation at church, Jesse knew what to do. He had always been better with actions than words. No one had ever taught him how to express himself with words, other than the angry kind.

So he would go for lunch. He *was* slightly curious about whatever had inspired his wife's kindness. Plus, little Angela, with innocent curiosity, had recently asked him, "Daddy, how come on Sunday we go to church and you stay home and watch football?"

Jesse had found himself defenceless. No reason seemed enough to answer his toddler.

That next Sunday, Jesse got up early and started getting dressed for church. He could feel Kathy looking at him quizzically while he prepared.

Then, off they went to church for the first time as a family.

At first he didn't really like the experience of attending church, but he kept going. His friend Rey assured him it was good for him.

Jesse hadn't anticipated what happened next—something began changing inside him. The things the pastor spoke about from the Bible seemed to speak right to him. After a sermon, Jesse often asked himself, *How did he know that about me?* It was like Pastor Ron knew the struggle inside him.

When Jesse wanted an opinion, he asked Rey. When he told Rey he wasn't sure why he should bother going to church, Rey just told him to keep going and pay attention. "You'll get something positive even if you don't like it," Rey had said.

And when Jesse was confused, he asked his friend Richard. Jesse was baffled at how he, who went to an entirely different church, was able to verify the things Jesse heard at Kathy's church. Kathy attended a Baptist church. Richard attended a Christian Missionary Alliance church. Jesse's basketball teammate attended a Pentecostal one. Jesse didn't understand the difference between these churches or why there were so many options. How did they all have the same stories if they weren't connected?

On their morning break, Jesse and Richard sometimes took quick walks down to the bakery on Burrard Street for croissants and coffee. During this time Jesse would ask questions. How did a person get to heaven? Why all the different churches? Who was the pope?

Richard always seemed to point Jesse back to the person of Jesus, continually and confidently assuring him that the Bible made it clear that only Jesus could give a person access to God, not the church you attended, anyone, or anything else.

One morning Jesse came into work angry. Richard listened as Jesse recounted the conversation he'd had with his wife's pastor the night before.

Kathy had invited her pastor over to their house to talk with Jesse about faith. Pastor Ron had asked if he were to get hit by a truck and die, where would he spend eternity? It forced Jesse to think about dying and where he stood with God.

That made Jesse mad. It felt like another reminder that he didn't measure up. He didn't like the pastor. What would happen if he died? Who would take care of Kathy and his girls? It felt personal.

Pastor Ron had made Jesse remember that he wasn't at peace with God, and he didn't like that at all. If nothing had ever been enough for his earthly father, Jesse couldn't imagine God ever being pleased with him.

Jesse was known for staying calm when people attempted to get under his skin—but not this time. Even the morning after that conversation with Pastor Ron, Jesse was still fuming mad.

Thankfully, Richard had a disarming way of talking about faith and helped Jesse understand that the pastor had asked him to consider where he wanted to spend eternity and how he would get there, not make him feel hopeless and condemned. Forever was a long time and Pastor Ron was convinced that Jesus was the only way for anyone to have eternal life.

Somehow, by the end of the conversation, Jesse's anger subsided. Richard's way of explaining things left him with some deep questions to ponder, without all the emotion. He still didn't like what Pastor Ron had said, but Jesse understood that the pastor had been trying to help him consider these weighty matters.

But Jesse never brought up his faith questions at home.

Much to Jesse's surprise, Kind Kathy, who had made her appearance the night he'd come home drunk, had in fact come to stay. And it made Jesse curious. Kathy rarely got angry with him anymore, and when she did she apologized. She seemed sincere. It was hard to be mad at someone who stopped being mad back.

Gradually and surprisingly, Jesse found himself listening, interested and even anticipating those Sunday services.

Each week Pastor Ron finished his sermon the same way, by inviting people to get right with God by receiving Jesus as their personal Lord and Saviour. At first Jesse watched in confusion as people got out of their seats, walked down the aisle, and bowed their heads to pray with the pastor who always stood in front of the altar. Then his confusion grew into curiosity.

Jesse was beginning to believe the words he heard week after week—that salvation and eternal life was a gift, not something he could ever earn. It felt like faith was growing inside him a little more each Sunday.

Then Jesse found himself wondering why he wasn't one of those people who chose to receive the gift of abundant life Jesus offered him. It was an invitation to get right with God, to have lasting peace and joy, something that Jesse was sure he'd never be able to earn on his own. And this righteousness was a gift.

All he had to do was receive it.

Pastor Ron explained that the way to do it was to have child-like faith and accept it just like you would a gift on Christmas morning. Pastor Ron always finished with a bit of urgency in his voice: "Don't wait. You don't know how much time you have. Today is the day of salvation."

But Jesse just wasn't sure.

At work that week, he found himself asking Richard more questions. Richard told him that his sin separated him from God (Romans 3:23), but God had demonstrated His own love for him by sending Jesus to die while he was still a sinner (Romans 5:8).

Richard assured him that anyone who was willing to believe in Jesus would not perish but have eternal life (John 3:16). This was the life Jesus had come to give him—an abundant one (John 10:10). Peace with God was only possible through Jesus (Romans 5:1).

Jesse had so much to think about.

Soon after, Jesse called Richard Navarro, a Filipino follower of Jesus who was also married to a Canadian woman. Despite the fact that Jesse had slept through the Saturday night Bible study Kathy had taken him to, he was sure Richard Navarro would be willing to answer his questions. Plus, Richard Navarro went to a different church, which would give Jesse a chance to verify what he'd been hearing.

Was it possible that it was all true?

Jesse was beginning to think that God might be trying to get his attention when Richard Navarro shared the exact same verses Richard from work had shared with him earlier that day. And they didn't even know each other!

Both Richards told him that beginning a relationship with God was simple. It wasn't about the words of the prayer, but about Jesse's faith. He shared a simple prayer as an example anyway.

Jesus, I know that I'm a sinner and that I need You to forgive me. I know that You died a painful death so that my sins could be washed clean. Thank You. I want You to be the Saviour of my life, and I will trust and follow You. Everything I have is Yours now. Be my Lord. In Your name, Lord, amen.

Though Jesse didn't feel quite ready to take this step of faith, he couldn't shake the feeling that God was somehow pursuing him.

He was running out of reasons to delay saying yes to Jesus. The previous Sunday, only three days before he announced his decision to his wife, he had almost taken the aisle during the invitation time. His right toe had made the slightest movement towards the altar, but he had hesitated. What would his family think? What would his coworkers think? Was he crazy?

He willed himself to stay in his spot, telling himself that the feeling would pass.

Then Monday came around and he couldn't shake the feeling that he needed to get right with God. By the time dinner clean-up rolled around, it was too much to bear and he announced his decision to Kathy.

Although she had thought she was being subtle, Jesse knew what she was doing in the bathroom: celebrating.

———————

Jesse could already feel something changing inside him as he pulled into the parking lot at work. After today, he was going to be right with God.

As he pulled on his coveralls, he glanced at the clock. 7:00 a.m. It was time to start work. He would call Pastor Ron on his break.

When Richard punched in at his usual time, a few hours later than the mechanics, Jesse called him over.

"I've decided!" Jesse exclaimed, a smile taking over his entire face. "I've decided to give my life to Jesus Christ."

Richard's eyes lit up with excitement as Jesse's announcement washed over him.

"I really want to pray with you to receive Jesus," Jesse said. "But I want to surprise the pastor."

"Jesse, I don't care who you pray with as long as you settle this with Jesus."

"Is this a good prayer?" Jesse asked, passing Richard the paper on which he had jotted down a few words. Both Richards had told him that it was more about meaning it in his heart than getting the words right.

But this was a big decision and he wanted to get it right.

Richard smiled. "That will work just fine," he assured him.

Jesse made his way over to the phone to call Pastor Ron to set up a meeting on his way home, but there was no answer. He tried again at lunch, and then again on his afternoon coffee break. He tried a third time at the end of the day.

Before leaving work, he picked up the phone to call Kathy and tell her about the change.

"I'm just coming home," he explained.

"Why?" she exclaimed, unable to hide her disappointment.

"I tried calling Pastor Ron on my morning coffee break. No answer. Lunch. No answer. Afternoon coffee. No answer. And now, still no answer."

He hung up the phone, then his coveralls, and headed out of the shop to his parked car to begin his usual commute home just like any other day.

# 11

*February 5, 1986*

# LEFT ON ALBION

*Before they call I will answer; while they are still speaking I will hear.*
—Isaiah 65:24

As he crossed the bridge that connected Vancouver and Richmond, Jesse couldn't shake the feeling that he shouldn't head straight home. But what would be the point? The pastor hadn't been at the church all day. Surely he wouldn't be there now.

He allowed his mind to wander as he continued south. *I wonder what's for dinner?*

The drive felt longer today, like it was passing in slow motion. Were there more red lights than usual?

The light turned green and he continued in the direction of home, still trying to shake the feeling. Of course he should go home. Kathy was expecting him. The twins would be waiting at the window to play like they did every day. He looked forward to cuddling his four-month-old baby.

Why was his heart beating faster? Why did the weight on his shoulders feel heavier?

He tightened his grip on the steering wheel and shifted in his seat as he realized the next street was Albion. The church was just around the corner. Maybe there was still a chance.

"Uh... God?"

His own words surprised him. What was he doing? He didn't know how to pray. The only prayers he'd ever said were the ones he'd memorized as a child.

Something compelled him to continue on anyway.

"I don't think you know me, but you know my wife Kathy. I have a problem… I've been trying to call the pastor all day so I can become a Christian, but he's not answering. If you're real, put him in the church. I'm turning left on Albion right now. Sincerely, Jesse."

He hesitated, unsure if that even counted as a prayer. But he found himself making a left on Albion.

This was it. A moment of truth. In less than two minutes, he would know if the God his wife knew so well would work for him, too.

He remembered the pastor saying something about faith and how you only needed a tiny bit. What was it again? A mustard seed. He wasn't entirely sure how small that was, but he hoped that whatever amount he had was at least that much.

Jesse turned off the ignition as he surveyed the empty parking lot and the dark building.

*See, no one's here.*

He lifted the keys back to the ignition to start the engine but instead found himself opening the car door instead.

*Just try.*

Reluctantly, he got out of the car, walked towards the building, and yanked on the door. Surprised to find it open, he stepped inside the quiet building. Was anyone here?

He spotted a crack of light coming from the pastor's office just to the left of the entrance. He walked towards the door and knocked softly.

"Come in," said a voice.

Jesse pushed open the door to see Pastor Ron hovering over his desk, jacket on, shuffling through the papers on his desk.

The pastor looked up, as surprised to see Jesse as Jesse was to see him.

"What're you doing here?" Jesse asked, his heart practically beating out of his chest.

"This is my office. What're you doing here?"

"You first," Jesse insisted. "I've been calling you all day and you haven't answered."

How much time had even passed between when he'd prayed and pulled into the parking lot? Why wasn't there another vehicle in the lot?

"I live across the field over there in the parsonage," Pastor Ron explained. "My wife was just getting dinner on the table when I remembered I needed to look over a piece of paper for a meeting tomorrow, so I popped over. That's why I still have my jacket on. What're you doing here?"

"I'm ready."

"Ready for what?"

"I'm ready to become a Christian."

Pastor Ron looked shocked. "You're ready to invite Jesus into your life?"

"Yes," Jesse replied in such a sombre voice that Ron could've sworn someone had died.

Tears began forming in the corners of Jesse's eyes, eyes that usually twinkled with a hint of mischievousness.

"Do you want me to lead you in a prayer right here?" Ron asked.

"No. I don't want to do something spiritual in an office. I want to do it there." He motioned towards the sanctuary. "I want to do it at the altar."

Pastor Ron led the way and turned on the back light in the sanctuary, giving the altar at the front only a faint glow.

Jesse rounded the corner formed by the last row of chairs and approached the altar. Pastor Ron then watched the grown man kneel like a child before God. He got on his knees, folded his hands, and bowed his head.

In Ron's many years of ministry, he'd never seen anything like it.

"Do you want me to pray with you Jesse?" he asked.

Jesse shook his head, trying to swallow the emotions that were suddenly welling up inside him.

"No," he answered softly. "I know what to say."

Emotion overcame Jesse as he prayed a humble yet powerful prayer acknowledging his need for forgiveness. He confessed his belief in what Jesus had done for him on the cross—dying to pay the price for his sin, then rising from the dead—and invited Jesus to be his Saviour and Lord.

Ron paused to take in the holy moment. He had been startled by the knock at his office door. He didn't normally leave the front door unlocked, but he had today given the quick nature of his business in the office.

He had been completely blown away when he saw that it was Jesse Morales. He liked the guy. And Ron knew Jesse was lost without Jesus.

Jesse had been in church more regularly with Kathy, but he'd given Ron no reason to believe he was ready for anything more than sporadic church attendance.

And whenever he was there, he looked sullen and uninterested. Ron had been sure it would take a lot more prayer and time.

This afternoon, though, Jesse looked so sombre that Ron had at first been certain his marriage was in trouble. Or worse, that someone had died.

But no, he was there to become a Christian. Ron was ecstatic.

When Jesse had finished praying, Ron quietly reached over and placed his hand on Jesse's shoulder.

"Lord Jesus, seal this decision in his heart today and fill him with Your Spirit," Ron prayed. "Give him the power to live the life You have created him to live."

When Jesse stood up, Ron couldn't help but stare. He was looking at a brand-new man. Jesse looked like someone had cut a thousand-pound weight loose from his shoulders. His countenance was bright. A visible peace shone from his face. He looked relieved to have finally settled the matter of eternity with his Maker.

He had finally surrendered his life to Jesus and couldn't stop smiling, his face brimming with joy.

Ron had just witnessed a miracle.

———

Kathy glanced up at the clock, unsure which emotion would win. Anger, disappointment, and worry battled furiously in her mind.

When she'd hung up the phone with Jesse, disappointment was the first to drop in. Of all the Wednesdays in the world, why had Pastor Ron needed to be out of the office today? This was the closest Jesse had ever come to becoming a Christian. Fear told her it was the closest that he ever would.

But then anger made a run at her: *He's late again. Great. He's probably at the bar drinking his life away.*

She was sure that given another night to sleep on it, Jesse would change his mind about Jesus. But at least the anger was less painful than disappointment. She could direct it somewhere.

Then, as she glanced at her daughters, worry popped in. What if something had happened to their dad? Her heart sank with guilt for having been angry. What if he had been in an accident? He should've been home by now.

Around and around these emotions went for a couple of hours. She felt tired from all the noise.

With dinner delayed, she gave in to a small snack, hoping to hold the girls off until Jesse got home for dinner. If he ever made it home. Angela was happily eating her orange slices and Christina was holding her orange in hand.

Kathy's thoughts were interrupted by the phone ringing. Was it Jesse? Or the police calling to tell her there'd been an accident?

"Hello?" she asked, hopeful.

"Hi, it's me." It was Jesse, and it sounded like he was smiling. Like he was having trouble talking because of smiling so much. Was that even possible?

Yes, there was definitely a smile in his voice.

Before she had time to say anything, he continued. "Sorry I'm late. I'm just leaving the church. I'll tell you the story when I get home."

He was sorry he was late? And he was leaving the church? This could only mean one thing. Her heart leapt as she returned the phone to its receiver.

Jesse must have become a Christian.

"Girls!" she shouted. "Your daddy is a Christian! He got saved today!"

She didn't need him to tell the full story to be sure; she already knew. She had been able to hear the marked difference in his voice.

The three-year-old twins joined their exuberant mom for a celebratory dance. Christina threw her orange in the air. They forgot how hungry they were. The three of them had been earnestly praying for the man they all loved for over a year.

"Daddy is saved! Daddy is saved!"

They all yelled and cheered until Angela stopped dancing. A worried expression took over.

"What's wrong, Angela?" Kathy asked.

"Daddy's saved," she said slowly, realization dawning. "But I'm not."

Kathy hadn't thought of that. She'd been so focussed on praying for Jesse, and the girls had been so eager to attend church and pray with her, that she hadn't thought about their faith.

"What would you like to do?" Kathy asked.

"If Daddy is going to follow Jesus, I want to too!" she decided thoughtfully.

"Me too!" Christina agreed.

Kathy smiled and led her daughters in a prayer confessing their need for forgiveness and asking Jesus to forgive them and be their Saviour and Lord.

*All in one day,* Kathy smiled, her heart overflowing with gratitude.

God had done not one but three miracles all on this one day. They now shared actual birthdays (December 25) and spiritual birthdays (February 5).

Those few minutes as they eagerly waited at the window for Jesse to arrive felt like an eternity. When they saw his car pull in, they shouted their usual "Daddy's home!" and began their descent from the living room down the stairs to the front entrance.

Jesse could barely open the door due to the exuberant welcoming committee crowding the small entrance.

"What happened? Tell me everything!" Kathy exclaimed. She hadn't met him at the door with this much excitement since the day she had been zapped.

His signature sly smile formed at the corner of his mouth. "Let me get my coat off. And take off my shoes."

Jesse was never in a hurry. Kathy was certain he didn't know how to hurry.

Instead of the usual routine of lying on the living room floor and the girls jumping on him and playing, he took a seat at the kitchen table, smiling mysteriously, like he had just won the lottery and hadn't told anyone yet.

"So?" Kathy tapped her foot, trying not to let her impatience show. "What happened?"

He chuckled. "I was driving down No. 4 Road and I talked to God."

Kathy was stunned. She hadn't known that Jesse prayed.

"It was the first time I talked to Him without a memorized prayer," he continued.

He went on to tell her about asking God to put the pastor in the church, and making a left on Albion. He recounted the empty parking lot and the dark building—and then, of course, the pastor being there when he wasn't supposed to be.

"He offered to pray with me, but I told him I already knew what to say. I showed Richard my prayer earlier today."

Kathy couldn't stop smiling. She was staring at a brand-new man, and together they finally shared the same faith in Jesus.

# INTERLUDE ONE

# 12

*May 2008*

## STAY

*Then I heard the voice of the Lord saying, "Whom shall I send? And who will go for us?"*

*And I said, "Here am I. Send me!"*

—Isaiah 6:8

"I think we should come home," I said to my dad over the phone.

The three hours of driving between our home and my parents was too great a distance to help with everyday challenges. And I knew the path ahead was only going to get more difficult.

Since getting the phone call, I wanted nothing more than to pack up our things, put a For Sale sign on the lawn of our new home, and put the remaining two years of my education degree on hold.

"Steph," my dad objected calmly, "you need to be wherever God has called you to be. You need to be on mission with Him."

I couldn't wrap my head around why God wouldn't want me at home. The need was great; I could help. The solution seemed logical and obvious: move home.

Plus, being where God called me involved me actually hearing from God. Every other time I'd fervently sought Him over a decision, it seemed like He was silent and I had to flip a coin when it was crunch time. I doubted that God would speak clearly to me.

Reluctantly, I prayed. "God, show me where You are calling me to be."

Much to my surprise, a clear answer pressed upon my heart. For the first time in my life, I was sure God had spoken and confident about what He'd said: *"Stay."*

"But what about Mom and Emily?" I wondered. "Who will take care of them?"

*"Trust Me."*

My dad's instructions to be where God had called us weren't merely words. From the day he had first put his faith in Jesus, his priority had been to follow Him no matter what it cost or how illogical it seemed.

To see what it looked like to go where I was sent, to stay where I was put, and give God what I had, I simply had to look in the rear-view mirror at the pattern by which my dad had always lived his life.

*Part Two*

# THE JOURNEY

# 13

*Thursday, February 6, 1986*

# THE ANNOUNCEMENT

*As for us, we cannot help speaking about what we have seen and heard.*

—Acts 4:20

"Hey Petar," Jesse said to his friend the next morning at work. "I have good news."

His new relationship with Jesus was the best thing that had ever happened to him. Nothing in his life had brought this kind of peace and joy. He couldn't stop smiling. Even after sleeping on it, the weight he'd always carried on his shoulders was still gone.

Jesse didn't want to tell everyone, but he had to tell someone. The spotlight wasn't his thing. He was much more comfortable in a one-on-one conversation than making a big announcement.

"But you have to promise not to tell anyone," Jesse clarified.

Petar raised his eyebrows as Jesse swore him to secrecy with a handshake. After all, he had thought his wife had joined a cult. What would Petar think?

Jesse lowered his voice. "I got born again last night!"

"That's your good news?" Petar laughed as he realized Jesse didn't have anything else to report and strolled back to his bay to get to work.

Jesse breathed a sigh of relief. Petar hadn't thought it was a big deal, so he definitely wouldn't say anything. His secret was safe.

"Hey everyone, gather round, gather round," Petar shouted at morning coffee break, his voice easily carrying through each of the work bays. One by one the other mechanics put down their tools, came out from under their hoists, and made their way towards him.

From two bays down, Jesse felt his heart start to pound. Though Petar had shaken on it, Jesse had a sneaking suspicion he knew where his friend was going with this.

"I have *good* news," Petar continued.

Jesse stayed put under the vehicle he was working on. Maybe he could just hide out in his bay?

"Jesse is..." Petar paused for dramatic effect "...born again!"

The mechanics all looked at each other, unsure of what to make of the morning announcement. Some laughed in disbelief, but most looked confused. The chances of Jesse becoming religious seemed pretty unlikely to them.

"Jesse, why don't you come over here and tell everyone?" Petar exclaimed.

So much for hiding out in his bay.

*I'll just say it's not true,* Jesse reasoned as he slowly made his way over to the impromptu staff meeting. But just as quickly as the denial came to him, so did the details of an Easter movie he'd once watched. What had Peter done again? He'd denied Jesus three times after promising three times that he wouldn't.

After all Jesus had done for him, Jesse didn't want to do that. So he swallowed hard, unsure of what would come out of his mouth.

Petar wasn't letting him off the hook. His twinkling eyes demanded an answer. "Well? Is it true?"

*Just deny it,* his thoughts shouted at him.

And then a gentle voice: *Just tell the truth.*

Which would it be?

Jesse looked around at all the guys staring at him, waiting for an answer. "It's true. I'm born again now."

"Yeah right."

"No way."

"Sure."

After a bit of laughing, the guys went back to work. The strange, impromptu announcement made no impact on them.

But Jesse was relieved. Inside, he sensed that God was pleased with him. He should probably thank Petar; now everyone knew he was born again and Jesse was off the hook.

# 14

*Spring 1986*

# THE SIGN

*But in your hearts revere Christ as Lord. Always be prepared to give an answer to everyone who asks you to give the reason for the hope that you have. But do this with gentleness and respect...*

—1 Peter 3:15

"I read a story in a magazine about a guy who started a Bible study at his work," Jesse said to his coworker Jack. "Apparently productivity changed, morale improved, and the boss really appreciated it. Can you imagine if there was something like that here?"

Jack just shrugged from the bay next to Jesse's. "I dunno."

"What're you guys talking about?" Petar asked, sauntering over to join the conversation.

"Jesse's talking about having a Bible study here," Jack offered.

Before Jesse could interject, the two were off to the races.

Petar snickered. "Like you'd go to a Bible study."

"Maybe I would. How do you know I wouldn't go?"

"Yeah right. If you go... I'll go."

Jesse could feel himself starting to sweat. What was happening? He had only been inspired by the story of the Bible study; he hadn't intended to replicate it. He loved reading the Bible, but it had only been, what... a few weeks? He wasn't qualified to teach a Bible study.

Before he could put the brakes on the conversation, Petar and Jack were shaking on it to see who would be a man of his word and show up to Jesse's Bible study.

Jesse hoped his coworkers would just forget about their bet, but these hopes were dashed when he walked by the break room bulletin board later that morning and saw the sign Petar had hung for all to see:

### BIBLE STUDY 6 AM FRIDAY
### JESSE IS BRINGING FREE DONUTS

*Oh boy,* thought Jesse, nervously running his hand through his thick black hair. *What have I gotten myself into?*

---

Jesse balanced the box of donuts and a stack of New Testaments as he walked into work Friday morning, earlier than usual. He didn't know the first thing about leading a Bible study. He had barely started reading the Bible himself and couldn't foresee this going well.

His own brand-new Bible topped the pile. Since he had decided to follow Jesus, he hadn't been able to stop reading the Bible, just as it had been with Kathy. His appetite for Scripture almost exceeded his appetite for food. For a man who was a bottomless pit, that said a lot.

The only problem was, Jesse hadn't owned his own Bible. He and Kathy had all but fought over whose turn it was to read her copy. Of course, this was better than their old fights! But finally she had marched over to the Christian bookstore and bought him his own.

When Jesse had announced to Kathy that he needed help with this break room Bible study, she'd felt about as qualified as he did. Jesse had recounted the conversation that had taken place at work and how it ended up with an announcement on the break room bulletin board.

He wrapped up the story with a desperate plea: "You've been reading it longer than me. I need your help!"

"I've never done anything like that. How could I possibly help?" Kathy exclaimed. "You should probably pay a visit to Pastor Ron."

Pastor Ron had been thrilled when Jesse told him about the break room bulletin board announcement. His enthusiasm was unaffected by Jesse's uncertainty that this was a good idea and lack of confidence in being the one to lead it.

But at least the pastor did give him some photocopied pages from a Bible study that Jesse could use as a starting point.

Pastor Ron knew the Bible a lot better than he did and kept assuring him that he didn't need to know everything there was to know in order to lead this study. The Holy Spirit would speak through him and that was more than enough.

He adjusted his grip on his load and took a deep breath as he headed to the break room.

# 15

*Spring 1987*

# TRAINING GROUND

*And without faith it is impossible to please God, because anyone who comes to*
*him must believe that he exists and that he rewards those who earnestly seek him.*
—Hebrews 11:6

*Is there even a point to all this?* The question stirred within Jesse as he made his way towards his parked car after a long week at work. Discouragement weighed heavily on him this particular Friday.

Early that morning, only Jesse had shown up for the Bible study, and the same had been true the past couple of Fridays as well. It felt like his efforts were in vain.

It had been more than a year since that first Friday morning Bible study when Jack and Petar had made good on their handshake and both showed up. Though they hadn't been regular attenders, without their seemingly inconsequential handshake, and the sign on the break room bulletin board, the Bible study would never have begun.

The sign had stayed up and people kept showing up at first. It didn't really matter to Jesse who or how many. It wasn't about the numbers. He was more than happy to share Jesus with anyone who would listen, even if it was just one.

After everything Jesus had done for him, Jesse was ready to serve Him with his life. But on days like this, he wondered if maybe he was doing something wrong. Is this what following Jesus was supposed to be like? Why did it feel so difficult?

He scanned the parking lot, trying to locate his car while he made sense of his discouragement.

Sometimes there had been five or six different guys crammed into the small break room, and occasionally there had been standing room only. Word had quietly spread throughout the dealership about this "Bible class," as some called it. Even those who weren't interested in Jesus wanted to know what had happened to Jesse. No one could deny that Jesse was an entirely different man than he used to be.

Whenever Jesse wanted to throw in the towel on the Bible study, he felt just enough of a nudge for him to continue.

A coworker would stop by his bay to apologize for sleeping in and missing the early morning Bible study and ask what he'd missed. Or while sipping his coffee at the morning break, Jesse would notice that the stack of New Testament Bibles in the break room now only had six copies instead of eight. People from other departments would occasionally stop by to ask him questions about faith.

People were curious even if they weren't consistent. The owner of the dealership, Mr. Andreassen, had even scratched the words "Keep up the good missionary work!" on his pay stub. The Bible study, though small in number, had had a mighty enough impact to garner the boss's attention. Mr. Andreassen had even made a few appearances, enthusiastic about what Jesse was doing. After all, it was having a positive impact on the employees.

Whatever form the nudge came in, it was enough for Jesse to show up again the next Friday. He needed these nudges, especially since Richard had left to attend seminary in the fall of 1986.

Then there was Herb Reesor, the kindest and biggest nudge of all.

Herb had come into the dealership for a used vehicle and somehow got wind of the Friday morning Bible study. He made his way down to the service department and introduced himself to Jesse. He then invited Jesse to join his monthly gathering of Christian businessmen called Faith in the Marketplace.

At first, Jesse had been reluctant to go. He wasn't a businessman and he was hardly sure whether his modest Bible study qualified him to be part of any sort of official gathering, or to even be called a ministry. But Herb insisted that he come for prayer and encouragement.

Jesse laughed and smiled easily. How had Herb known he was discouraged? Though Jesse didn't know it at the time, Herb felt that his personal assignment from God was to encourage those who felt discouraged in their faith. Jesse definitely qualified in that regard.

Jesse didn't know what to expect from this gathering. With his brown paper lunch bag in his oil-stained hands, he followed Herb's instructions on foot to the nearby Bentall Centre, a few blocks from his work, and located the conference room where the meeting was to be held.

Jesse swung the doors open and immediately noticed the extravagant chandelier, plush carpet, and a room filled with men in fancy suits.

Before he could decide to stay or go, someone spotted him. "You must be Jesse. Welcome!" The man gave him a giant hug.

These men didn't seem to notice his oil-stained fingers or dirty work clothes. They embraced him as family, a fellow brother in Christ with the same goal they had: to live out their faith at work.

At these gatherings, Jesse always found timely encouragement for his new-found faith. Month after month, he went in his same work clothes—with his same brown paper lunch bag, in his same oil-stained hands—to be fuelled up to continue living out his faith at his workplace.

Between those monthly gatherings, Herb periodically stopped by the dealership to invite Jesse for a walk around the block during morning coffee break. If it was around lunchtime, Jesse would bring his lunch bag and they'd pause on a bench on Hornby Street to pray and talk.

Though these visits were never on the calendar, they were always timely. Whatever Herb had to say turned out to be what Jesse needed to hear. How did Herb know how to speak directly to Jesse's doubts and discouragements? It was almost as if God had put him up to it. How else would a complete stranger know what to say?

"Don't worry about attendance," Herb would tell him. "Just do what God tells you and leave the results to Him. Keep it simple. Share your faith simply and love people. Don't give up. Just keep going. Following Jesus means just doing whatever He tells you to do."

Herb was almost two decades his senior. His kind and gentle disposition and no-nonsense nature felt fatherly. It was impossible not to feel the love of God in the man's presence. For Herb, there was no separation between his faith and the rest of his life; he was outspoken about his faith in Jesus and one couldn't be in his presence without it rubbing off at least a little.

Jesse had already seen God at work around him and through him. He'd also experienced the truth about what the Bible said about the Holy Spirit. God had given Jesse opportunities to share and words to speak.

A worker from another department began asking questions about his faith. Though she never attended the Friday morning study with the mechanics, Jesse was able to tell her what the Bible said about how to have a relationship with God. She had prayed with Jesse to receive eternal and abundant life through Jesus Christ.

But when no one showed up, he wasn't sure he had it in him to continue. He had read in the Bible that he had been saved by grace through faith to do the good work God had prepared for him, but was this it? Shouldn't good work have better results? What was even the point to this?

*"This is your training ground,"* a voice spoke to him.

While reaching into his pocket for his car keys, Jesse looked up, startled. There was no one else in the parking lot, but he had for sure heard a voice speak straight into his heart.

He mulled over what the voice said as he drove back to Richmond that day. Was God really speaking to him? This was his training ground? Training for what?

When he got home, he asked Kathy what she thought it might mean. Her guess was as good as his. Neither of them had any idea what he was training for, but whatever it was, Jesse figured he'd better not quit. He decided to take Herb's advice and leave the results to God.

He went back to his Bible, the pages beginning to feel familiar and worn, and back to his knees in prayer to see what God wanted him to say next Friday to anyone who showed up.

This was his training ground, even if he had no idea what it was for.

# 16

*Spring 1987*

# THE CALL

*So we keep on praying for you, asking our God to enable you to live a life worthy of his call. May he give you the power to accomplish all the good things your faith prompts you to do.*

—2 Thessalonians 1:11 NLT

"Where's Jesse?" Cindy asked when she got home. Cindy was Kathy's friend from university who had recently returned from New Zealand and needed a temporary place to live. Since Jesse and Kathy's house on Berry Road had an extra room in the basement, Cindy had moved in while she looked for a more permanent place.

"He's gone to the evening service at church," Kathy replied.

"I'll be home the rest of the night. Why don't you join him?"

Kathy glanced at her watch and thought about it for a moment. The twins and baby were already in bed, so she still might be able to catch the end of the service. She thanked Cindy, grabbed her keys, and headed off to join her husband at church.

She chuckled to herself as she drove the few blocks to the church, thinking about how much had changed. Two years ago she hadn't been able to drag Jesse to church—and when he did go, the chances of him falling asleep were high. Now Jesse was eager to go to church, even on his own sometimes.

The only thing that rivalled Jesse's new spiritual appetite was his physical one. For his small stature, the man could put away an incredible amount of food.

People always thought he must have hollow legs. And spiritually, it was the same. He couldn't seem to get enough of God.

They still weren't sure what Jesse was training for, but their hearts had been primed with the words of encouragement Jesse received in the parking lot that day. They were both listening.

Instead of going out for drinks with the guys after work, his desire was to be present with his family. He no longer turned on the TV after taking a power nap after work.

On a recent visit, Kathy's sister had said, "Something's different! The TV is off."

Jesse had changed so much that she had started calling him "New Creation" instead of her usual terms of endearment. Life wasn't perfect, but there was a peace between them that hadn't been there before. It was like he didn't need constant noise and activity anymore.

Kathy smiled as she pulled into the church parking lot. She snuck quietly into the back of the building and scanned the sanctuary to see where Jesse was sitting.

Just then, he turned around and spotted her. His eyes widened and his expression told her that this wasn't just any ordinary evening service.

She quietly made her way towards him, searching his face for any clues as to what was going on.

"I was just sitting here thinking, *I wish Kathy was here,*" he whispered to her when she sat down. "I feel like we need to go forward and ask the church to pray for us. I think God might be calling us to go into ministry."

Kathy marvelled at the way God was always working all things together for good, evidenced in the simplest thing like getting her to church that night. She'd had no idea this was stirring in Jesse when Cindy had offered to babysit the sleeping children, but of course God was at work. He always was.

Together they walked to the front of the church and told their small spiritual family all that they understood at the time: they were training for something, maybe ministry, and whatever it was, they were all-in.

# 17

*Summer 1987*

# THE FLEECE

*The one who calls you is faithful, and he will do it.*

—1 Thessalonians 5:24

A lthough they were all-in, neither knew quite what they were all-in for. So they decided to take a few days to get away without the kids and pray about it.

"What do you think about seminary?" Jesse asked as they strolled through Stanley Park.

Their church was part of a larger family of churches that had recently opened a seminary in Cochrane, Alberta. The thought of getting more training had piqued Jesse's curiosity, though he doubted that age forty was the ideal time to start a new endeavour, especially an academic one. It had been almost two decades since he'd been a student, and he had never completed his studies.

Jesse enjoyed his work as a mechanic, but restlessness was growing within him. Plus all the noise at work had damaged his hearing. He wanted a change. Maybe this was God's way of ushering him into something new?

But he was certain he wouldn't be able to work full-time to provide for his family while trying to carry the academic load of a full-time student. This was a problem for a man like Jesse who worked hard to provide for his family.

"What do *you* think about the new seminary?" Kathy asked, throwing the question right back at him.

"I think it might be the thing God is calling us to do. But I know I would be out of my league, and I know I couldn't work and study at the same time. How would we live?"

"I don't know, but if God is telling us to do it, I'm sure He has a way to provide," she replied confidently.

In her few years of walking with God, Kathy had already checked off lots of answered prayers in her journal. This included everything from a new dress she wanted but couldn't afford to Jesse choosing to follow Jesus, and much in between.

God had brought them this far. Surely He wouldn't stop being faithful now.

"Someone told me we should put out a fleece," Kathy said. "They said it's in the Bible."

Jesse looked at her quizzically before they both broke out laughing, realizing that neither of them knew what it meant to put out a fleece. They were still relatively new at following Jesus and reading the Bible.

"Let's look," Jesse replied.

Kathy pulled out her Bible and together they found the story of Gideon and the fleece in the book of Judges. Gideon hadn't known what he was supposed to do in battle so he had put out a fleece and asked God to make it wet to confirm that he was hearing the right instructions. And when he still wasn't sure, he did it again, this time asking for it to be dry. Then he asked a third time, to make it wet again.

"Maybe we could try that," Jesse suggested. "But what would be our fleece?"

Kathy pondered the question carefully. "If you're saying that you don't think you'll be able to work, then let's ask God to show us that He will provide the money to live on—if going to seminary is what He wants us to do."

Together they bowed their heads and prayed, telling God they were willing to go, and asking Him to confirm this by showing how He would provide for their family.

———

A few days later, the phone rang. Kathy answered, "Hello?"

"Hi Kath, it's Mom. I'm calling because Dad was offered a short-term contract in the Philippines and I think we're going to take it. Since it's only two years, we don't want to sell the house. We thought you guys might like the chance to save some money."

As Kathy listened to her mother Evelyn's idea, all she could think about was the fleece. The suggestion was for the family to move into Kathy's parents' house since they could rent it for less than they could earn by renting out their house on Berry Road. The difference would end up in their pockets.

Kathy hung up the phone slowly. It had only been a week since they'd prayed for God to show them how He would provide.

*I think we might be going to seminary,* she thought to herself.

She couldn't wait for Jesse to get home so she could tell him. She wasn't entirely sure what the whole wet fleece was supposed to look like, but she was pretty sure this news could be the beginning of it.

# 18

*Summer 1987*

# THE YACKLES

*And God is able to bless you abundantly, so that in all things at all times, having all that you need, you will abound in every good work.*

—2 Corinthians 9:8

After taking some time to process the offer from her parents, Kathy and Jesse decided to stay put in their home on Berry Road. Bill and Evelyn's house was bigger, but the street was busier, making it less ideal for their young family. Their three girls were all under five. It didn't make sense to uproot them.

Since their "fleece" had been asking God to show them how He would provide, anything they collected over and above the $700 her parents wanted for rent would become their seminary savings. With the help of Kathy's friend's realtor husband Jerry, they put a rental ad in the newspaper. Jerry had warned them that it would be difficult to rent, given the location; nevertheless, he suggested listing it high since any potential renter would surely negotiate the price down.

The house had seemed like their answer to prayer, but reality kept bursting their bubble of hope. They got no bites. The idea of the seminary fund didn't appear to hold much promise.

But now someone was interested.

"Hi Kathy, it's Jerry," the realtor said over the phone one day. "Are you available tonight? There are some people who are interested in renting the house."

Kathy felt hope rise in her heart as she got ready for Jerry to pick her up. Since this was the only interest anyone had shown, Jerry's advice was to meet them and try to get a contract signed as soon as possible before they changed their mind.

As they made their way up the front walk and entered the home, Kathy immediately noticed the words staring back at her from the front hall: "May the peace of Christ that transcends all understanding guard your hearts and minds in Christ Jesus." Her heartbeat quickened. There was a Bible verse splashed on the wall? These were the only people who'd expressed interest in renting?

Jerry immediately wanted to get on with signing the contract, but Kathy couldn't keep her curiosity to herself.

"Are you a believer?" Kathy asked.

"Why, yes!" exclaimed Mrs. Yackle. She explained that her husband had been a doctor on the mission field and they had just returned to Richmond and were in the market for a home to live in with their two young boys. "Are you?"

Kathy nodded, not quite sure what was unfolding in front of her.

Mrs. Yackle continued. "When I told my husband we had to inquire about this ad, he asked me why. This was a house for rent and we were looking for a house to buy. I told him I didn't know why, but it caught my eye and something told me we just needed to do it. So tell me, what's the story here?"

Kathy sat down at the kitchen table with Mrs. Yackle. The story about Jesse giving his life to Jesus, the call to seminary, and putting out the fleece spilled out of her like they were old friends.

"Do you two know each other?" Jerry asked, puzzled, impatient, and slightly curious. He was eager to get the contract signed.

"No, but it sure feels like we do!" Kathy exclaimed.

Their instant connection and fellowship could only be explained by their common faith in Jesus.

Mrs. Yackle assured Kathy that she would get back to her as soon as she and Dr. Yackle had further discussed it.

As Kathy and Jerry headed back to the front entrance to say goodbye, the Yackles' parrot squawked, "Boys, brush your teeth!" And then, "You must be born again!"

———————

Every time the phone rang for the next few days, Kathy wondered if it would mean a renter for her parents' house and the beginning of their seminary fund.

"Hello?" Kathy asked as she answered an incoming call.

It was Mrs. Yackle. "Kathy, we've decided we are going to put off buying a house. My husband and I talked, and it's obvious that God is in this and we want to be part of what He's doing. We're going to rent the house for $1,200 a month. We'll give you postdated cheques for the next two years, $700 to your parents, and $500 to you and Jesse."

Kathy could hardly believe her ears as she hung up the phone.

"Jesse, we're going to seminary!"

Jerry was shocked that a couple with kids who played outside would want to live on that busy street.

Soon after this experience—having witnessed the fellowship between Kathy and Mrs. Yackle and God's miraculous provision—Kathy led the realtor to receive Jesus's gift of salvation.

God's plan was beginning to take shape. It was becoming easier for Jesse to embrace his training ground now that he knew what he was training for.

# 19

*September 1989*

# THE HURDLE

*And hope does not put us to shame, because God's love has been poured out into our hearts through the Holy Spirit, who has been given to us.*

—Romans 5:5

K athy glanced out the kitchen window as she heard a car pull into the back parking area at their new home in Cochrane. Jesse was home from his first day of seminary!

God had paved the way for them to come here. She was sure of that. How else could a person explain a mechanic now studying theology? Everyone had seen the 180-degree transformation in Jesse since the day he had surrendered to Jesus only three and a half years earlier.

They had saved $500 every month for the past two years thanks to God providing through the Yackles. Kathy smiled, remembering how seamless it had all been. Nothing had gone wrong with the house during the family's entire tenancy. Nothing had even required maintenance.

Kathy still couldn't believe they had been willing to rent and put off buying a house, all for the sake of joining in the work God was doing in Jesse and her.

God had even provided a house for them in Cochrane. The Richmond real estate market was doing well, so their house on Berry Road sold easily. The lower market in Cochrane brought down their costs considerably. The money they had saved was enough to cover their living expenses for the first year, affording Jesse the opportunity to focus solely on his studies.

Jesse's sister travelled with her family from Texas to assist with the move.

Jesse and Kathy's church family at Towers, whom they had grown to know and love, had thrown a big celebration to see them off into this new chapter. Kathy had bawled her eyes out, as she often did when her heart was full of emotion.

Kathy was so grateful that God had provided a spiritual family for her as she'd begun her faith journey. Pastor Ron and his wife Jaylene had been instrumental in growing her faith and encouraging her as she prayed and loved Jesse.

When Ron and Jaylene had moved on to their next assignment, God had brought Henry Blackaby to Towers as interim pastor. Henry had met with Jesse every Wednesday morning at 6:00 a.m. and taught Jesse all about experiencing God in day-to-day living. He'd always encouraged Jesse to believe that God was continually at work around him, and to join God in whatever He was doing. A crisis of belief, as Henry called it, required faith and action.

Jesse had grown so much in his faith through his time with Henry.

By the time they departed for Cochrane in 1989, Pastors Ray and Patsy Woodard had come to lead the church.

Kathy was overflowing with gratitude for the family of God. In many ways, she felt like these people God had brought into their lives had helped to raise them, spiritually speaking—not unlike the way she and Jesse were raising their own daughters.

Kathy had prayed and trusted that God would bring the same kind of family in the new place He had called them to. And with that, they loaded their life into a U-Haul and headed east.

Their kids made instant friends with their neighbours. Kathy prayed for the family next door—Barb, Jim, Natalie, and Hailey. Who knew? Maybe it would be the beginning of faith and a lifelong friendship.

On the first day of school, the twins reported all their excitement, and Kathy couldn't wait to hear how seminary had gone for Jesse.

But as she peered out the window and noticed his furrowed brow and sunken shoulders, she suspected that his first day hadn't gone as well as the twins'.

*Uh-oh*, she thought as he made his way to the back door.

The fact that God had obviously called Jesse to seminary hadn't erased his apprehensions about the academic world. But Kathy had been optimistic.

As Jesse entered the back door, Kathy's worries were confirmed.

"What was I thinking?" Jesse muttered as he tossed a pile of seminary textbooks and syllabi onto the counter. His day had been completely overwhelming.

At forty-two, Jesse was older than all his classmates—and he was the only one who had been out of school for more years than he'd been in it.

While smart and capable, Jesse hadn't exactly applied himself to studying in his earlier years. Most children in the Philippines didn't begin school until age six or seven, but at the age of four Jesse had told his older brother Bert, who was fifteen at the time, "I want to go to school."

"Okay, let's go," Bert had said.

When the teacher had seen Jesse's intelligence, she'd admitted him even though he was younger than the starting age.

Jesse had always loved learning, but by the time he entered high school he had grown more interested in his friends. School often got in the way of Jesse's fun, so he simply skipped it. The movies were far more enjoyable.

His lack of consistent attendance quickly caught up to him. Four years of high school studies took him six years to complete. Jesse's carefree habits only angered his father, adding more tension to their already strained relationship.

Jesse had had every intention of getting an education. He'd enrolled in political science courses at night on his own dime and continued working in his father's shop during the day.

But after finding success and stability in automotive mechanics, he had put the academic world behind him. Because of that, Jesse had never learned how to write a paper or study.

Now, all these years later, he was feeling the consequences of being a delinquent student.

Kathy hadn't seen this dejected side of Jesse for some time, but she had seen the slumped shoulders and defeat in his eyes so often in their early years of marriage. It seemed like anytime he felt like a failure or went up against a task for which he felt ill-equipped, feelings of inadequacy worked their way to the surface.

But since becoming a follower of Jesus, Jesse hadn't lived in defeat, and for the most part defeat hadn't made too many appearances.

At this moment, defeat was written on every part of him.

He slumped down, his elbows on the kitchen table and his forehead resting on his fingers as he massaged his temples.

Kathy searched for the right words. Faith and fear wrestled inside of her.

They had given up everything to follow God to seminary. They'd left both of their extended families, Jesse's stable job at the dealership, and uprooted their life. They had even sold their home, leaving their friends and everything that was comfortable and familiar. Every egg was now in this one basket—even their family. They knew they wanted to add to their family, but they'd decided to put that on hold until seminary was done.

Had they heard wrong?

Maybe Jesse could get a job as a mechanic here. Maybe there was still an exit ramp.

Kathy shook her head as if to loosen the doubts beginning to take root in her mind and sat next to her discouraged husband.

"I can't do this," Jesse moaned.

Kathy saw the sullenness and defeat descending over his face like dusk. This was the part she feared. When something in life pressed on his woundedness, he shut down. She never knew it was happening until she found herself on the outside of his closed and locked door. Once it happened, it often felt too late.

Words spilled out of her before she could think about their impact. "Jesse, it's too late. We're already here. No going back now!"

It was immediately obvious that these words weren't helpful.

"What can I do to help?" she asked.

He sighed, feeling helpless.

"Do you want to pray?"

The look on his face told her he wasn't in a position to receive help or prayer. *Sorry I asked,* she thought to herself. But she would pray as she always did.

They had gone through more hopeless times than this. Her journey with God, which had become their journey with God, had always been full of moments of promise and hope followed by discouragement and obstacles. Would this life of faith ever get easier?

Fortunately, the pain and messiness always seemed to carry her straight back to the Lord, the same way it had all those years ago. God would be faithful, even if Kathy couldn't see how.

# 20

*Fall 1989*

# THE TUTOR

*Two are better than one, because they have a good return for their labor...*
　　　　　　　　　　　　　　　　　　　　　—Ecclesiastes 4:9

"**H**ey Jesse!"

Jesse looked up from his study table in the small seminary library to see his classmate Kevin Trick wave and walk towards him. The younger man was carrying a pile of papers.

The weightiness Jesse had felt during the first week of classes had only gotten heavier with each passing day and lecture, but he'd kept it hidden inside. On the outside, he was still Jesse—friendly, gentle, energetic, and easygoing, enjoying meeting new friends and professors in this new season of his life.

He rubbed his temples. How was he going to do this? As Kathy had so kindly reminded him, there was no going back.

When he had surrendered to Jesus, a weight had been lifted from his shoulders and he had experienced the peace of God like he hadn't before. He still knew he had peace with God.

That didn't mean life didn't feel weighty. Jesse had always had a strong desire for integrity and doing the right thing. It simply wasn't a light load. But this was the path God had called him to. Jesse knew there was no going back, but he certainly couldn't see the way through. He'd only started reading the Bible three years ago. Studying it at this higher level felt like a big challenge.

As Pastor Henry had taught him, following the call to seminary was a crisis of belief that required faith and action. Jesse had faith and had taken action on this call.

But was it up to Jesse to figure this thing out? That's what it had been like in his dad's shop back in the Philippines. Jesse had been expected to know what to do and do it perfectly. Mistakes hadn't been allowed.

Surely this wouldn't be the same. Surely God would help him even now.

Jesse hoped so. Studying felt like death by a thousand cuts. There was the language barrier with the professors, the speed at which they lectured, and just the sheer volume of new information.

He leaned back in his chair, pushing his thoughts aside and gesturing for his friend to sit down.

Kevin took a seat, set the papers down on the table, and slid them across to Jesse.

"What's this?" Jesse asked, scanning them for clues.

Kevin shrugged. "Every day after classes I go home and type out my notes. I just thought I'd print two copies. I wasn't sure, but I thought this might be helpful?"

Relief washed over Jesse. He was drowning and Kevin had thrown him a life preserver. Jesse was holding a few pages of succinctly typed summaries of every class he'd attended in the past week. He'd been scrambling in class to listen while taking notes, trying not to forget anything.

For the first time that week, he felt like his head was above water. The weight he'd felt since that first day of school began to lift.

"Thanks, man," he offered, feeling like his words were inadequate to express the gratitude and relief he felt. "I'm in way over my head. I knew I needed help but didn't really know where to go."

"I thought you were looking a little overwhelmed this week," Kevin said. "You mentioned that it's been a while since you've been in school. I do this anyway for myself, so I thought it might help."

Jesse felt at home around Kevin. His brother Doug had been a translator of the Bible in the Philippines and his affinity for Filipino people and culture had made Jesse feel comfortable. It had made Kevin's offer to help study for tests and write papers easy to receive. Jesse had turned out to be a tutor and friend all in one.

Kevin's typed summaries were a continuous gift. They freed Jesse to listen and understand during lectures rather than focus on recording everything. He could read the notes over and over again until the information stuck. When Jesse had questions, he could simply ask.

God had called Jesse here. He alone was the one who had initiated and invited Jesse on this adventure—first to a relationship with Jesus Christ, to a brand-new life, to his training ground, and now to seminary.

When Jesse paused to glance in the rearview mirror, he could see that God had always provided. There was no room for pride or figuring things out on his own.

For this specific leg of the journey, God had provided the finances, and now He had provided this friend. Jesse didn't know what was next, but it was becoming more and more obvious that God's specialty seemed to be showing up when Jesse came to the end of himself.

Whatever God wanted to accomplish through him, he would continue to cooperate. God would see him through.

# 21

*January 1990*

# GOING HOME

*For I am not ashamed of the gospel, because it is the power of God that brings salvation to everyone who believes: first to the Jew, then to the Gentile.*

—Romans 1:16

Kathy listened to her husband's long-distance plea with the corded kitchen phone tucked between her ear and shoulder.

"I have the gospel," Jesse began, "and these people need to know how they can know Jesus. But I don't know how to share it in my dialect. Please pray!"

Jesse's father Zachary had passed away somewhat suddenly, sending Jesse back to the Philippines for the funeral. He was connecting with family members and old friends, many he hadn't seen since immigrating sixteen years prior. And he might never see them again.

Jesse wasn't sure where his father had stood with Jesus when he died, but Jesse was hopeful. He was the first person to drive his father's car after his death and the radio had been set to a Christian station. Perhaps his father had heard the gospel and responded to Jesus's gift of salvation.

Kathy heard urgency in Jesse's voice, fuelled by his unwavering conviction that Jesus was the only way to live truly and fully alive. Yet he was unable to communicate about Jesus clearly. Not every word from English translated clearly into his dialect, Pampango.

Having a relationship with God through Jesus Christ had completely transformed Jesse's life. The moment Jesse had trusted in Jesus's life, death, and resurrection for his salvation, a miraculous exchange had taken place.

Jesus had taken Jesse's sin—everything wrong he'd ever done and the wrongs done to him—and in exchange given Jesse his own perfect, righteous, and spotless life. This meant that Jesse had peace with God. When God now looked at Jesse, He saw Jesus. In Christ, Jesse didn't only have the promise of heaven when his time on earth was done, but the opportunity to live abundant life in the present.

And it was all a gift. Jesse had received it with humble gratitude, not asking Jesus how much he owed for it. It was real and personal, not because of what he had read or been told but because of the change he'd seen in his wife and himself.

Since that February day, Jesse had been different. Everyone around him knew it.

Though several years had passed, Jesse still couldn't stop telling people about this good news. His warm smile, non-threatening stature, and easygoing personality engaged and disarmed people in everyday conversation. His conversations naturally turned to Jesus, no different from how one would effortlessly share good news about a new member of the family.

This news was too good not to share. If anyone would listen, Jesse would tell them about Jesus. How could he not? It came as naturally to Jesse as breathing.

In English, at least. It was the language in which he'd first heard the good news, and thus far the only language he communicated in about faith.

But here Jesse was in the Philippines, amongst hurting and grieving people searching for answers, with the greatest news ever but unable to share it in a language his people could understand.

Kathy rallied all the praying people she knew and relayed Jesse's plea. Together, their community of faith asked God for help.

———

Kathy continued to pray, as did those she shared the request with, having no idea how God was going to work it out. She prayed continually and waited expectantly.

Sure enough, the next phone call from Jesse came with good news. Kathy listened with joy as he relayed the surprising answer to their prayer for help.

Jesse had found himself in a conversation with an elderly gentleman in the community. Through a broken mixture of English and Pampango, he had attempted to share the good news about having eternal life through faith in Jesus Christ with this man who was willing to listen.

"Wait," the man said, interrupting Jesse with a raised hand. "I think I know what you're trying to tell me."

The elderly man's daughter was a born again believer in Jesus Christ, and she had shared the gospel with her father many times. Though the elderly man had never decided to follow Jesus, he knew all about it. His daughter had communicated to him so clearly and so often that he was able to relay the good news to Jesse in Pampango with perfect clarity.

This was becoming a pattern. Humility, accessed by acknowledging their own insufficiency, combined with a mustard seed of faith, consistently preceded demonstrations of the power of God in and through their lives.

With God, all things were possible. Their lives held so much proof.

Jesus seemed to delight in bringing what was dead to life when humility was combined with faith. When Kathy acknowledged her own dead efforts, Jesus moved in powerfully. The wisest thing either of them could do was quit trying to do anything on their own.

When they couldn't see a way, God always made one. And once again God provided. Their weakness was God's strength, just like the Bible said.

God had answered their prayer in the most unexpected way—through a man who wasn't even a follower of Jesus. With humility and faith, God had moved another mountain.

# 22

*1991*

# THE POSITION PROVISION

*Now he who supplies seed to the sower and bread for food will also supply and increase your store of seed and will enlarge the harvest of your righteousness.*
—2 Corinthians 9:10

Kathy relayed to Jesse the message she had picked up off the answering machine when he returned home from classes that day. Martin Schmitke, manager of the Town of Cochrane, had called.

"What did he want?" Jesse asked, brow furrowed. He had built a detached garage at the rear of their house earlier that year. Was it not to code? Was there a problem with the colour of the siding?

Kathy shrugged. "He didn't say, only that he wanted to talk to you and to please call him back."

Jesse nervously dialled the number. They couldn't afford a mistake like that right now.

But thankfully, the voice he heard on the other end of the line sounded friendly. "Hi Jesse. I heard you and your wife Kathy speak at the Valentine's banquet at Cochrane Alliance Church not too long ago."

"Yes, that's right."

The town manager had been in the audience? So far so good. Maybe this wasn't about the siding.

"I'm calling because I want to offer you a job," Martin continued. "I want you to work for the Town of Cochrane part-time as our in-house mechanic. Until now, we've always contracted mechanics. Are you interested?"

Jesse was stunned. The way God had taken care of them was a story in itself.

As the first year of seminary had come to an end, so had their seminary savings fund. Jesse and Kathy had gotten back on their knees, asking God for a way to provide.

In the summer of 1990, with his first year of study behind them, Jesse and Kathy had travelled back home to Richmond to visit family and friends. While visiting, their three girls had attended Vacation Bible School (VBS) at Towers and Kathy volunteered. Pastor Ray then invited Jesse to preach.

A few weeks after returning home, the phone had rung. It was Pastor Ray.

"A woman named Sara Levy from Mississippi was in the audience the day Jesse preached," Ray explained. "She had been visiting her daughter, and her grandson was in Kathy's VBS group. She wants to provide textbooks and tuition until Jesse graduates."

Kathy had almost dropped the phone. A complete stranger had just happened to be visiting from another country the same Sunday Jesse had just happened to be guest preaching? And she was going to pay the remainder of Jesse's seminary expenses?

It had seemed too good to be true, but a few weeks later Kathy held the cheque in her hands. The remaining years of seminary had been provided for in their entirety.

Nothing seemed to be impossible for God. If God could do this, surely he could provide a job for Jesse. Sure enough, he found work as a small engine mechanic in the fall of 1990 and adjusted his academic load for the second year of studies so that he could steward both responsibilities well.

But then, as Christmas approached, Jesse had been unexpectedly laid off. He and Kathy hadn't had any idea what to do, or how they were going to buy gifts for their girls.

One afternoon during Jesse's post-school power nap on the living room floor, the doorbell had rung.

Since Jesse slept like a rock and didn't move, Kathy answered. To her surprise, she'd found a small group of women dressed as elves. They were from the Cochrane Activettes and had come bearing boxes of food and gifts for the girls.

Christmas had been provided for.

As the calendar turned over to 1991, Kathy had continued her routine of cleaning houses and teaching piano. God had faithfully provided, but Jesse still needed a job. By the time they spoke at the Valentine's banquet, they had been unsure of how they would make ends meet.

And now here Jesse was being offered a job—a job that hadn't even existed the day before.

"How did you know I was looking for a job?" Jesse asked, surprised and puzzled.

"I'm not exactly sure how," Martin said slowly. "I just felt like the Lord lead me to create a part-time position for you."

Jesse hung up the phone in awe. Working for the Town of Cochrane meant a stable job with a salary and benefits. His kids could finally go to the dentist!

Though he was still unable to fully grasp what had happened, he relayed the good news to Kathy. God had provided yet again and they were utterly amazed at His goodness.

# 23

*1992*

# THE SPARK

*But you will receive power when the Holy Spirit comes on you; and you will be my witnesses in Jerusalem, and in all Judea and Samaria, and to the ends of the earth.*

—Acts 1:8

"Watch for Filipino people," Jesse reminded his daughters as they got out of the van.

Ever since his trip back home for his father's funeral, Jesse had felt his heart growing to reach Filipino people with the good news of Jesus. Sharing Jesus with his own people had lit a flame in him.

The only problem was, Jesse didn't know any Filipinos in Cochrane. Unlike their previous home in Vancouver and Richmond, Cochrane wasn't exactly a place of diversity. When they'd moved there three years earlier, Jesse had been one of only three non-Caucasian adults living in the town—and the only Filipino.

When Angela and Christina had begun Grade Two, they'd been teased as they walked home for being "Chinese." The children at their school had never seen classmates with black hair and darker skin.

Jesse smiled, remembering how his girls, almost seven at the time, had handled themselves. Tired of the taunting, Angela had turned and chased them down. One boy got away, but she had caught and pinned down the other in the alley, two garages away from their house.

"Go get Mom," she'd told Christina. "She will know what to do."

The boy escaped, but the damage was done. By the time both girls made it to the house, they were in tears, hurt and unsure of why they had been the object of scorn. After lunch, Kathy had walked them back to the schoolyard and asked them to point out the boy.

No longer confident and cocky, the wide-eyed boy had listened attentively as Kathy firmly but lovingly explained, "My daughters are not Chinese. They are half-Filipino, because their dad is from the Philippines. And even if they were Chinese, that would be no reason to make fun of them."

The boy nodded enthusiastically, and from that point on he became the educator.

"See those girls over there?" he would say when the twins walked by. "They're half-Filipino. Their dad is from the Philippines." He seemed proud to hold this insider information.

Jesse wanted to reach Filipinos, but how would he do it if there weren't any around? Maybe the family could move back to the Vancouver area once he finished seminary.

But Jesse's recent field education project for seminary had awakened his heart to the possibility that there was a mission field in Calgary, not far from his new home. They had been instructed to survey the spiritual beliefs and needs of a desired group, and Jesse had focused on Filipinos. He'd brought the survey everywhere he went in the hopes of meeting Filipinos and making relational connections.

Watching for Filipino people had become a regular practice for the entire family. While they were running errands or getting groceries, they'd stop to make conversation with Filipino people they met. Filipinos were always thrilled to make a connection to their life back home. Jesse would ask questions about their spiritual beliefs and if they felt there was a need for an evangelical church for Filipinos in Calgary.

Often while in conversation, God would nudge Jesse's heart to not only survey but also share the gospel of Jesus. When people responded in faith and received eternal life, he was thrilled.

But the more people that said yes to Jesus, the more Jesse began to sense that God might be calling him to reach Filipino people in Calgary. Only Jesse didn't know the first thing about starting a church or leading one. His faith was only as old as his youngest daughter.

However, from his six years of experience following Jesus, Jesse knew that God's specialty was making a way when he couldn't see it. Though he couldn't see how starting a Filipino church in Calgary was possible, Jesse knew his only responsibility was to listen and obey.

# 24

*1992*

# BROTHERHOOD

*A friend loves at all times, and a brother is born for a time of adversity.*
—Proverbs 17:17

Jesse always seemed to find himself outnumbered by women. Growing up, he had been surrounded by sisters. Even though he had two brothers, there were eleven years between him and his older brother Bert, and seven between Jesse and his younger brother Lope, leaving plenty of space for all three of them to be sandwiched by sisters.

He and Kathy had only daughters. And now Jesse found himself leading a Bible study entirely made up of women.

Each May, seminary students were invited to different churches across Canada to preach, and Jesse had preached at Cambrian Heights Baptist Church in Calgary.

When Jesse had finished preaching, he was approached by a Filipino woman named Merlyn. She asked for his help leading a Bible study at her downtown apartment.

Jesse agreed. Every Sunday afternoon, his family piled into the van to drive the forty minutes to downtown Calgary.

Whether at home or Bible study, it always seemed to be Jesse and the girls. He loved his family and those God had called him to serve, but it wasn't the same connection that brotherhood carried.

At seminary, Jesse experienced the positive impact of having friendships with godly men. He and Kevin and their small band of brothers, who had all begun seminary at the same time, were in the trenches together trying to figure out how to be godly husbands and fathers, and to lead well in ministry. Jesse and Kevin had forged an authentic friendship as they studied and repaired broken-down minivans together.

He and Kevin talked openly about their pasts and the desire not to repeat them. They both wanted to be better husbands and fathers than what had been modelled in their lives. Neither was entirely sure how, but at least they were in it together. As they exchanged notes and wrenches, they talked about the challenge of learning to love their wives as Christ loved them and what it meant to raise their children in a loving home.

Jesse was hungry to know how to be a godly husband and loving father. Neither came naturally to him. Verbal affirmation and affection weren't a natural part of Filipino culture, yet that seemed to be what his wife and daughters desired from him. There were so many things in his life Jesse needed faith for, including this one.

Even though Jesse knew he had a new identity in Christ, old tapes occasionally played in his head telling him he wasn't good enough and not up to the task. The Bible told him of a very real enemy who was on the prowl seeking to devour, and Jesse was learning to recognize the spiritual battle that often began in the mind.

Though it was a struggle, Jesse wasn't deterred from following Jesus in his role as a husband and father. It didn't come naturally, but he wanted to learn to love like Jesus. And that began in his home.

Neither Kevin nor Jesse had answers, but asking the questions together somehow connected them. They were fellow travellers, or perhaps fellow strugglers headed in the same direction.

Kevin's full course load and Jesse's reduced one meant that Kevin was going to graduate one year ahead of Jesse. This had only grown in Jesse a greater desire for more authentic relationships like the one he had experienced.

But the current Bible study group had only women, no brothers in the faith.

It was then that Jesse and all his girls—his family and the women in the Bible study—started praying that God would send them some men.

# 25

*1992*

# THE ANSWER TO PRAYER

*He fulfills the desires of those who fear him; he hears their cry and saves them.*

—Psalm 145:19

"Jesse, I want you to meet someone," his coworker said, gesturing towards him.
Jesse looked up to see a Filipino man, probably a bit younger than him, walking towards him with his coworker.

*This must be the guy he was telling me about,* Jesse thought. *Could he be the answer to our prayers for men?*

"Kumusta," Jesse said to the stranger, offering the usual greeting of their culture. It meant "Hello" and "How are you?" all in one.

The man introduced himself as Greg. He had immigrated to Calgary with his family in 1989. He had two children and his wife was expecting. He had been working at a job site removing scrap building materials when he'd met Jesse's coworker, who had insisted that he and Jesse meet.

After exchanging pleasantries Greg asked, "Why did you move your family to a rural community? Filipinos always live in the city when they immigrate."

"I'm studying at the seminary here and I hope to start a Filipino church in Calgary someday," Jesse explained.

"I'm not a born again Christian." Greg went on to explain that when he had worked in Saudi Arabia, he'd attended a Bible study but never made a decision to give his life to Jesus.

"Can you buy rice here?" Greg asked

Jesse laughed comfortably and shook his head. "Not the kind we like."

Rice was a staple in their culture, and the stuff at the local grocery store wasn't authentic. Jesse explained that they made frequent trips into the city, especially if they needed to purchase Asian groceries, including rice.

Their shared culture gave them an instant connection and they exchanged phone numbers, planning to get together with their families. Jesse invited him to the upcoming Sunday afternoon Bible study at Merlyn's apartment.

Jesse couldn't wait to tell Kathy about his new friend. Greg wasn't a follower of Jesus yet, but Jesse had seen what was possible when God pursued a person who was willing to receive Him. Jesse had a feeling this might be the beginning of an answer to prayer.

# 26

# A CHURCH IS BORN

*...not giving up meeting together, as some are in the habit of doing, but encouraging one another—and all the more as you see the Day approaching.*

—Hebrews 10:25

Jesse sat in the front row, beads of sweat escaping his temples as he tried to calm his pounding heart by taking slow and deep breaths.

It was Easter Sunday in 1993 and approximately eighty people sat in the temporary rows behind him, filling the fellowship hall adjacent to the sanctuary at Cambrian Heights Baptist Church.

Greg, who had recently become a follower of Jesus, was almost finished leading the opening set of worship songs, which meant it was almost time for Jesse to stand up in front of all those people and preach.

A few weeks after meeting Greg and inviting him to Bible study, Kathy had glanced out Merlyn's apartment window one Sunday afternoon and exclaimed, "That guy's here and he brought his guitar!" A few of the other women peered out the window to see Greg and a friend approaching the apartment building.

God was answering their prayers and bringing men. Jesse was going to have some brothers in Christ, and they were one step closer to starting a church. As God drew Greg's heart towards Jesus, Greg was inviting his friends in whom God seemed to be working.

The Bible study quickly outgrew the apartment, so the group moved to the fellowship hall of the building where Jesse had preached only a year earlier.

One of the members of the Bible study had then suggested the idea to have a Filipino worship service to celebrate Easter. Their excitement grew as they made plans.

Studying at seminary was teaching him a lot, like how to prepare a sermon, but not how to avoid sweating buckets minutes before it was time to deliver it! Jesse felt like a rookie.

How had this all happened again? Leaving Richmond, going to seminary, the Bible study at Merlyn's, meeting Greg... and now here he was, preaching? Now Jesse could lead a Bible study in a small group comfortably. Sharing Jesus was like breathing. But preaching? He felt like his daughters when they had first been learning to walk—unnatural, awkward, and easily tripped up.

"Dad, it's not hot in here," I said from the next seat. "Why are you sweating so much?"

I sat on my hands, swinging my legs under the seat, clearly unaffected by the nerves that had worked their way through his entire body.

"It's okay." He tried to sound casual. "Don't worry about me."

He looked up to see all of Greg's sheet music fly off his music stand. Jesse breathed a sigh of relief. At least he wasn't the only nervous one. Together, with God guiding their steps, they would figure it out.

He breathed a quick prayer, offering his sweaty and shaky self to God for His purposes, and stood up to preach his first official sermon.

# 27

## *1994*
# THE RELUCTANT LEADER

*So Christ himself gave the apostles, the prophets, the evangelists, the pastors and teachers, to equip his people for works of service, so that the body of Christ may be built up…*

—Ephesians 4:11–12

Pastor Jesse. He wondered if he would ever get used to being called that. Jesse didn't feel like a pastor. The men who had been his pastors—Pastor Ron, Pastor Henry, Pastor Ray, and his current pastor, Hamish—were the pastor type, wiser and more qualified than he.

When the Bible study had first started, the women in Merlyn's apartment had just called him Jesse. As it had grown, they'd begun calling him Brother Jesse.

He hadn't been called this since his days at the dealership. His coworkers had started calling him Brother Jesse the day the announcement was made that he was born again. It was always said fondly, yet with a hint of mockery. The name stuck until his last day of working there when Petar, the spokesperson for the group, bid him farewell on behalf of all the mechanics with a heartfelt letter, expressing how proud they all were of him.

When the first person called him Pastor Jesse after the impromptu Filipino Easter worship service, he had been caught completely off-guard. After a minute of pondering, he'd reluctantly responded, "Well, if this is a church, I guess I'm the pastor."

Jesse knew God had called him to seminary and then to start a Filipino church. But being a pastor felt like a much bigger task than what Jesse could offer.

The only thing he knew for sure was that he didn't know the first thing about being a pastor. His faith was vibrant but still only eight years old. He shared Jesus freely and loved people fiercely, but he wasn't convinced he was a pastor. He wasn't the kind of guy who set out to blaze trails. He was simply saying yes to Jesus, his Saviour and Lord.

Kathy, who knew him best, always called him the reluctant leader. Surely God was the one behind all this, because somehow a church had started and Jesse had found himself the pastor. There was no other explanation for how Jesse, an immigrant from Dau, Mabalacat and mechanic from Vancouver was now pastoring a church in Calgary.

Jesse's sister-in-law had once said to his daughters, "When we first met your dad, the last thing we ever thought he would be was a pastor!" Jesse couldn't have agreed more. He hadn't even known what a pastor was a decade ago! It was the last thing Jesse had ever seen himself becoming.

But that didn't seem to matter to God. Reluctant or not, God was clearly at work.

Following that first worship service, the people wanted to begin to meet weekly. Jesse had said no. At the time, he'd still had his final year of seminary to finish.

Kevin had graduated around the same time as that service, though, and Jesse wondered how on earth he was going to make it through his final year without his tutor and friend.

"You're going to be okay," Kathy assured him.

Kevin had taught him well, and Kathy was convinced Jesse was ready to tackle his final year.

Prepping a sermon was an incredible amount of work for Jesse. He couldn't imagine doing it every single week. He had never been good at managing his time, especially when the task was one he didn't feel confident in.

Yet only one year after someone had first called him Pastor Jesse, he was standing before the congregation at the first official worship service of the Filipino Canadian Baptist Fellowship as their pastor. Jesse had the privilege of baptizing his new brother in Christ, Greg.

"Greg, have you repented of your sins and received Jesus Christ as your Lord and Saviour?" Jesse asked his friend as they both stood waist-deep in the waters of the baptismal tank at Cambrian Heights Baptist Church.

"Yes," Greg answered with one hand raised to publicly profess his newfound faith and life in Jesus.

"Then, Greg, I baptize you in the name of the Father, the Son, and the Holy Spirit. Buried with Christ." Jesse leaned his friend backwards, immersing him in the water for a split second, and then bringing him up out of the water. "Raised to new life in him."

As the congregation sang, Greg began splashing the water up all around him, unable to contain the joy exploding from him. Water flew out of the baptismal tank, hitting the stage and coming close to the people in the front row. There was no containing his joy... or the water.

This outward expression of an inward transformation never got old to Jesse. New life was what Jesus offered anyone who would believe. He'd died on the cross, taking the power of sin, guilt, shame, and fear to the grave, only to overcome it three days later when He rose from the dead. Jesus had buried Jesse's sin, guilt, and shame and now he was seeing the same powerful gospel at work in Greg.

When they'd first met, neither Jesse nor Greg knew the storm that was about to sweep into Greg's life.

At the time, Greg's wife had given birth to a baby girl. They had been shocked to discover she had serious disabilities and would not survive.

Jesse had been at the hospital to visit his new friend and congratulate him when he learned the tragic news. Greg and his wife wrestled with the thought of letting their beloved baby go when Greg had remembered the scrap piece of paper his wife's hospital roommate had pressed into his hands earlier that day. He took it out of his pocket and read: *"Read Isaiah 41:10. Whenever it says 'you,' read Katie."* Katie was the name of his new daughter.

Jesse had marvelled at the way God worked, positioning this woman in the hospital to offer hope to Greg and his wife as they grieved.

Though Greg hadn't owned a Bible, he remembered the one he had found at a city dump a few days earlier. He'd tossed it in the trunk of his car because he hadn't thought it belonged in the trash bin.

After receiving the prompting to read Isaiah 41:10, Greg dug out the Bible and read: *"Do not fear, for I am with Katie; do not be dismayed, for I am Katie's God. I will strengthen Katie and help Katie; I will uphold Katie with my righteous hand."*

After crying, he and his wife decided to give Katie to the Lord and they experienced incredible peace.

Jesse visited them many times during those difficult weeks and offered for the pastor of Cambrian to officiate the funeral. He watched as God met Greg in his grief. Greg accepted the invitation to come to the worship service at Cambrian Heights, the church the Filipino group had joined when they didn't have their own weekly service. That Sunday, he simply stopped fighting and walked down the aisle to receive Jesus as his Lord and Saviour.

Whether or not he was the pastor type, Jesse couldn't deny that God was at work. People were coming to know Jesus and being transformed. They were receiving the gift of salvation and being moved from darkness to light. They were finding a place to belong in the family of God, and they needed someone to lead them.

Jesse had nothing to brag about. He knew he had been called to live by faith, beyond what he was capable of in his own strength. But as long as he lived, he would brag about Jesus. He believed the words Jesus had spoken to Paul, words that he might as well have said to Jesse:

> But he said to me, *"My grace is sufficient for you, for my power is made perfect in weakness."* Therefore I will boast all the more gladly about my weaknesses, so that Christ's power may rest on me.
> —2 Corinthians 12:9

Jesse had that much going for him—a whole lot of weakness. But if that was the meeting place of God's power, he would simply keep following Jesus whether as Pastor Jesse, Brother Jesse, or just plain Jesse.

Jesus had rescued him from his sin, so Jesse would do anything He asked.

# INTERLUDE TWO

# 28

*May 2008*

# SOMETHING SOLID

*Surely there is something,* I thought as I frantically rummaged around my house. I was desperately looking for anything my dad had given to me over my twenty-two years.

Since the diagnosis a few weeks earlier, the ground beneath my feet had felt like it was shaking and slowly but surely crumbling. There was nowhere to run or hide from the diagnosis, nothing to stand on or grab hold of.

As this realization washed over me, I was overtaken by a desperate urge to find something I could physically hold in my hands. I had to find something and I had to find it now.

My search turned up the promise ring my dad had given me for my thirteenth birthday and the portable CD player he had given me for my birthday during my first year of college basketball.

Gifts were not his love language.

As I stared at the small pile with only two options to grasp—an obsolete music player or a tiny piece of jewellery—their futility dawned on me. Holding either of these wasn't going to help or comfort me.

The greatest gift my dad had given me wasn't stored in the bottom drawer of my desk or in a small velvet green case in the depths of my closet. It was much greater.

The next time I was at my parents' house, I headed downstairs to my dad's home office. My eyes scanned the built-in bookshelves until they located what I was looking for. Somewhere in his collection of notebooks and journals, the written record of the time he spent with God in prayer and reading the Bible, I would find something that represented his greatest gift to me.

I pulled them off one by one, quickly flipping through the pages and scanning to see what dates were recorded at the beginning of the entries.

Finally, my eyes landed on what I was looking for. I grasped the black leatherbound journal in my hands with the words *June 2003* scrawled on the first page.

It wasn't just the journal I wanted, but what it represented. This would show me how to not only have but hold onto the only thing that could get me through the darkest nights—the promises of God.

This was something my dad had done before. I had watched his dark and desperate season from a distance. Now I wanted and needed to know how he had held on to his faith.

Because I wanted to, too.

*Part Three*

# THE SLIPPERY SLOPE

# 29

## *Spring 1995*
## TENNESSEE

*Because we loved you so much, we were delighted to share with you not only the gospel of God but our lives as well.*

—1 Thessalonians 2:8

"D o you know what I'd love to do?" Jesse asked.

"What's that?" his new friend Brian asked from the passenger seat.

"A church camp."

A church camp would be a more immersive version of the revival that the church was experiencing this week.

Revival week turned out to be far more than Jesse could've imagined, both for his congregation and for himself. Nightly, the church gathered for praise, prayer, and to listen to the guest preacher from Nashville, Tennessee. Hours of fellowship followed late into the evening. No one was in a hurry to leave even though people had to get up for work the next morning.

Jesse loved having fun and sharing life, but more than anything he wanted people to trust Jesus as their Saviour and learn to follow Him as Lord. He took seriously the responsibility to shepherd the flock.

This revival week couldn't have come at a better time. It was helping to strengthen the people's faith, and it gave Jesse a break from carrying the leadership load by himself.

God had brought more people, particularly men, to their growing church. A new brotherhood had formed over hours of conversation, sharing meals, fishing trips, picnics, camping trips, and recently a road trip to Seattle for a Promise Keepers men's conference. This was Jesse's wheelhouse.

The church grew rapidly. People who were new to having a relationship with Jesus were inviting their friends who didn't know Him. It was an exciting time and God was on the move.

But this rapid growth presented a new challenge: their church was starting to feel more like an orphanage than a family. They needed spiritual mothers and fathers to help raise up all the spiritually new babies. Jesse and Kathy could only do so much.

Jesse was asking God for help. How would all these new believers grow in their faith?

Thankfully, their growing church was part of the Canadian National Baptist Convention, an organization that existed to connect, serve, and strengthen their family of churches. Jesse contacted the office and requested a guest preacher for their upcoming second-year anniversary service.

Of all his pastoral responsibilities, preaching by far took the most out of him.

To Jesse's delight, he was connected to Jim Powers, a veteran pastor from Nashville, Tennessee who was willing to come and preach. He and another man, Marvin, were happy to serve. Unbeknownst to Jesse, the Tennessee Baptist Convention was emphasizing missions to Canada around that same time, which meant they were ready and willing to partner with ministry needs and requests.

Jesse was so relieved and grateful that Jim would do all the preaching for a week of consecutive nightly worship services in the week leading up to the anniversary service. This weeklong break from the pulpit freed Jesse to do what came most naturally to him—dialogue with people, share life, love them, and talk about Jesus.

As a mechanic, Jesse's work had been clear cut: diagnose the vehicle, fix the problem, and get it back on the road. There was an obvious start and finish to the job and the workday. If the job wasn't finished, Jesse just clocked out, went home, and picked up where he'd left off the next day. The job was done when the car was fixed and he only fixed vehicles between 7:00 a.m. and 4:00 p.m. from Monday to Friday. The boundaries were clear.

Being a pastor was different. The work week, responsibilities, and boundaries were harder to define. During his time with the Bible study, he'd been juggling his load as a seminary student, part-time work as a mechanic, and taking care of his growing family. He'd squeezed in ministry wherever and whenever he could.

Though the seminary load had been off his plate since graduating the previous spring, his plate still felt like it was at capacity.

The middle of the week was filled with part-time mechanic work, being a husband and father, pastoral visits to people from his church, and leading Bible study. These were all life-giving to Jesse.

Then there was preaching. Of all his responsibilities, preparing his weekend sermon by far took the most out of him. Each week he worked a little longer and pushed a little harder. On Saturdays, he always found himself going over his sermon notes late into the night, seeing what he could improve. Since the church had transitioned from meeting monthly to weekly a year and a half earlier, Jesse had been questioning whether he could do it all. He knew God was the one to speak, but Jesse never felt ready for Sunday morning. He struggled to manage his time.

When Jesse picked up Jim and Marvin from the airport, there was a third man with them—Brian. In time, Jesse and Brian came to find out just how much they would share each other's loads in the days to come.

Jim and Brian had only briefly known each other, while Marvin and Brian were longtime friends. Marvin had stopped by Brian's farm two weeks before departing on his upcoming trip to Canada.

"I sure wish I could do something like that," Brian said after listening to Marvin excitedly describe the trip.

"Why don't you just come?" Marvin suggested. "We already have accommodations and work to do while we're there. All you need is a ticket."

Two weeks later, Brian was boarding the plane with Jim and Marvin.

Each night during their visit, Jim, Marvin, and Brian piled into Jesse's tiny car and drove from Cochrane to Cambrian Heights Baptist Church in Calgary where FilCan (the nickname for Filipino Canadian Baptist Fellowship) met. Brian, the largest in stature, was always offered the front passenger seat.

On these nightly drives, Jesse felt like he was talking to an old friend. Jesse was forty-seven; Brian was twenty-seven. Jesse was a Canadian immigrant from the Philippines; Brian was from Tennessee. Despite their differences, Jesse felt so at ease as they talked. They laughed. They understood each other.

Amongst their cultural differences, they found commonalities. Brian and Jesse's wives were both due to give birth in the next couple of months—Brian's firstborn and Jesse's fourth.[4] They shared excitement and nervousness over being new (and new again) dads.

They also shared a love for sports, namely basketball and football.

But most of all, they shared a heart to know Jesus and make Him known. Neither man felt particularly drawn to speaking in front of crowds, but they relished the opportunity to get into one-on-one conversations.

Brian felt called to start a church back home in Murfreesboro, Tennessee and plans were underway for him to do just that in the fall. Jesse's church was still in its infancy. Neither felt like they knew what they were doing.

So tucked into this revival week was a hidden gift: an unlikely friendship.

---

4  Between seminary and starting the church, there hadn't been an ideal time for Jesse and Kathy to once again expand their family. At forty-seven and thirty-seven respectively, they decided no time would ever be better to have their fourth baby.

# 30

# FAMILY CAMP

*In his defense Jesus said to them, "My Father is always at his work to this very day, and I too am working."*

—John 5:17

The first FilCan family church camp blew Jesse's expectations out of the water. The lives of his congregants were changed and challenged. They experienced God. And once again, it hadn't been up to Jesse to make it happen.

God was at work drawing hearts back to Him and into fellowship with the church. Many who hadn't previously been interested were asking questions about Jesus. Others said yes to following Jesus and committed their lives to God. Men were filled with spiritual courage. New believers were encouraged in their faith.

What God was doing couldn't be explained by Jesse's own talents or abilities. It was the Holy Spirit's work.

Jesse's new friend Brian came to help direct the camp and his team from Tennessee helped run it. The Tennessee crew did almost all the cooking for the one hundred fifty people who attended, but of course they had a bit of help to add Filipino flavour to the menu. No one went away hungry, physically or spiritually. It was everything Jesse wanted for his people to experience at camp—arts and crafts, Bible lessons for the kids taught by loving adults, dramas, singing, Bible studies, hikes, and adventure games. God seemed to meet and minister to all ages at the nightly worship service.

Most importantly, the team loved every single attendee at camp, from the adults down to babies, and encouraged their faith, many of them still fairly new at it.

Jesse had gotten more than just a church family camp; he had gained a brother in Christ.

Despite their age difference and lack of ministry experience, Brian made him feel less alone in the journey. And they had stayed in touch and allowed their unlikely friendship to grow.

Brian's encouragement had a way of lifting Jesse's spirits, which often felt heavy with the load of ministry. Brian's enthusiasm was contagious, always igniting and reigniting Jesse's. Their friendship somehow lessened each other's burdens and made the journey as new pastors and new fathers more enjoyable, even across the many miles.

Jesse had plenty of friends and plenty of brothers in Christ, but this was different. For this season, he had a fellow traveller.

The church that had started accidentally was growing fast, and lives were being changed. But Jesse could feel himself growing tired. He couldn't do it on his own forever.

# 31

*1998*

## TOO BUSY

*Not that we are competent in ourselves to claim anything for ourselves, but our competence comes from God.*

—2 Corinthians 3:5

"Steph, what's new in your life?" my dad asked, glancing across the car at me. I was normally brimming with enthusiasm. Out of his four girls, I was easily the most talkative. Usually it took only one question, if that, and I was off, happily chattering on at a million miles a minute.

But I was unusually quiet on this morning drive to school, staring out the window without making eye contact with him.

When I finally turned to face him, there was fire in my eyes rather than my usual sparkle, and a trembling lip in place of my usual smile. I was trying to resist the emotion that threatened to overtake me.

"You *never* have time for me!" I said angrily. "And now you want to know what's new in my life?"

I returned to staring out the window, crossing my arms over my heart as if to say, *You can't come in here.* My dad didn't say anything. He just turned his eyes back to the road. He kept on driving with a stunned expression on his face.

As soon as I had been old enough to toddle, I had been my dad's little apprentice—so much so that he had gotten his sister to sew me a pair of coveralls.

Mostly I just liked to be in my dad's presence. I happily joined whatever he was doing. This began in Richmond and continued in the garage he built in the seminary days in Cochrane. Since moving to Calgary the previous year to be closer to the growing church, the quality time we spent together seemed to have become less and less frequent.

We had always been close. But that was then. Now, he was too busy for me. I had been replaced.

I had no warm pleasantries to offer as he dropped me off at school, leaving him with only his surprise to keep him company.

———

*Where did that come from?* Jesse pondered as he drove to his office at Cambrian Heights Baptist Church, the place FilCan still met for their weekly worship services. Was it true? Did he not have time for her?

Jesse had always tried to make his family a priority, but spending time with his girls had seemed simpler when they were younger.

As his girls got older and Jesse found himself busier, connecting with them proved more difficult. The older three, now thirteen and sixteen, didn't want to play or apprentice anymore.

Thankfully, the youngest—little Emily—did. Jesse loved every minute of fun with his four-year-old.

All his girls had taken up basketball, and Jesse was so pleased that they shared his love of the game. The court provided a place he could continue to connect with them. No matter how busy he was, Jesse made it a priority to be at every basketball game and drive them to school in the morning.

But was it enough?

As the church grew, so did his load of responsibilities. Jesse had quit his job at the Town of Cochrane after Emily was born and become a full-time pastor. Sermon preparation, leading the seniors Bible study, evening visitation, giving people rides, and leading prayer meetings filled his weeks.

The family moved from Cochrane to Calgary in January 1997 to be closer to the church. This saved Jesse a lot of drive time each day. Oftentimes he had so many things on his plate that he couldn't focus long enough to get anything finished. He wasn't a strategic thinker by nature; he simply shared Jesus, loved people, and shared his life with them.

Jesse sighed as he drove away from the school that day. Even though the verbal onslaught had caught him off-guard, deep down he knew there was some truth to it. Ministry had become his whole life... and his family was footing the bill.

He had to do better.

# 32

*May 10, 1999*

# JIM

*I will give you a new heart and put a new spirit in you; I will remove from you
your heart of stone and give you a heart of flesh.*

—Ezekiel 36:26

What was Jim Messner doing here?

Jesse hadn't expected to see his old neighbour and friend at the
going-away party for Pastor Hamish, Jesse's former pastor and friend through
their seminary years and early church-planting days. Hamish and his wife Cindy
were moving on to a new assignment and the Cochrane community had come to
celebrate their ministry and see them off.

From the years of casual conversations on the lawn between their yard or
over the fence, wandering over to each other's open garages and borrowing tools,
Jesse knew that Jim believed in God but didn't want to turn his life over to Jesus.
Though his wife Barb had decided to follow Jesus just over two years earlier, Jim
hadn't been eager to embrace her newfound faith.

But Jesse knew God was at work.

From the early FilCan days, Jim and Barb had allowed their daughters to tag
along to church with the Moraleses many Sundays and for Vacation Bible School
(VBS), the weeklong Bible camp the church often hosted for children in the summer. Their daughter, Hailey, had been the first one in the Messner family to give
her life to Jesus at the first VBS FilCan held during the summer of 1994. A few
years later, as Jesse and Kathy were preparing to move their family to Calgary to

be closer to the church, Barb showed up on their doorstep. She needed to process her marriage struggle with Kathy, who had often been a source of encouragement to her.

Kathy assured Barb that her and Jesse's marriage experience had been the same when they'd tried to do it their own way. Though there was still conflict, like in any marriage, Jesus had made all the difference. Living His way had saved Jesse and Kathy and their marriage. Barb, now realizing that all the worldly wisdom she had tried using to improve her life wasn't working, was finally ready to try Jesus.

Since praying to give her life to Jesus, Barb had been changing from the inside out. Jim wasn't sure how to feel about the changes in his wife. Barb had begun attending the church Jesse and Kathy had attended while in seminary and joined them in praying for Jim and her other two children.

A few months earlier, Kathy had received a late night phone call from Barb. She and Jim had been at the local pub when spiritual questions poured out of Jim.

"Is it all right if I invite Kathy?" Barb had asked her husband, feeling ill-equipped to answer them. "She knows so much more than I do about the Bible."

"She's married to a pastor," Jim said. "The guy runs a church. There's no way she'll come to a bar."

But he agreed.

He was shocked when half an hour later, Kathy sat across from them, listening to all his questions and answering them according to the Bible. He wasn't ready to give his life to Jesus, but he was touched that she would meet him and answer his questions on his own turf.

That summer, the Holy Spirit had continued to work in their hearts. Barb's eldest daughter, Natalie, decided to give her life to Jesus at the FilCan family camp, run by Brian's team. When Kathy asked twelve-year-old Natalie what had finally convinced her to give her life to Jesus after so many years of hearing about Him, she said softly and tearfully, "It's like I have a new mom."

Though the Moraleses had moved to Calgary, the two families remained close friends and continued to share their annual Messner/Morales Christmas dinner together and many other parts of everyday life.

And Jesse had continued to pray for Jim's salvation.

And tonight Jim was here at the going-away party. Was God up to something?

Jesse looked over at his friend, standing quietly by the back door and waiting for the program to conclude. Jim, a former RCMP officer and current race car driver, looked like the weight of the world sat on his shoulders.

After the program ended, when Jim finished saying farewell to Pastor Hamish. Jesse then went over to greet his old neighbour.

Jesse listened intently as his friend spilled out the events of the day. Jim had been driving at 125 miles per hour, breaking in a new engine in his race car.

Without warning, the engine exploded.

Jim was shaken to the core, overwhelmed at the thought of the cost of repairing the engine, the responsibility he had to the race sponsors, and the fact that he had just narrowly escaped death.

After coming home to an empty house, Jim had felt like someone was grabbing him by the neck, urging him to head to church.

Unable to resist the urge he felt deep inside, Jim had headed over, sceptical that there would even be a place to park his truck and racing trailer, which was still in tow. Despite the large turnout at the crowded church, the curb right outside the building had been wide open, with ample room for Jim to park his rig, as if someone had cleared the way for him.

As Jesse listened to his friend, still reeling from the day's events, he felt the familiar prompting from the Holy Spirit to share with Jim how to have peace with God. Jesse simply followed the prompt. He told Jim that God loved him so much that He'd sent Jesus to live, die, and be resurrected from the grave to pay for all of Jim's sin and give him abundant and eternal life. But it wasn't enough for Jim to know about this gift—he needed to receive it.

"Jim, do you want to receive Jesus as your Lord and Saviour?" Jesse asked.

Jim nodded, silent tears beginning to form in the corners of his eyes. Jesse bowed his head and led Jim in a simple prayer confessing that he was a sinner in need of a Saviour, and that he believed Jesus had lived, died, and rose from the grave. He invited Jesus to live inside him and be his Lord and Saviour.

When the two men said amen, a miracle had taken place in the spiritual realm. Jesse looked at his old friend but was staring at a brand-new man. Instead of the weightiness that had plagued Jim only moments earlier, there was new peace and joy.

This refreshing opportunity to witness a transformed life turned out to be food for Jesse's weary soul. Telling people about Jesus never got old. There was no greater joy. It didn't matter if it was a stranger at the coffee shop or his next door neighbour and friend. Whenever someone was willing to listen, Jesse would tell about Jesus. He couldn't imagine ever losing the joy of giving Jesus away.

But he also had no idea what was around the corner.

# 33

*2000*

# STUCK

*Come to me, all you who are weary and burdened, and I will give you rest.*
—Matthew 11:28

hy did he feel so stuck? Jesse finished typing his email to Brian. When it came to feelings, writing seemed easier than talking.

Saturday, June 20, 2000
Hello Brian,
I got your message from Kathy yesterday. The church line is now in the church office. I am planning to go to Austin, Texas on the second week of August. My sister is giving me her car. I will fly down and drive back. It will probably take three days to get back to Calgary.

I heard your concerns about people leaving your church. I can identify with you on this issue. I always ask the Lord this question: what can I do to address this concern so that it does not negatively impact the church? Believe me, I battle with this all the time. I will be in prayer with you.

Pray for me.

It seems my inner struggles are always related to the kind of behaviour I adopted from my past. At the same time, I know there is a new person inside of me and I possess a new identity and the Holy

Spirit. The potential to grow is already built into me. Does this sound familiar to you?

My prayer and question to God is: Lord, what is it that is stopping me to be the kind of husband and father you want me to be? Or a friend to my wife?

I say this because I feel like I know what I need to do. I have heard enough about what a Christian marriage ought to be. About relationships. But there is something blocking me on the inside. Whatever it is, it needs to be unlocked. I feel sometimes I am trapped in a maze and I can't figure the way to get out.

Please pray for me as I try to seek God's guidance and counsel. Thank God for our friendship. I feel blessed to have a friend to share my personal struggles with. Hear from you again.

In Christ,

Jesse

He hit send, feeling both relieved and grateful to put words to the inner struggle plaguing him. Though Jesse made friends easily, this depth of vulnerability wasn't easy or possible with everyone.

But with Brian, it was.

In whatever form they communicated, there was easy laughter, the comfort of old friends, and an unspoken but shared understanding of the pastoral weight they both carried. He and Brian didn't need to pastor one another; they were simply brothers in Christ, fellow travellers on the journey of wanting to be faithful to the call of God on their lives. That made it a safe place to be honest about their struggles.

Brian never tried to fix him, even when he was trying to fix himself. They listened to each other without judgment. And thanks to email, staying in touch was easier than ever.

But finding words to describe his feelings was the most unnatural thing Jesse had ever tried to do. No one had ever taught him how. He didn't understand his own emotions, let alone his wife's or daughters'.

Jesse had never come across a car he couldn't fix, though. Sometimes it took a phone call to his brother Lope to troubleshoot together, but at the end of the day the steps were simple. Diagnose. Find the necessary parts. Repair. Get the car back on the road.

But when the struggle was from within himself, it wasn't so simple—especially when it came to struggling to be the kind of husband and father he desperately desired to be.

Jesse had always loved kids, including his younger siblings during his childhood. His mom had always said he could take care of kids better than any woman she knew.

So when his girls were younger, connecting with them had been simple. As babies he cuddled and bathed them. As little girls, they played or tagged along with him in the garage or as he puttered around the yard.

But as they got older, connecting with them proved to be more difficult. And they wouldn't be at home much longer.

He knew post-secondary education was on the horizon for his daughters—as well as weddings, at some point—and he worked hard to provide, picking up automotive jobs on the side. He wanted them to take advantage of every opportunity to further their education.

And then there was his wife. He loved Kathy so much, but his efforts always seemed to come out wrong.

He washed the vehicles, filled them with gas, and fixed them when needed. He mowed the lawn. Did the dishes. Took out the garbage. Yet it felt like his acts of service weren't enough to push through the cement blockade that kept him from feeling deeply connected to those he loved most.

Why did it feel like his efforts didn't count? Why did he feel like he was never good enough?

He could still remember his dad's angry voice from the old days they'd spent together back in the Philippines. That voice seemed etched into his soul. He thought the voice had disappeared forever when he'd encountered Jesus, but he was starting to hear it again, and more frequently than he cared to admit. It always told him to try harder, be better, and do more. It told him he was never okay. He pushed the voice down, deep down.

He sighed, weary, wishing God would just fix him.

*Lord, what's stopping me?* he silently pleaded.

There was no audible answer, only silence.

# 34

# THE CUT

*Brothers and sisters, if someone is caught in a sin, you who live by the Spirit should restore that person gently. But watch yourselves, or you also may be tempted.*

—Galatians 6:1

Had he done the right thing? The church was haemorrhaging and the weight of what had been done pressed heavily down on him.

Jesse was growing increasingly uncomfortable with what the congregation told him they had seen. Was it possible they were right about what was happening? He hoped and prayed it wasn't true.

Jesse sighed heavily, wishing that exhaling could somehow release the weight that pressed down on him.

As a pastor, he wanted the people in his church to grow in their faith and become spiritually mature. He wanted them to experience freedom from sin. He wanted everyone to become a contributing and reproducing member of the body of Christ. He wanted to protect them from the influences of evil. He wanted them to grow in holiness and love and experience transformation. He wanted them to live life to the fullest. And he wanted the leaders to set an example.

Instead there was an allegation of a leader having an affair.

There had been no seminary class on how to lead through this kind of situation. Jesse had sought the Lord fervently in prayer. He kept the details confidential, even from Kathy. He saw no need to burden her.

He'd sought godly wisdom in the confidence of his weekly conversation with his friend and fellow pastor, Hamish.

"We're having trouble," he had said to Hamish. "Honestly, this is hard for me."

He had known the sin had to be addressed. It had to be dealt with. It could not remain in the camp.

Jesse wanted this leader to be restored. He wanted restoration for all the families affected. Restoration for the church. Restoration of trust. Restoration of broken fellowship.

The leadership team had called a meeting to confront the allegations. Jesse had believed wholeheartedly that God could work all things together for good, including what the enemy clearly meant for evil. He'd prayed there would be humility and confession.

But instead it was like a bomb went off. Instead of clarity, there had been only more confusion—and a lot of anger.

Jesse replayed the sequence of events. He'd handled the situation the best way he knew how and it hadn't gone according to plan. Was he responsible? There was no one to tell him otherwise.

He came home from the meeting feeling—and according to his wife, look-ing—beat up, battered, bruised, and more burdened than ever before. And that night he didn't yet know the rippling effects of the explosion.

Kathy was surprised and confused when she received a phone call the next Sunday morning informing her that the leader and his family would not be com-ing back to the church. She felt the absence of the empty chairs that morning, not fully understanding what had caused them.

And the following Sunday, a few more people left. People they had loved, invested in, and grown to think of as family. They were gone, just like that, with only the empty seats and murmurings in the congregation to tell the story. This painfully slow dagger to the heart cut a bit deeper each week.

Jesse wasn't exactly sure what story was being told and what story was being spread, but he had an idea. People talked, even if Jesse didn't. He kept silent each time he heard more of the slander, the same way he had kept silent under his father's verbal barrages. He wanted to shout the question that plagued his heart, the same one he had asked his father the one time he had talked back: "Why are you doing this?"

He didn't understand. Jesse loved the people he had the privilege of pastoring. He wanted life for them. Why were they doing this to themselves? To their families? To the church? To him? Was he somehow responsible?

*If I was a better pastor, maybe this wouldn't have happened,* he thought. His life seemed to hold proof that he was missing the mark.

He wished he could call for a sub, but there was no coach to recognize his exhaustion. There was no one to call a timeout. The game was still going and the team needed him. His wife needed her husband. His girls needed their father. What was left of the church still needed its pastor.

He would find a way to keep going.

On the outside, he smiled. He remained calm. He shrugged casually anytime anyone shared what was being said about him. He never defended himself. He never spoke ill of those who had hurt him. He never shared the details of what had happened. He continued to write sermons and care for his people.

He had nowhere to unload the heaviness he felt, so he did the only thing he knew how to do: he limped along, unaware that he was slowly bleeding out.

# 35

*Fall 2000*

# TRY HARDER

*My prayer is not that you take them out of the world but that you protect them from the evil one.*

—John 17:15

A small part of Jesse began to dread Sunday morning. When he got up to preach, the increasing number of empty seats shouted at him, *You're not good enough.* Attendance seemed to decline a little more every week.

But it wasn't just the decline in attendance. Jesse had always believed Jesus was the head of the church and was responsible to grow it. There were seasons of pruning. So whenever Kathy felt emotional over someone leaving, he gently reminded her, "Kathy, God will grow the church."

He could sense an increasing division in those who remained. These hurting people were doing that which is most common: they were trying to find allies.

Jesse took action, trying to get more organized personally and pastorally. He needed to figure out how to equip more leaders so they could become contributors, not just consumers, in the kingdom of God.

Brian helped over email, all the way from Tennessee. Jesse scanned the email he had recently received.

Monday, September 11, 2000

Jesse,

Thanks for faxing your schedule. Looks like you have a full week. I'm wondering if you could focus on one priority each day? You remember the four we talked about—relationships, leadership, communication, and health. I try to focus on one priority each day as I do my message prep and other pastoral duties.

If you could next week, beside each day write which priority you will be focusing on. I notice Monday night and Wednesday night and Saturday night are open. I would like to challenge you to go ahead and schedule time for your family on those nights. If you don't plan for it, someone else will. Remember: nothing becomes dynamic until it gets specific.

I'm interested in what you will share with Pastor Richard on Tuesday.

Give me some details on the plans you discuss with him. I look forward to hearing from you.

In His harvest,

Brian

Jesse struggled with organization. When the church had been beginning, he had thrived in the small group setting—caring for people, speaking into their lives, and sharing Jesus with their friends and family.

He felt like he started more than he could finish. His best intentions didn't necessarily become plans. He didn't know how to surround himself with people who had gifts that complemented one another in the same mission.

He loved caring for people and sharing Jesus, but all the administrative responsibilities weighed on him. He was juggling so many things that didn't come naturally to him, and the result was that he was dropping things left and right. He hated to admit it, but it seemed he most often dropped his time with his family.

At least he had Brian to keep him accountable.

Thursday, September 14, 2000

Brian, thanks for checking me out.

I have a tendency to just make a schedule at times without praying, thinking and looking closely at what the priorities are and what

God wants me to accomplish on a day to day basis. Thanks for checking me out. I am determined to stay in this accountability principle.

Let me share with you what Richard and I discussed the other day. My objectives for taking my leaders, or at least twenty-five people in the church, on a retreat are:

- to find out what God wants to accomplish through us in the next three years, maybe set some goals.
- to find out if we are particularly on the same page.
- to emphasize unity in our strategy for fulfilling the five purposes of the church.
- to develop a vision statement.
- to come away with a sense of togetherness.
- to have key people take responsibility for the goals we want to achieve.
- to get these key people to form teams for accomplishing the set goals we have come up with.

I want your comments on these thoughts of mine. Hear from you soon, Brian. Thanks, bro.

In His steps,

Jesse

If Jesse could get the church on the same page, maybe the bleeding would stop and they would start growing again.

# 36

*Winter 2001*

# BE BETTER

*Do not let any unwholesome talk come out of your mouths, but only what is helpful for building others up according to their needs, that it may benefit those who listen.*

—Ephesians 4:29

Jesse loved his wife. Even before Kathy had encountered Jesus, she had been loving and kind to him. And once Jesus had come into her life, her love for him had only grown. No one had loved him like Kathy.

But he'd never seemed to get it right when it came to loving her back. Jesse was forgetful when it came to special occasions, especially when he felt overwhelmed. He was often at the mall on Christmas Eve. If it weren't for his daughters' reminders, Valentine's, anniversaries, and birthdays would all sail by without a thoughtful gesture from him.

He did try, but it often didn't look like it.

The recent marriage seminar they'd hosted at church had helped him begin to understand the disconnect—Kathy's love language was words of affirmation and Jesse's was acts of service. For him, speaking words of affirmation felt about as natural as pulling teeth.

Words of affirmation were not part of Filipino culture. Parents loved their kids by providing, not verbally professing their love. And it especially hadn't been part of Jesse's family. If his parents had felt proud, they never said it to their kids, only about them to people in the community.

Jesse had never been on the receiving end of affirming words. So it was hard for him to say the words he never really heard: "I love you" and "I'm proud of you."

But even though it was hard, it was what his wife and daughters needed—and what God had commanded.

God was answering his prayer and beginning to unlock his heart, removing the barriers that prevented him from being the kind of husband and father he wanted to be.

He had to at least try.

Jesse picked up his pen. If he couldn't express his feelings in spoken words, maybe they would find their way out in writing.

January 30, 2001

Dear Kathy,

Time has flown since we first met. You have been a great companion and a loving wife to me. I know I cannot redeem the time that has gone by, but there is still time for me to make up in my relationship with you. I realized that my relationship with you has not been the way it should be. I have difficulty sharing my feelings with you. Please forgive me for all the pain I have caused in your life. My pledge before God today is to begin a fresh approach with godly attitudes in my relationship with you. I love you. I want to be with you till the day God takes me home.

Jesse

# 37

# PRAY

*And pray in the Spirit on all occasions with all kinds of prayers and requests.
With this in mind, be alert and always keep on praying for all the Lord's people.*
—Ephesians 6:18

"*Pray for your safety.*"

*That's weird,* Angela thought as she loaded her laundry basket into the back seat of the car. Where had that voice come from?

Her college basketball games were finished for the weekend and she looked forward to spending a couple of nights at home. There were multiple ways to make the hour-and-a-half drive from Prairie Bible College in Three Hills to their home in Calgary. The new stretch of highway between Linden and Acme was open, she remembered as she shut the back door and climbed into the car. She would take that route. It would shave a few minutes off their drive.

"*Pray for your safety.*"

The urgent prompt from the strong voice did not leave as she thought about the drive home. Without knowing why, she prayed, "God, keep us safe. I pray that we're okay."

The unsettling urgency to pray stood out in Angela's mind as she started the car.

She glanced around the vehicle. Christina loaded CDs into the six-disc changer. Emily stowed her toothbrush and homework in the pocket behind the passenger seat, then slid to the middle and fastened the seatbelt around her small frame. Emily was always careful to follow instructions, whether it was her Grade One teacher's homework assignment or her mom's instructions to brush her teeth in case she fell asleep on the drive home.

Only one sister was missing. At the last minute, I had stayed home, still unable to put weight on the ankle I had injured at basketball practice a few days earlier.

Sure that all her passengers were safe, Angela pulled out of the parking lot and headed for the new highway that would take them home.

---

*"Pray for your girls' protection."*

The thought took Jesse by surprise. Pray for his girls' protection? Jesse's girls were his everything. Were they in danger?

He prayed for his girls regularly, but this felt different; it was urgent. Jesse glanced around the crowded room filled with mingling pastors and their wives, searching for a quiet place to pray.

With one more night remaining, the weekend ministry retreat had already provided Jesse with much-needed refreshment. He had puttered into the weekend on emotional fumes. Ministry felt especially heavy these days. The pastors and wives retreat was just what he and Kathy had needed.

Jesse could never figure out how to unload the weight he constantly carried around for all the people he cared about. This retreat had given him permission to set the weight down, freeing him to more fully enjoy being with his wife. Jesse was anticipating going home the following day with a full tank.

The weekend had been one of the few times Jesse had missed one of his daughters' basketball games. In every season, no matter which daughter or what age, Jesse scheduled his life around cheering them on.

He glanced at the clock. Angela's game would be finished by now and they were likely already on the road.

Jesse spotted the bathroom door and excused himself from the conversation, heading towards it. Over the years, Jesse had learned that it was best to obey the promptings of the Holy Spirit rather than try to understand them.

He closed the door behind him and in the quiet of the bathroom did what he sensed the Holy Spirit urging him to do: he prayed fervently for his girls' protection.

———

"I'm tired," Emily announced to her twin sisters, her energy and enthusiasm fading quickly. Maybe it was all the cheering she had done at her big sister's game. Plus, it was far past her six-year-old bedtime.

Angela glanced back in the rearview mirror as she drove carefully down the pitch-black highway, the headlights the only thing lighting up the back country road.

"Move over so you can lean against the window," Angela suggested.

Emily unbuckled, quickly sliding over to the seat where she could rest against the window, and reached behind to pull the shoulder strap across the front of her body.

"Check your seatbelt," Angela reminded her, keeping her eyes on the road. *Click.*

"What's happening!" Emily suddenly screamed, her newly fastened seatbelt locking as the road beneath them seemed to slide.

"What's going on? What're you doing?" Christina grabbed onto the handle on the door for dear life.

"I'm not playing around... I can't control the car!" Angela's body tensed up, panic rising within her.

A second ago, she had been able to see the road ahead, and now a cloud of dark dust blocked her view as the car swerved. What had happened to the ground beneath them? Were they going to die?

Emily's screams pierced Angela's ears, joining the chorus with her own.

Christina braced herself. *This is it,* she thought, tightening her grasp on the door handle, the only thing she could hold onto as the car changed directions.

They were going over the edge of the road. She felt a *thunk*, then tumbling, another *thunk*, more tumbling, another *thunk*, more tumbling, another *thunk*, more tumbling... and then a final *thud*.

———

Christina's senses told her she was upside-down. And if she was upside-down, the car wasn't squished. So she wasn't dead.

Emily was suspended in her upside-down position by the seatbelt she had clicked in only seconds ago, surrounded by the laundry that had formed a protective pile around her small body.

The next few moments were a blur. Christina could hear Angela telling them that they had to get out of the vehicle. What if it caught on fire—or worse, blew up?

Adrenaline made the next series of decisions that their shocked minds and bodies couldn't make for themselves. They unbuckled, releasing their bodies from their suspended position, and crawled out of one of the car's shattered windows.

Christina paced around the dark valley, trying to get a signal on her old cell phone. Why did it never work? She could hear Emily protesting about having to leave the vehicle without her toothbrush or homework. And one of her shoes was missing. Angela was trying to reason with her.

"Your teacher won't care," Angela urged. "We need to go now!"

The only light that pierced the darkness was from the headlights of the upside-down car and the distant yard light of a nearby farmhouse.

"Good thing I just invited Jesus into my heart last week," said Emily. "We almost went to heaven."

———————

"I'm so sorry for your loss," said the impound lot attendant the next day.

Jesse surveyed what was left of the car, the events of the previous night replaying in his mind.

Last night's news had been incredibly unsettling, even for someone like Jesse who was characteristically calm and even-tempered no matter what was in his path.

After praying for his girls, Jesse had returned to the social and soon after received word of every parent's worst nightmare—his girls had been in a car accident. On the phone, he was told they were all okay, but Jesse still had to get to his girls and see them with his own eyes, especially when he heard Angela's voice burst into sobs on the phone.

Friends from Three Hills were going to pick them up from the farmhouse near the accident site. The kind owner of the home had seen the headlights swerving and go off the highway.

Jesse had moved into action, packing up their things and trying to console his emotional wife as he ushered her to the vehicle. At the time, the focus had been on the fact that the girls seemed to be okay.

Only seconds after Emily had clicked in her seatbelt, the car had hit gravel at highway speed with no warning. There hadn't been any warning sign that the highway, still under construction, had a break in the pavement. Their negligence kindled Jesse's anger. It wasn't right.

Upon hitting gravel, the car had swerved over the centre line. It then rolled sideways down a steep, unguarded embankment, before landing upside-down at the bottom of the small valley.

It was beginning to dawn on Jesse what a miracle this truly was. Had they really literally walked away from this? This twisted heap of metal screamed that the accident should've had a different ending.

Staring at the vehicle, the realization of what could've happened felt very real.

The county had quickly moved to action, towing the car first thing that morning after an overwhelming number of those passing by had called 911 to report the terrible rollover.

His mind returned to the present moment. The impound lot attendant had just expressed remorse for his loss.

"Actually, my girls are all okay," Jesse replied, barely able to believe the miracle himself. "God protected them."

The impound lot attendant raised his eyebrows, as if to say he'd never heard of someone, let alone three people, walking out of any vehicle in this condition.

"When I saw this car, I was sure there were casualties," the man said in disbelief.

The sight of the twisted heap of metal made Jesse's stomach turn. He inspected the totalled vehicle more closely. The left side of the vehicle had been hit worst, and Jesse could see now why Angela's pain was more severe. And Emily's move to the right from the middle seat had likely saved her life.

It was clear that the back left side of the car had hit a boulder on its tumble into the valley. This was the only part of the vehicle that bore the marks of the trees, bushes, and boulders of the embankment.

Fortunately, no one had been sitting in that spot, and the spilled laundry had protected Emily from the shards of flying glass. The roof of the vehicle had caved in, except for the area right above where Emily had been sitting.

*"Pray for your girls' protection."*

149

Jesse was already convinced of the power of prayer, but this vehicle offered undeniable proof of one thing: God could be trusted to protect his girls, even when Jesse couldn't.

# 38

*Spring 2003*

# THE TEARS

*Record my misery; list my tears on your scroll—are they not in your record?*

—Psalm 56:8

I woke up, confused. Was that the sound of someone yelling? Yes. Mom and Dad were fighting.

I had never heard my parents fight before. Were they going to split up? What was happening? I didn't know how to interpret this.

I intentionally made a bit of noise as I made my way to the bathroom to alert them that there was a witness to their argument.

Their voices quieted, but I couldn't shake the unsettled feeling now churning in the pit of my stomach.

I managed to keep the lid on my emotions as I got ready and climbed into the car with my dad. He started heading towards the mall to drop me off for my all-day Saturday shift. It felt like there was an elephant sitting between us.

The car was often our place of conversation over the years—good, bad, or otherwise. These short drives together were when I had my dad all to myself. And they were often when I was able to be the most honest.

As an elementary school kid, he had picked me up in his Town of Cochrane flatbed truck, putting something down for me to sit on so I wouldn't get dirty. We would drive to a nearby park for a picnic and tennis game on his lunch break. This was a "special time," as our family called it—a one-on-one outing of the kids' choice. The tennis game would be brief, turning into a nap on the grass under the tree for him and solitary swinging at the park for me. I was happy to keep an eye on him.

As a resentful teenager, the car was where I let the cap come off the head gasket when I felt like my dad no longer had time for me. The car was where he asked me what God was doing in my life and I replied with a sulky, "Nothing." It was where he spoke these words I will never forget: "God is *always* doing something in your life. You're just not paying attention."

The car was where he had recently asked what I wanted to do with my life, as my high school graduation was on the horizon. When I told him I wanted to become a teacher, he tried to persuade me to become a lawyer instead.

On another occasion when he was flustered at our lateness to get someplace, and the red light that was slowing us down, I looked at him and said, "You being mad isn't going to get us there any faster." I held the eye contact, and my conviction, until he slowly broke into a smile.

"You're right," he said, laughing and shaking his head.

In all his busyness, the car was often where we connected.

But not on this day. The sun was the only thing shining during this silent drive to the mall. He said nothing. I said nothing.

I wasn't sure what to make of this version of my dad. There was no sign of his usual easygoing nature, or his ability to laugh and the humility that allowed me to speak my mind, even when I was out of line. There were none of the usual jokes that only he found funny. Only sad silence.

Was it just me or did he look more tired than usual? I couldn't take it anymore.

"Dad?" I asked carefully. "Are you and Mom okay?"

As I watched tears fill his eyes, I knew his answer wasn't going to put me at ease.

"I just don't know how to make her happy," he said softly, tears escaping his eyes.

I had no words, only feelings, as he dropped me off at the door and I headed into the longest eight-hour shift of my life.

I buried my feelings in the pile of denim I busied myself folding at my job. Thankfully, no one in the large store seemed to notice I was on the brink of tears. Or if they did, they didn't ask.

On my lunchbreak, I wandered over to the store where my boyfriend Mike worked, in need of some stability and comfort.

Four years earlier, Mike had come to our church basketball tournament at the invitation of a friend. Pastor Jesse, the persistent evangelist, had then invited him to come to our annual youth camp and he'd said yes.

But then Mike had backed out, having no idea the loving persistence he was about to encounter. My dad proceed to call Mike every day for a week until he agreed to come.

My dad's friend Brian served as the camp pastor, and my dad happily served in the kitchen, always putting on a pot of rice for the Filipino campers even though it was never on the menu.

That summer, Mike gave his life to Jesus. The running joke would eventually become that my dad handpicked him for me.

Mike studied my face as I tried to force a smile and suppress the tears that were trying to find their way out.

"You okay?" he asked, careful not to burst the dam.

I inhaled slowly, keeping my forced smile in place. "I don't know what's happening."

My parents were fighting. My dad was crying. I didn't know what to make of my dad crying. My dad never cried. He was small and mighty. Tender and tough. Kind and strong. I had never seen him like this.

That was my one and only clue that something wasn't right.

# 39

*2003*

# I JUST CRY

*Those who sow with tears will reap with songs of joy.*

—Psalm 126:5

K athy could feel her frustration mounting. Managing time had never been Jesse's strong suit. Over the decades they had been married, she'd changed her expectations revolving around time. It was the only way to prevent herself from going completely crazy every time he was late coming home or they were late leaving to go somewhere.

The running joke was that he was always on Filipino time, but he was such an in-the-moment kind of person that he could easily forget the next place he was supposed to be or the person he was supposed to pick up.

But this was a new level, even for Jesse.

He was needing to spend yet another Saturday night in his basement office, on top of the forty hours he'd already spent there this past week. He got so caught up in whatever was right in front of him that he forgot everything else that needed to be taken care of, sacrificing even his time with family on the altar of ministry.

He had made promises that they would do something together as a family, but once again his intentions weren't turning into actual plans. The lack of follow-through made Kathy feel like she and the family didn't matter to him as much as ministry did.

She knew Jesse had been trying to get organized. Brian was trying to help him ensure that his priorities were reflected in the way he spent his time. But clearly something was going wrong and Kathy wanted to know what it was.

With this latest broken promise, she wasn't going to let it go.

Since becoming a pastor almost a decade earlier, Jesse had always struggled with boundaries. Ministry was continuous and he wanted to make himself available to people. But sometimes he was so available to everyone else that he ended up too busy for his family, with the exception of basketball games. He didn't seem to have an off switch.

Kathy searched for patience within herself and found none. She threw her hands up in the air, exasperated.

"What do you do all day?" she demanded when Jesse eventually came in through the door.

Whatever the answer was, it was costing them their time together.

Jesse sat quietly, his head hanging. Only silence.

Her eyes narrowed. Really? Did he have nothing to say? She wasn't letting him off the hook this time.

"You've been at your office all week! Your sermon should have been done by now."

When he finally looked up, Kathy was surprised to see tears in his eyes. "Sometimes I just put my elbows on the desk, hold my chin in my hands, and cry."

Kathy's heart softened as she felt her anger instantly drain away. She blinked, confused. Cry? Jesse went to his office and cried all day? She knew the past few years of ministry had taken a toll on him, but she'd had no idea it was this bad.

This was not normal.

She moved towards her husband, absorbing his weak and weeping body in an embrace.

"We're going to get you some help," Kathy assured him.

# 40

# THE CONFESSION

*Answer me quickly, Lord; my spirit fails. Do not hide your face from me or I will be like those who go down to the pit. Let the morning bring me word of your unfailing love, for I have put my trust in you. Show me the way I should go, for to you I entrust my life.*

—Psalm 143:7–8

I sat, stunned, uncertain of how to interpret what I was seeing and hearing. The ground that had felt unsteady beneath my feet a few months earlier was finally giving out.

My dad, the superhero, the rock of our family, fearless enough to squish a bee between his bare fingers, was broken and weeping—and publicly, standing before the church he had planted and pastored for almost a decade.

My dad was depressed? Impossible! How?

Normally when he stood before the church it was to preach a sermon, always biblical and with a good dose of Jesse. I turned a profit on this anytime he used a story about me without permission. One dollar was big money in the early 90s! As youths, we often giggled when he preached a sermon about the wheat and the weeds. His thick Filipino accent made it impossible to know if he was talking about "da wheed" or "da wheeds."

But on this day, there was no laughter. Nothing easy about it.

I unsuccessfully tried to blink back tears. I was no match for my emotions. He would be taking a sabbatical from the church. I wasn't privy to any details of the difficulties of ministry my dad had endured. As far as I knew, ministry had been peachy.

But the ground beneath my feet was crumbling.

I had always been thankful for my uneventful life. Nothing tragic had characterized my upbringing. Life had been safe and predictable, and so was my faith. My dad was the dad all of our friends wanted to hang out with, despite the fact that half of them struggled to understand his accent; it didn't matter, because he was kind. He was the cool dad, always reaching out and connecting with our friends on whatever level he could. He simply loved.

I was weeks away from leaving for college for the first time, and suddenly things in my life didn't feel as they should be. I felt untethered and uncertain, having to trust God for real, not just in theory. I needed Him to heal my dad.

On September 2, 2003, I wrote in my journal,

Thank You, Lord, for all the ways You are working... I'm thankful that You are bringing Mom and Dad through this time and that it never got really bad with Dad. Thank You for taking care of us. I think I'm okay because I know that You're in control. Help Dad to heal during this time.

This was my first lesson in experiential trust with God—entrusting the man I loved, respected, admired, and relied on into His healing hands.

# 41

*August 2003*

# BROKEN

*The Lord is close to the brokenhearted and saves those who are crushed in spirit.*

—Psalm 34:18

Jesse hit send on the email, barely able to believe he had been writing about himself.

Tuesday, August 12, 2003

Hello Brian,

Here is an update in regards to what I have been sharing with you. The church unanimously approved a four-month sabbatical for me last Sunday. This includes a one month holiday due for me. This time off will begin on August 26. Please pray that God will inspire many people to come to the plate to serve and that He will raise up godly leaders to lead the church. My doctor recommended three months off. He is convinced that I am clinically depressed. My medication is helping a bit. I will keep you updated.

Thanks for your prayers,

Your friend,

Jesse

Clinically depressed. That's what the doctor had said.

After he'd told Kathy about crying in the office, she had begun making phone calls. One was to Bob, the leader of church health at the Canadian National Baptist Convention. He was also a friend and had walked through his own burnout and depression in ministry. As a result, he was passionate about helping pastors "enjoy the journey, stay the course, and finish well," as he used to always say.

When Jesse sat down in his friend's office, Bob immediately recognized the defeated look in Jesse's eyes. It was the same look he had once seen in the mirror.

Bob helped walk Jesse and the church through this season. He stood beside Jesse on that Sunday when they'd announced his diagnosis to the church, sharing what would happen next and what their pastor desperately needed. The congregation was shocked and saddened that their beloved pastor was burnt out and depressed and more than willing to give him the time off he needed.

In 1986, at the start of his faith journey, Jesse had been so full of life. Almost two decades later, he just felt tired. And it was more than his usual need-a-nap tired; his soul was tired.

Jesse sighed, remembering how simple it had felt in the early days. In the process of caring for his people, he somehow ended up neglecting the care of his own soul. He took responsibility for everything that went wrong, even if it wasn't his to take. This had been deeply ingrained into him since the days in the Philippines with his father.

But now it was too much.

The exasperated and angry voice that accused him of not being good enough had come back with a vengeance, its volume turned all the way up. Jesse couldn't seem to hear anything else these days. What had happened to the sun? Where was the voice of truth?

The angry accusations had once sounded like his father's shouts, but now the voice sounded just like his own. How could he resist the sound of his own voice? He found himself agreeing with it. He didn't have any fight left in him. He felt like he was being swallowed by darkness.

Jesse wasn't sure how his own struggles fit into the pastoral picture. His journal was the place where he often got honest with God—more honest than he could be with any other human, since he was quiet by nature and a very internal processor. Most of what he wrestled with never came out in the open.

For many years, the church hadn't been in a position to hire another full-time staff member to help carry the load. Thankfully God had brought a new youth pastor to the church, as well as a couple who was passionate about evangelism and administration. They were helpful, but much of the damage had already been done. It seemed like Jesse's soul had sprung a leak, much like the vehicles he worked on.

He asked the Lord to make it clear if there was someone better suited to shepherd this flock. He needed rest—deep, refreshing, soul-level rest. How did God feel about all this? Was He disappointed in Jesse for allowing this to happen?

Jesse prayed, asking God to fix what was broken in him. No matter what Jesse did, there always seemed to be more in need of fixing. But he was beginning to realize he didn't need to be fixed; he needed to be healed.

# 42

# THE ROAD OF RESTORATION

*He will yet fill your mouth with laughter and your lips with shouts of joy.*

—Job 8:21

W arm familiarity washed over me as I watched my dad laugh. He slapped his knee, doubled over, and laughed from the deep recesses of his gut. I couldn't recall the last time my dad had laughed like this. How long had it been?

The depression had descended like a sunset over years, my dad's easy laughter slowly disappearing without saying goodbye or announcing if and when it planned to return.

But hearing him laugh felt like the sweet relief of turning onto your very own street after a long journey. It felt like home.

*He's back,* I thought.

———

Jesse smiled, something he wouldn't take for granted anymore. Smiling had once come so naturally to him, but in this season of depression smiles and laughter had been few and far between.

He had spent the first two weeks of his sabbatical sleeping. It was as if his body got the memo that it was finally safe to power down.

Now, with some months of rest and healing behind him, he flipped through his journal entries from the darkest months. Sadness washed over him as he was reminded of just how tired and weary he had gotten.

June 17, 2003. Oh Lord my God, speak to me. I am tired and weary. Give me emotional energy. Revitalize my spiritual life. Give me a renewed mind. Come and help me, oh God. Rescue me from depression and discouragement.

June 18, 2003. I have had enough pressures in life, physical tiredness and burdens. Lord, renew my faith. Reenergize my spiritual life. Show me how to return to my first love for You. Fill me with Your supernatural spiritual power so I can move forward. The journey is too much for me. Give me strength, fresh passion for ministry, and a mind that will seek You first and Your rule over my life. I need a fresh word from You.

June 20, 2003. Lord, help me to trust You even when I don't understand. I know You can do all things; no plans of Yours can be thwarted (Job 42:2). Forgive me for not trusting You, ignoring Your counsel, and overlooking the blessings You have given me—financial stability, a godly wife, good children, ministry, and the opportunity to serve You. Lord, show me how I can have Your perspective on every circumstance that I face and every situation I have. Thank You for loving me, protecting me, teaching me, guiding me.

June 21, 2003. Lord Jesus, I realize that my life has not been pleasing in your sight. Forgive me for my sins and cleanse me and remove every guilt I have chosen to carry. Thank You for freeing me from the load of guilt. Give me a new start. A fresh beginning.

June 24, 2003. Oh God, forgive my ungodly thoughts. Purify my heart. Clean me from my impure motives.

June 26, 2003. God wants me to love life, not waste it. Life is precious to God. It is a gift from God. He wants to use my life for His own purposes. I can cry out to God and He will deliver me from my troubles.

July 7, 2003. Someday soon, Jesus will rescue me, change me, and restore my hope, joy, and passion for Him. Lord Jesus, thank You for speaking to me.

July 10, 2003. I am thankful for the faith of R.D. In all my struggles and complaints I voiced to the Lord, the problems I encountered in my ministry are nothing compared to what R.D. is going through. To know that a fellow pastor is willing to remain faithful in ministry despite all of the pain and heartache has caused me today to be thankful to my God. Help me and show me every day how I can allow Christ to live His life through me.

August 20, 2003. Lord, I am crying out to You today asking forgiveness for my shortcomings, such as not intentionally making changes in my life, taking the privilege You have given to me [ministry] for granted, not taking time to spend time with You daily. Help me and show me how to walk closely with You. For my life is so brief and short. For I am only here on this earth for a brief period of time. I didn't bring anything into this world. You simply allow me to work for the things I enjoy. I know everything belongs to You. So what is the most precious and valuable thing to do? Take my life as I give it to You. I am Yours, Lord. Use me to further Your kingdom and to make a difference in people's lives. Hear my prayers. Don't ignore my pleas. God, I know You have responded to my plea. You have given me this opportunity to take some time off. Spare me, extend my life, give me more years of physical strength, emotional stamina, and spiritual stability. I want to smile again. Thank You, Lord, for speaking to me through Psalm 39. How fitting the message of this passage to my present condition. In Jesus's name, amen.

August 22, 2003. Lord, I often forget that You already delivered me from hell. You have given me a new life that began on February 5, 1986. You have helped me to understand the purpose You have given me. You have given me ministry responsibilities which I have taken for granted. Forgive me, Lord, for not intentionally learning and doing the things I knew to do to become a good leader. Lord God, I know I lack discipline. Help me to develop a disciplined mind. Show me how I can renew my mind daily. I want to live a life of integrity. In Your name, amen.

The depression surrounded him like a cloud, blocking his view of reality. He wasn't able to see that God was with him. He wasn't able to see the love that surrounded him in his family. His mind knew God would never leave him alone, but his heart wasn't confident.

Rereading his words made him remember how desperate he had felt and how the unhealed wounds of the past had contributed to his present pain.

August 27, 2003. My negative emotions have narrowed my focus. I was looking through the eyes of hopelessness. The body, mind, and spirit work in relation to one another. The body and mind share the effects of depression.

August 28, 2003. Depression is a gift from God. God uses depression to draw me closer to Him. Depression should serve as a constant reminder that I need to stay close to God. I have failed to treat, to love, to value the most important people in my life—my wife, my kids, and my church people. Lord, help me to change my thought patterns and angry emotions. Lord God, in my heart, I want to know You. I want to walk with You and love You with all my heart. I must forget what is behind—the unhealthy emotional past and bad, negative experiences—so that I can press on and move on.

September 9, 2003. This truth implies Jesus can resurrect my spiritual life and can give me new hope. God is with me. He is mighty to save me from depression (Zephaniah 3:17). He will quiet me with His love and rejoice over me. He was able to still me.

December 1, 2003. God's mercy for me endures forever. His mercy was there when I cried out on February 5, 1986. With God, things can get better. Lord Jesus, don't let me fall back into my old way of life. Give me courage to do what is right, a renewed mind that can view myself differently and see myself the way You see me. Help me to begin with a fresh start.

December 4, 2003. Dear God, help me know in my heart that I love You. My years of life are in Your hands. I pray that You will extend my life for Your purposes. I will feel fulfilled when I see You using me. Conform and transform my character. I desire to change.

Jesse had been desperate for God to restore him so he could be used by Him. In this way, he felt like his life was of value. As God had been healing him, he was learning that being loved by God was greater than being used by God.

He wanted his life to count. He wanted to spend his days on what would matter in eternity.

God's perfect love had begun to drive out Jesse's fear from the deep places where it had taken root. Fear, the Bible said, had to do with punishment. This freedom was fuelling more love in Jesse for God and his family.

December 6, 2003. God is constantly revealing Himself to me. I do not lack revelation from God. His presence is with me and He speaks through my daily life routines. I desire to hear a fresh word from You daily. Today You gave me a perfect verse to memorize—1 John 4:18. There is no fear in love. Perfect love casts out fear because fear involves torment. Fear can capture my inner man and keep me from loving people. God loves me, this I know. God wants me to keep loving people so that I may experience freedom from fear.

December 12, 2003. I was discouraged and depressed and had lost my passion. God intervened and allowed me to have [physical] rest and a break from ministry.[5]

---

5   This was written in response to his entry on June 17, 2003.

December 17, 2003. Lord, thank You for rescuing me from the dark valleys of life. Thank You for causing me to realize I was depressed. Last April at the prayer conference in Richmond, B.C. I shared with Henry Blackaby how I was feeling about ministry. I remember telling Henry I was losing my passion and love for people. He simply said my focus had shifted away from God. On June 17, in my prayers, I honestly said to God that I was very tired, weary, depressed and had no spiritual life. I asked God to revitalize my spiritual life. I prayed through Psalm 38. Teach me to do Your will. Revive me, oh Lord, for Your name's sake. I desire to make You known to others.

January 4, 2004. Search me, oh God, and know my anxious thoughts. See if there is any offensive way in me. Oh Lord, in my heart You are making me aware of the things You want me to change in my life. Your work in my life is immeasurable. I desire to humbly walk with You, be fair in my dealings with the world, love mercy, and live it out in my own life. Thank You for adopting me as Your child. Teach me daily to live what I believe. I know I must bear fruit worthy of repentance.

January 13, 2004. Lord, heal my emotional wounds. Lord, heal my deaf ear. Without faith I will not see the wonders and miracles of God. I must trust Jesus to step into deeper waters. Faith is always accompanied by actions.

A year ago, passion and vision had been strangers to Jesse. All he had been able to think about was sleeping and taking a break.

Slowly but surely, he felt his heart stirring for something fresh. God was planting something new inside him; he just needed to keep leaning in to know what it was.

The sabbatical was extended to one year, and Jesse was beginning to wonder whether God was going to send him back to the same role he had been in. He was getting a clearer sense of how God had wired him and what he had been created for.

January 19, 2004. Ministry work has to be shared with others. God will speak clearly to me in certain places. Lord, give me a sense of anticipation that You will speak to me today or in the coming days.

January 23, 2004. Lord, thank You for Your clear instructions. Make me aware of your presence in my life. I am determined to live a life of integrity and humility.

January 27, 2004. God provided Moses with helpers to do the task and provide for his weaknesses. Lord God, this is one of Your confirmations for me to have helpers, coworkers, for my next assignment. I praise and thank You for speaking to me today.

February 2, 2004. Lord, You have done so much for me in the past. Help me to always remember the great things You have done through me.

February 4, 2004. Oh Lord, I want to bless Your name. I don't want to forget all Your benefits. You redeemed me from destruction. You have forgiven all my sins, saved my soul. I want to follow Your plan for my life. Unfold Your plans for the ministry You have entrusted to me.

February 26, 2004. I must have faith to apply what I know from Scripture. The purpose of knowing Scripture is to develop my faith.

February 27, 2004. Lord, help me to overcome my unbelief.

March 3, 2004. God, thank You for rescuing me from depression, keeping me emotionally and spiritually alive, providing for my needs, showing Your love for me through the church.

March 4, 2004. What God told me today—fast one day a week and spend more time in prayer. Do some studying and planning.

March 7, 2004. Lord, my days and years are in Your hand. Keep revealing to me Your ways and Your will. Help me train my ears to hear Your voice and give me a specific vision of this new church plant You are leading me to do.

March 10, 2004. Speak to me, oh Lord, through life circumstances through Your word and through the Holy Spirit. Give me ears to listen and discern Your voice wisely. Lord, it's my deeper desire to receive a word, instructions from you every day. Help me to renew my mind daily, confess my sins constantly, and pray regularly.

March 13, 2004. God wants me to value excellence—do my job right, do careful planning, do critical thinking, and do intensive and intentional studying.

March 16, 2004. God show me how to be a tree of life. I desire to be a source of encouragement, a high impact person for Your glory. Let Your presence in my life make a difference in people's lives.

March 18, 2004. God will meet my needs. He knows how much we need to survive. God knows how much money we need to support my girls in education.

March 23, 2004. Oh God, help me to realize in a deeper way the value of spending time in Your word.

With this renewed passion and restored hope, Jesse was just as excited to share Jesus as he had been when he'd first become a Christian. But now he would be travelling a little lighter. He had been weary and heavy-burdened and God had given him rest for his soul. God was also showing him a new way to work, alongside Jesus with His easy yoke and light burden.

Jesse had seen God answer this specific prayer numerous times in the past, and he was excited about seeing God continue to answer it in the future.

April 2, 2004. I ask that You make my spiritual life rich. Bring those people whom You have prepared for the gospel of Jesus Christ.

April 10, 2004. Lord, You have chosen me to be Your instrument, ambassador, spokesperson for your good news, Your servant. Thank You for saving me from eternal damnation, for giving me a purpose to live for, and an everlasting life that I can anticipate to enjoy with You.

April 11, 2004. God, I know I am not to trust in my own strength, abilities, wisdom, and understanding. I can't even hide anything from You. Jesus knows the thoughts of men. You've made me realize that everything in me is transparent before You. I know that at times I allow impure and ungodly thoughts and ideas to linger in my mind. Give me a powerful mind to take captive every thought and make it submissive to Your will. For I know the power of Your word is enough to overcome and defeat ungodly and evil thoughts.

# 43

*Spring 2005*

# SOMETHING NEW

*He put a new song in my mouth, a hymn of praise to our God. Many will see and fear the Lord and put their trust in him.*

—Psalm 40:3

Jesse could feel his heart rate beginning to speed up. Beads of sweat formed on the edges of his forehead.

It felt like he had come full circle. After more than a decade, here he was again, sitting in the front row on a Sunday morning preparing to give a message.

Only this time, it wasn't the first message. It would be the last at this church.

Towards the end of his sabbatical year, Jesse had sensed God calling him to start new work. His beloved church had blessed him to leave the senior role and become the church-planting pastor. The past year had been filled with this new part-time ministry role, and picking up automotive mechanic work on the side to provide for his family.

Jesse took a deep breath, hoping to swallow the emotion he felt rising up in him. It was time.

Humour would relieve the tension he felt. He grabbed the roll of toilet paper sitting on the seat next to him and stood up, holding it high in the air.

"I brought this for a different purpose. Just in case that box of tissues isn't enough for my wife, I brought this," he said, chuckling. The congregation laughed. "This morning my daughters reminded me, 'Dad, don't forget to bring tissues today.' 'Why?' I asked. They said, 'You know our mom, how emotional she gets.' I told them, 'Okay, I'll bring a backup.'"

"Thanks, dear," Kathy called out from the audience with an easy laugh.

"I believe today is a time to celebrate," Jesse continued, speaking with a sense of calm sincerity and optimism. "I was struggling about what I was going to share. I said, 'God, what is it You want me to speak about?' Acts 13 kept popping up in my mind. But before I share this message, I want to thank our church for setting this Sunday aside as a special day for all of us—a commissioning Sunday."

There were many smiles in the congregation as he looked out and already saw a few tears.

"Let's pray," Jesse said as he bowed his head. "Lord, when we look back in our lives, even for the last year or so, even if we go beyond that, ten or twenty years ago, we can really see the work You've done in our lives. And we know it only convinces us about Your work when You bring things to pass. And today, as we look back a little bit and think about moving forward, we know that You will still be very much involved in our lives in the process, and particularly in doing kingdom work. Help us to draw insights from Your word today and may we learn something from Your word today that we can apply in our daily lives and something we can take with us from this point on. In Jesus's name I pray, amen."

Jesse looked up.

"Open your Bibles to Acts 13." Smiling, he added, "Blessed are those who brought their Bibles today."

A small ripple of laughter went out throughout the congregation as he began to read from Acts 13. They were used to it. Pastor Jesse always encouraged his people to bring their Bibles to church.

As he read the story of Paul and Barnabas following God's leading from Acts 13, he paused, allowing a moment for the truth to settle over the congregation.

"Sometimes when we read a passage like this, it's easy to assume, 'Wow, they were praying and the Spirit of God spoke and they took off.' We think, 'How did the Spirit of God speak with an audible voice? How did they know it was the Spirit of God?' We don't know that. What's important for us to know is that God spoke. It's not how he spoke. The Bible says, 'They took off!' Wow, what faithful men these are! Just like that, they took off and followed the leading of God's Spirit.

"But I'm telling you, because they're humans like us, I'm sure they struggled in following that call. Like many of us. When God speaks to us, we struggle in responding and doing the right thing. All of us go through that, even on a daily basis.

"I remember when we were planning to move to Alberta many years ago. I thought, 'Is this just about me who wants to walk away from pulling wrenches? Or is it really God leading me?' We struggled, but we took a step of faith and moved to Alberta.

"As I read this passage, I came out with this question: what would Paul and Barnabas have missed if they had chosen not to obey? If they had chosen not to go where the Spirit of God was leading them to go? They would've missed the power of God working through them.

"They encountered a man who was a sorcerer and Paul rebuked this man, causing him to get blind. It wasn't Paul or Barnabas who did that, but God doing it through them. Had they stayed and not followed God's leadership, they would've missed seeing this man, the proconsul, coming to faith in Christ. Scripture says he was an intelligent man.

"So I end up asking myself, 'What would I have missed if I stayed in Richmond B.C. and not moved to Alberta?' Well, I can name a lot of things. I would've missed working with people in this church who love the Lord and love the Word of God.

As Jesse preached, he felt emotion surfacing in the back of his throat.

"I would've missed being with a group of men going to Seattle, going to a Promise Keepers conference, and having a great time. Brother Orly, I remember that, and Norbert. I would've missed baptizing people in the lake in Sicamous. I would've missed the Word of God in the lives of the people in this church. How we changed a lot of people in the church. I would've missed the work of God in David Cay's life. I pray for these young people as I see them responding to God's Word and to what I sense the call of God is on their lives. I began to pray, 'God, these young people will face a lot of temptation. God, would You guide them and not allow them to stray away from the Bible and the values their parents taught them?' I feel blessed when I see three young people in this church in Bible college and sense the call of God on their lives.

"I would've missed the great wedding yesterday, had I not moved to Alberta. We've had a lot of fun. I would've missed seeing a man who was a law enforcer who had nothing to do with God when I met him. Little did I know, God was at work in his heart. I would've never thought that this man would be with me side by side doing ministry work. I would have not met people like the Duggans, Bishops, and the Sheltons.

"What would Paul and Barnabas have missed if they had not taken that step of faith? What would you have missed if you had not responded to Jesus Christ?

"You know, I've never met or heard anybody who resented and said words like this: 'I wish I was not a Christian. I wish I had not become a born again Christian.' I've not met somebody who said that to me.

"Over a year ago, when I knew that God was leading me in a new direction, I knew my passion was doing church planting and starting new work. We told the leadership team in the church that we wanted to have some recommendations along with Bob Shelton. I knew in my heart I was prepared to take any response that they would give me.

"After walking away from that meeting, I felt humbled by the Spirit of God, saying to myself, 'Who am I to deserve that kind of support from this church?' Because they said, 'Jesse, we're with you. We're going to help you. We're going to pray for you. We are going to help you financially. We believe in you. We believe this is what God is leading you to do.'

"I walked away and said to myself, 'Lord, I don't deserve this treatment from these people. But I recognize that this is Your work. It's not about me.'"

Jesse couldn't fight the overwhelming emotion that was choking him up and pouring through his voice. He continued, able to sense the Holy Spirit speaking through him.

"So after seeking the Lord's guidance and talking with some people I knew for ten years, God began to bring people into the group. I knew I wasn't going to do it by myself because I see in Scripture that God desires for His people to do work with a team effort.

"I didn't read that when I began this church. I did it by myself and my wife. We were at least a team, the two of us. So as we began to dialogue, I didn't exactly know where this area might be where we would see a church one day—perhaps even a building. After dialogue and much praying and discussion in our group meetings, a member of the church-planting team, Pat Duggan, said to me one day, 'Jesse, you might want to see the new areas out there. There's going to be lots of houses and people out there and there are no visible, physical churches out there. Maybe that's where we ought to go.' That's where we feel God is leading us to focus on."

Jesse sat down as a video played about the Symons Valley area in Calgary, the area where he felt called to start this new work. As the video summarized, fifty-four thousand people would be moving into the valley in the next two years. And there was only one visible church in the entire area.

As the video ended, Jesse stood back up.

"In my opinion, one of the most exciting things a Christian can experience is to see the work of God in a person's life. I saw that in Jim Messner's life. I would like Jim to come up and share his journey with God since he came to know Jesus Christ."

He smiled at his friend as Jim took the stage.

"For twenty-seven years I was in law enforcement," Jim began, gesturing towards Kathy and Jesse. "I don't think I ever shed a tear. Since I met this couple, I can't count the tears I've shed!"

His honesty elicited laughter from the audience.

"In 1989, they moved in next door to us after they'd taken that huge step of faith. I'll never forget the day I met Jesse. In 1997, they moved to Calgary to be closer to this church. In 1999, I prayed to receive Christ with Jesse. That was ten years of patience on his part, let me tell you. It seems God brought us back together again as we became part of a new church plant. Symons Valley is where God is leading us—there's no doubt in my mind. I know people here might be sad, but I'm excited. But I still had tears of joy when Jesse was talking.

"Right now we are a small group of people. We get together each Sunday, read the Bible, share, and pray. I get excited when I see new people coming to our church, but I get really excited when I see people coming to know God.

"Jesse and Kathy are people who allow themselves to be used by God to impact and change the lives of others so they too can have the abundance and pleasures of life as God meant it to be.

"I always thought I had to give up something to follow Jesus. I'm still not used to what I've gained. When I think about people who are really genuine, who care about God, family, and other people, I think of the whole Morales family."

Jim choked on his words, remembering how his family had been changed one by one.

"Our family has seen how they help, and I don't want to see that end. I've seen so much of this in our previous community in Cochrane. Like you are to them, to us, they're family. In the next year, I suspect we will see several small home study groups in the Symons Valley area. In the next three years, we will see

God at work with the firm foundation of people's families, individuals, and youth in Symons Valley. Jesse is a true church planter like I've never seen. He's not shy about his faith and he is sensitive to people.

"After Symons Valley, I'm not sure where God will lead them. There will be people impacted by their lives all the way through. I'm glad we can all be a part of that here today. Thank you."

With that, Jim once again took his seat.

Jesse stood back up and continued to speak. "The day I landed in Cochrane, the very next day I got out of the house and unloaded my stuff from this five-tonne truck. I saw a police car pull up. I thought, 'Oh no, I better be on my toes now.'" he chuckled. "But you know you don't really know or even understand in a lot of ways the work of God in people's lives. I would have never thought that Jim Messner would be with us in ministry.

"But who did all of that? It was God who allowed us to meet for a specific purpose. He allowed me to meet Greg Villabroza at the town yard where I used to work in Cochrane. One day I was standing there just about 4:00 in the afternoon. Here comes this guy introducing himself as Greg and we chatted for a few minutes. As he is leaving, he says, 'By the way, when I was in Saudi Arabia I joined some Bible study there.' That just clued me in that there's something in this man. I better build a relationship with this man. Through Greg, I met a lot of people. Dom. Mark. And through Greg and many others, we began this church. We were all rookies. We didn't know what we were doing.

"I remember the first worship we had. Greg was leading worship. I was sitting and all the papers were everywhere. I was sweating like crazy... but I was glad I wasn't the only one who was so nervous. But that was also God's work. To Bob and to John, from the bottom of my heart, even though there is this physical disconnection from this church here, it doesn't mean we will be spiritually disconnected. We won't be too far from you. But I'm going to miss a lot of good people here who love God and taught me a lot about ministry that I never would've learned in seminary classrooms or Bible college.

"I want to thank you for allowing us to serve you for those ten years and for walking alongside us. And during those tough times and great times, I look back and consider the hand of God in those times and moments. We can see that it was all part of God's plan for a greater purpose, because He wants to accomplish something so wonderful and valuable through your lives and in our own lives. May that be the part that you never forget as you walk away from this place today."

Jesse sat down.

Now it was Kathy's turn. She was already full of tears as she stood up and arranged her notes on the podium. Jesse jokingly handed her the roll of toilet paper. She and the congregation erupted in laughter.

When Kathy began, her words were already wrapped in tears.

"It seemed like such a short time ago that Angela, Christina, and Stephanie were in elementary school," Kathy said. "Every Sunday afternoon after church we would drive from Cochrane to downtown Calgary to Merlyn's tiny apartment to have a Bible study. At that time, the group of six ladies was nicknamed Jesse and the girls. He was the only male. Look around—that group has grown!

"Early we decided that Jesse needed male company, so we specifically started praying for men. You heard how God brought Greg to meet Jesse in Cochrane. I remember the day we were gathered for Bible study and someone looked out the window and said, 'Look, there are two men, and one has a guitar!' We saw Greg walking up. God had answered our prayers."

The emotion was too much for Kathy. She was unable to hold back the dam that was about to be released.

Jesse stood up and offered her the toilet paper roll. By laughing, she was able to find the strength to continue.

"We were no longer Jesse and the girls. God began to add people one at a time," she continued. "You're all very special to us. Today God is opening a new chapter in our lives. I have a mixture of great sadness and great joy. What a privilege it's been to serve the Lord here and raise our four children. Emily was born here. It takes a whole village to raise a child. This has been a safe and loving place for our children.

"In the very beginning, we were Jesse and Kathy. And then they called him Brother Jesse. And then one day someone said Pastor Jesse and I said, 'Oh yikes, if he's the pastor, I'm the pastor's wife!' I had only been a mechanics wife until that point.

"It was a scary and exciting day. We were fairly new Christians. God had just fast-tracked us off to seminary. We were in ministry and didn't know too much. Thank You, Lord, for sending Bon and Vangie Vedoya and everything I learned from her about shepherding people. God called them to Edmonton. It was a sad day to say goodbye, but I thought, 'Maybe I'm going to be okay now.'

"This summer, we will be starting again. We have two churches coming from Tennessee. Brian Harrell is bringing a team for the first two events in the community and we're praying that God's going to connect us to people just like you. Pray that God will continue to use us to continue to introduce people to Jesus. More churches will reach more people.

"Last year when Jesse was getting weary, you graciously gave him the time off he needed. He slept for the first two weeks, and when he finally woke up I saw a spark come back into his life. He would come home and say, 'Guess what? I was at the coffee shop and got into a conversation about the Lord.' I saw life come back to Jesse. God had wired him to get out and share Jesus.

"I just want to say thank you for being a hundred percent behind us with this decision to leave the church. God already had new leadership in place as we were sensing this call to start something new. Thank you from the bottom of our hearts."

Kathy took a deep breath and smiled, grateful to have made it through what she wanted to say.

The opening of a new chapter meant the closing of another. New beginnings weren't without pain, but she and Jesse had committed their lives to following Jesus, and this was where He was leading them next.

# 44

*May 2005*

# A PERFECT FIT

*...for God's gifts and his call are irrevocable.*

—Romans 11:29

*L*ord, *is this from You?* Jesse wondered.

The new opportunity seemed almost too good to be true. He could spend his time sharing life with people who did not yet know the love of Jesus, without the burden of administration and organization.

The call from Gerry Kraft, founder of Outreach Canada, had come as a surprise. He still wasn't sure how Gerry had gotten his number, but he was grateful. The founder and CEO of Outreach Canada wanted to meet with him!

The offer to work as a corporate chaplain with Outreach Canada was a dream job Jesse hadn't known existed. It seemed like the perfect fit.

When he met with Gerry, Jesse knew immediately that they shared the same heart to tell people about Jesus. The man's eyes sparkled as he spoke of the privilege of getting to tell people who were separated from God about the good news of eternal life, peace, and joy that was available to them through faith in Jesus.

"Some people think we shouldn't be aggressive about Jesus and only share if we're invited," Gerry explained.

Jesse smiled. "I like to look for opportunities to answer people's life struggles with Scripture and tell people about Jesus."

"You are the kind of chaplain I want, the perfect guy for the job," Gerry said. "Someone who genuinely desires to meet people where they're at, help them, and point them to their Saviour, Jesus."

*The perfect guy for the job.* Those were Gerry's exact words. Jesse had never felt like the perfect guy for anything before.

Jesse wasn't threatening in any way, either in stature or his approach to people. His warm personality made it easy for even those who were roughest around the edges to open up and share their story before they even had time to realize it was happening.

This was the most excited Jesse had ever felt about a job. He could see the chaplaincy ministry growing in the future.

Among his conflicted feelings, however, there was also a major hurdle: every employee of Outreach Canada had to fundraise their own salary.

When Gerry told him this, Jesse burst out laughing.

"I'm not good at that," he said. "And I don't know anyone with lots of money!"

If there was something Jesse struggled with, it was asking for help. It was difficult for him to accept gifts, let alone ask for them.

Years ago, when the transmission had gone in the family minivan, a generous offer had come from someone up north to pay for a replacement. Initially Jesse had respectfully declined.

"Jesse, God has called some people to ministry, and others to earn money to support the work of ministry," the man had told him. "Don't rob me of my gift."

Only then did Jesse reluctantly receive the money. He didn't want to stand in the way of another man's obedience to God.

Reluctantly receiving an offer was one thing, but intentionally asking? How could he possibly ask people he knew and loved for their hard-earned money?

Surprisingly, this didn't seem like a dealbreaker for Gerry. He offered to introduce Jesse to some people who could help him raise support. Jesse wasn't sure how this would change the reality, but he agreed. He was always happy to meet people.

*But what about my current work?* he asked himself.

Since transitioning to his new part-time role as church-planting pastor a year ago, he had started picking up extra mechanic work on the side.

The previous summer—at the same time he had gone from full-time senior pastor to part-time church-planting pastor—had been an exciting and expensive one for his family. Jesse had walked Angela and Christina down the aisle, three weeks apart on sunny Saturdays in July, giving them away to his new sons-in-law, Jordan and Frankie.

Jesse was so proud of his daughters and their pursuit of post-secondary education and college basketball.

Thankfully, he was still skilled with wrenches! After all, weddings and tuition came with hefty price tags. Jesse had listened to Tradio, regularly scanned the *Auto Trader*, and every Thursday picked up a copy of *The Bargain Finder*, scouring for any opportunities to buy, repair, and sell in addition to the work he did for other people.

He loved the simplicity of cars—he could diagnose the problem, repair it or replace parts, and then return the car to the road. There was a clear beginning and end, and always something to show for his labour.

Vehicles always needed fixing. People always needed a vehicle. He wasn't afraid of hard work, so he would always have a way to provide.

It was a miracle that his daughters were able to graduate without any debt and that he and Kathy were still able to help with wedding expenses. God always provided for his family in ways Jesse couldn't begin to explain.

Their family hadn't been on an airplane together until five years earlier when Brian's church had hosted a spaghetti dinner fundraiser to pay for his family to enjoy a vacation in Tennessee and Florida.

He and Kathy had always wanted a Christian education for their daughters but hadn't been able to afford it. But in its inaugural year, Bearspaw Christian School allowed ministry families to attend one year for free.

They planned to return their girls to the public system when Kathy got a phone call from a friend and board member, announcing the board's surprise decision to allow ministry families a discounted tuition rate.

The Christian school their oldest daughters had attended for their Grade Twelve year had also allowed Jesse to work in the cafeteria. The twins had even been allowed to clean in order to help offset their tuition cost.

On another occasion, Angela was due to take a missions trip to Romania, but she couldn't pay for her expenses. Then she found a cheque in the mail for the exact amount that was needed.

Each and every time the family had a need or an unforeseen expense, God provided. Often it came just as the need was getting down to the wire.

More times than he could count, Jesse had seen the promise in Matthew 6:33: *"But seek first his kingdom and his righteousness, and all these things will be given to you as well."* Jesse's priority was to follow Jesus—and to this point, God hadn't failed to provide.

His mechanic work was how God had allowed him to provide for his family while continuing the ministry God had called him to. But Jesse knew he couldn't do it all—church-planting, chaplaincy, and mechanic work. The last decade had taught him that.

Jesse had been a chaplain for Allied Trucking for a couple of years. Seeing God at work in the lives of the truck drivers had been an incredible blessing in the midst of his burnout. He loved the work, but it had only been part-time. Jesse hadn't had any idea there were so many businesses willing to hire chaplains. He hadn't known this world existed.

Ultimately, Jesse wanted to do the will of God, not his own thing, so he took time to pray about the Outreach Canada opportunity. Jesse took all his questions to the same place he always did—to the Lord. God knew all things, including the beginning from the end.

So he got out his pen and his questions and wrestled with them on the pages of his journal:

May 18, 2005. God, I thank You for the great work You have done and have been doing in my own personal life. You redeemed me from the hand of the evil one who once had a stronghold in my life. You brought me to a place where life is abundant in a country of opportunities. You gave me a new life and a purpose that is worth pursuing. You delivered me from depression. You satisfy my inner emptiness. You fill my thirst. You sent Your counsel to heal me and You rescued me from depression. Lord God, I thank You for the ways You have demonstrated Your work in my life. Lord, help me to be consistent in my walk with You. I desire to have a clearer understanding of the things and the blessings You have shown me. I know that Your love towards me is enduring and uncondi-tional. Show me ways of how I can express Your love to other people.

May 20, 2005. Oh God, would You teach me to focus on your nature, goodness, mercy, love, and faithfulness? I want to discern Your will about this ministry being offered to me with Outreach Canada. Oh God, I can see this chaplaincy work growing in the near future. Con-firm with me through real life experience if You are leading me to be part of the Outreach Canada team. Lord, are You asking me to trust you for the Outreach Canada offer to me? Help me decide about this Outreach Canada ministry opportunity. Lord, I want to be emotionally well. I desire to be fruitful in the work You have given me. Lord, show me what I must do in this chaplaincy work with Outreach Canada and this church-planting work. What is it with Outreach Canada that You are trying to do and accomplish? Are You showing me that I have a role to play with Outreach Canada? Give me a clearer understanding about Your activity there. Lord, speak to Your servant about this corporate chaplaincy work.

May 27, 2005. Adonijah took the initiative to anoint himself as king of Israel without consulting the man of God [Nathan]. It's unwise to make decisions without inquiring from the Lord. Lord, confirm with me this new ministry direction with Outreach Canada. Lord, speak to Your servant about this corporate chaplaincy work. This new ministry opportunity looks very positive. Lord, I trust You would reveal to me the next step.

Jesse was still trying to figure out how God had worked this whole thing out. Gerry invited him to share his heart for evangelism with the board of Outreach Canada, and he evidently also told them about Jesse's reluctance to fundraise.

The next conversation with Gerry was not one Jesse could've predicted. Gerry had formally offered him a part-time position as a corporate chaplain with Outreach Canada, and by some miracle Jesse wouldn't have to fundraise his salary.

May 30, 2005. Lord, let me think differently today instead of thinking wrongly about what You constantly provide for me. Help me think of those things I enjoy as blessings that come from You. I can think of automotive work I frequently do, the privilege of doing ministry with pay, and the new chaplaincy work I will be doing with OC. Lord, help me think always that these good things come from you. James 1:17 says, *"Every good and perfect gift is from above..."*

June 6, 2005. What areas in my life has God continually proven faithful to me, yet I remain reluctant to trust Him? Work... finding ministry.

God, I want to experience more of Your supernatural power in my own life. How do I begin to walk with You in a fresh way? I repent of my sin and accept Your forgiveness today.

June 8, 2005. Jesus tells me to bring His presence into the workplaces.

June 13, 2005. I thank You for creating me and for the new life You gave me. Will You cure my emotional illness, my emotional wounds from my past? I praise You for not letting Your anger fall on me. All my days, planned by You, are written in Your book.

August 15, 2005. Life can end abruptly and unexpectedly. Lord, would You teach me how to use the resources You give to me in a way I would see good results? Give me the ability to understand Your ways and Your activities.

# 45

*April 6, 2008*

## CELEBRATE

*The Lord has done great things for us, and we are filled with joy.*
—Psalm 126:3

"When I die and you have my funeral, I don't want it to be sad," Jesse said without a trace of sadness. "I want it to be a celebration of life."

This declaration, made as the van travelled south on the highway, didn't come entirely out of the blue. We were travelling home from Angela's mother-in-law's funeral in northern Alberta. After battling cancer on and off for several years, she was finally at home with Jesus in heaven, healed and whole.

Funerals have a way of bringing the brevity of life to the forefront of one's mind. All humans must face death, and since my dad was human, I suppose I knew it would eventually happen.

But I pushed the thought away, far into the future where I thought it belonged.

A few months earlier, we had celebrated my dad's sixtieth birthday. The family had all hid behind upright menus at a restaurant and yelled "Surprise!" when my mom brought the unsuspecting celebrant in. He had smiled, grateful though not one to love being the centre of attention.

By all measures, life was good. In addition to his wife and four daughters, Jesse now had three sons-in-law—Jordan, Frankie, and Mike. His first grandchild, Ethan, the boy he had always wanted, had turned two at the beginning of January.

He had recently been promoted to big brother when Maia was born a few weeks after his birthday. Papa, as he wanted to be called, couldn't stop snuggling and kissing his new granddaughter on our short trip up north.

Having twelve-year-old Emily at home kept him young, as did working in his sweet spot as a church-planting pastor and corporate chaplain. Since healing from burnout and depression, the past several years had been especially full of life and new beginnings.

He was a picture of health, still playing basketball in the driveway with Emily and still just as regularly referring to himself as the Filipino Isiah Thomas, the former Detroit Pistons Hall-of-Famer known as the little man with the big smile. As the story went, the players in Jesse's former Filipino league had given him this nickname. We called him on travelling frequently, teasing him for thinking he was airborne while in reality he was taking far more than the allowable one and a half steps on the ground.

In the grand scheme of things, he was still young. I was certain he still had decades left before we'd need to start thinking about planning his funeral.

"I want it to be a celebration of salvation that comes through Jesus Christ," he declared.

We promised him that when it came time to celebrate his life, we would, in fact, celebrate.

"We need to stop in Grande Prairie and find a car wash," he said without skipping a beat. His tone grew more serious. The weather during the funeral had been nothing but rain and the combination of the water and gravel roads had left the exterior of the van completely covered in mud.

"Why?" I pressed. "It's so out of the way, and the van is just going to get dirtier while we drive."

It was still raining, but that didn't matter to dear old dad.

He laughed, not budging an inch from his conviction. "Having all that mud on the outside will decrease our gas mileage."

"Seriously?" I asked in disbelief.

But from years of experience, I knew it was pointless to argue. For all his love, humility, hard work, and humour, my dad could be as stubborn as a mule. We tried but quickly gave up trying to reason with him and took the one-hour detour to wash the van.

For the five minutes the van stayed clean, our fuel efficiency was quite stellar.

# 46

*Spring 2008*

## IF

*I have told you these things, so that in me you may have peace. In this world you will have trouble. But take heart! I have overcome the world.*

—John 16:33

"If anything ever happened to my dad I would not be okay," I said, the dam of tears suddenly releasing in front of my unsuspecting husband.

Mike stole a surprised glance at me before returning his eyes to the road.

"Your dad is fine," he replied, reaching across the car and giving my hand a reassuring squeeze. "Nothing is going to happen to him."

His second glance told me he was confused about what had triggered my thought as we drove from Calgary back to our new home in southern Alberta.

I couldn't control the wave of emotions that came over me. I sobbed, unable to see the road through my tears. The very thought of anything ever happening to my dad felt devastating, and I was certain it was the one thing I wouldn't be able to survive.

# INTERLUDE THREE

# 47

*May 2008*

# CONFIDENT

*See what great love the Father has given us that we should be called God's children—and we are! The reason the world does not know us is that it didn't know him.*

—1 John 3:1

"**I**t's *my* daughter," I heard my dad say over the phone. "I have to take this."

My heart swelled with pride and my eyes with sadness all at the same time. The acknowledgement of being his daughter hit me with a range of emotions.

"Hi Step," he said, his accent still going strong.

"Hi Dad." I barely managed to get the two words out before the tears began to flow.

As a husband and father of four daughters, he was no stranger to tears. Knowing how to respond to us wasn't his area of expertise, but he always tried... even if he was unsure what to do.

Neither of us broke the loaded silence for a few moments.

"What's going on?" he finally asked, careful not to sound hurried.

That simple question was so loaded. So much was going on inside me. It had only been a few weeks since the phone call that had changed everything. Raw emotions and fragile feelings had very much been the norm since May 5. Tidal waves of sadness, shock, and anger took turns barging in and finding their way out without warning.

"I'm just calling because... I can," I said, failing in my attempts to choke back the tears. "I just wanted to hear your voice."

For the time being, I could still pick up the phone and call my dad, or find him in the garage when I visited home. This meant I had access to wisdom, protection, provision, and presence. And it gave me a sense of security. Whether I needed to hear his voice, have him listen to the funny noise my car made, or get his advice, having access to my father assured me that I would always have what I needed.

Knowing that this wouldn't be the case forever, or for much longer, was unsettling.

I had so many questions for God about the future. Three to five years didn't seem like enough. What about when Emily graduated? What about my mom? Who was going to take care of her? What about when Emily got married? Who would walk her down the aisle? What about my future kids—they would never get to meet him? What about when I went home for the weekend and didn't hear tools clinking in the garage?

God answered so many of my questions with a gentle but strong invitation in return: *"Will you trust me?"*

But there was a question he answered more directly, one that was at the root of every other question. I asked, "What about when I need my dad and he's not there?" Asking this question meant acknowledging that the clock was ticking. We were closer to the final buzzer than we wanted to be.

Who would I call to talk to? Who would give me wisdom for life? Whose shoulder would I cry on? Who would keep pointing me back to the Word of God? Who would take care of me?

The answer from God was swift and certain: *"I was his father. I will be yours too."*

Every girl needs her dad. Every child needs a father. And I would still have one. God's answer was sufficient for me. He had just promised that even though I was going to lose my dad, His presence was most assuredly going to fill in the aching and gaping space that was slowly being vacated. It didn't stop the tears or the sadness, but I believed God was going to take care of me.

I was losing my dad, and finding my Father.

*Part Four*

# THREE LIFE-CHANGING LETTERS

# 48

*May 5, 2008*

# THE NEWS

*They will have no fear of bad news; their hearts are steadfast, trusting in the Lord.*
—Psalm 112:7

Jesse sat down and Kathy took the seat to his left. Across from them and behind his desk sat the neurologist with a pad of paper in front of him.

"Why are you here?" he asked, not wasting any time beating around the bush.

Jesse began to explain the loss of strength he had noticed in the one finger on his left hand beginning on January 15 and how it seemed as though the weakness had spread to the one beside it.

"I see… follow me," the neurologist said, his expression remaining neutral. He gestured towards Kathy. "And you can come, too."

The couple followed the neurologist to an examination room, where he instructed Jesse to change into a hospital gown and have a seat. Kathy sat on the extra chair in the corner of the room. She couldn't wait for Jesse to get a diagnosis and prescription for whatever treatment he needed so things could get back to normal.

The loss of strength in his fingers was making it difficult for him to work on cars. He'd called it a night early not too long ago when the frustration got to him. Quitting before the job was done was out of the ordinary for Jesse.

He had complained that something was wrong with his finger, but he'd dismissed Kathy's suggestion to go to the doctor. He waved her off, saying it was nothing serious.

But eventually he went to see Dr. Hanlon, their longtime family doctor, who tested him for carpal tunnel and arthritis. These tests had come back negative.

In fact, they were only here at the neurologist's office because Dr. Hanlon, at Kathy's recent appointment, had asked how Jesse was doing. She'd reported that he was fine, but then relayed the latest strange story that Jesse had recently told her.

Jesse had been sharing his testimony at a weekly Christian businessmen's Bible study when all of a sudden it had felt like his tongue stopped working. For the last thirty seconds of his fifteen-minute story, Jesse struggled to get words out.

By the time he'd called her, his tongue had gone back to normal, but it had been strange nonetheless.

At her report, Dr. Hanlon froze, his entire countenance changing. But Kathy thought nothing of it.

"Have Jesse come in and see me *tomorrow*," he urged when he finally spoke again.

After Jesse's visit, Dr. Hanlon's office had called to explain that Jesse had an appointment with the neurologist in September, but that he was on an urgent wait list in the meantime.

Within a day, the neurology department at Rockyview Hospital called and asked Jesse to come in on May 5.

So here they were, minutes away from the answers that would fix Jesse. Then they could be on their way. Kathy was planning to carry on to watch Emily's track meet after this and Jesse would be heading back to work.

While waiting to see the doctor, Kathy pulled out the small Bible she kept in her purse. Since it was May 5, she opened the book to Psalm 5 and read: *"Listen to my words, Lord, consider my lament. Hear my cry for help, my King and my God, for to you I pray"* (Psalm 5:1–2).

Her thoughts were interrupted by a soft knock, signalling the neurologist's return. Kathy quickly tucked her Bible back into her purse along with the thought that had just entered her mind: *Am I going to need help?*

The neurologist entered the room, closed the door, and Kathy watched as he began a physical exam of Jesse.

"I see some muscle-twitching in your cheeks," the neurologist observed, pointing towards Jesse's face.

198

Kathy looked closer. Sure enough, the muscles in Jesse's cheeks were ever so slightly twitching. Seeing this triggered a memory.

"That happened to his arm a while ago," she said. "Remember, Jesse?"

He nodded and Kathy recounted to the neurologist how while lying in bed one night she had noticed Jesse's upper arm muscles twitching in the same way. She had watched it for a moment before pointing it out to Jesse. He could see it but not feel it.

At the time, he had shrugged it off. "Maybe yours is doing it, too."

They had both climbed out of bed, stood in front of the mirror, and compared arms. Kathy's muscles were still and Jesse's continued to twitch for a few minutes.

Once it stopped, they'd both dismissed it as nothing.

"It's the same thing," the neurologist confirmed, his expression still even. "Any other unusual symptoms?"

Jesse shrugged. Kathy racked her brain and then told the story about the time when Jesse's tongue had stopped working.

After finishing the quick five-minute exam, consisting of a few pricks and prods, the neurologist asked Jesse to get dressed and said he would be right back.

When the neurologist re-entered the room, he looked at Jesse, who was leaning against the examination table.

"I think you should sit down," the neurologist said.

Kathy felt her heart begin to thump. Why did Jesse need to sit down? Was something wrong?

The neurologist wasted no time. "I'm sorry. I have bad news."

Jesse let out an easy laugh. "Well, Doc, I've spent my life telling people the good news. How bad could it be?"

The neurologist's expression remained even, hinting that this was no laughing matter. "You have ALS. It's a fatal illness. The average life expectancy is three to five years. There is no treatment and there is no cure."

*Three to five years? I'm going to see my Lord sooner than I thought,* Jesse concluded silently. Only seconds early, he had been convinced he still had decades.

During his regular prayer time, Jesse regularly asked God to extend his life. He was ten years older than Kathy but still young by all earthly measures, in body and spirit. His Filipino genes had been fairly kind to his aging process and most people thought he was younger than he was. He was barely sixty, but looked and acted like forty.

There was still so much life ahead—watching his children become parents, leading their small but growing church, and taking care of the growing number of employees at the different businesses where he served as a chaplain. Emily still had many years before she would leave home, and naturally Jesse hoped he would have at least a few more boys in the mix of grandchildren surely to come in the next decade.

He had recently started saving to buy a new pickup truck. He had never owned a brand-new vehicle and had always looked for the mechanics' specials. Though he loved working on cars, he welcomed the idea of not having to fix something on a weekly basis.

When people asked about his retirement plans, he always joked that he couldn't find retirement in the Bible. However, he and Kathy had talked about travelling to the Holy Land and possibly interim-pastoring in their golden years. As long as Jesse had breath in his lungs and life in his body, he would serve the Lord and tell people about Jesus.

Kathy blinked, confused, trying to process what she had just heard. The neurologist must be mistaken. Her strong and healthy husband couldn't possibly be dying.

After letting them absorb the news for a moment, the neurologist continued. "I can only ever be ninety-nine percent. The only way to be a hundred percent sure is with an autopsy. But you have several classic symptoms."

He went on to connect all the dots between the symptoms Jesse and Kathy had thought were unrelated oddities—the loss of strength in his fingers, the sporadic muscle-twitching, and the loss of movement in his tongue.

"I'll refer you to Dr. White, the ALS specialist in our neurology department," said the doctor. "You can schedule a follow-up appointment at the front desk on your way out."

With that, the neurologist turned and walked out, leaving Jesse and Kathy in stunned silence.

Never in a million years had either of them suspected this. Their world, which had seemed a prescription away from perfect only minutes ago, had been shattered by three letters they'd never heard in such a fatal combination.

Kathy couldn't stop her tears as a wave of questions slammed up against her. What exactly was ALS? Had the neurologist said fatal? Jesse was dying? Had she heard that right?

Her wave of questions was soon joined by a wave of sobs as she dialled her parents. Meanwhile, Jesse returned to the waiting area to schedule his follow-up appointment.

As Kathy heard the sound of her own voice relaying the news, reality broke through the protective layer of shock and denial that had formed around her. She barely managed to get the words out and could hardly believe them: Jesse had ALS and a life expectancy was three to five years.

"Do you want us to come?" her parents asked with deep concern.

There was no reason for the elderly couple to hop on a plane, but Kathy promised to call later. She then hung up and dialled her longtime friend Barb.

"I was thinking it might be ALS," Barb said sadly. "But I hoped I was wrong."

Kathy looked up to see Jesse making his way back towards her. "He's coming now," she said, recruiting all her energy to compose herself. "I'll call you later."

Slowly, with their arms around one another, Jesse and Kathy silently made their way down the hospital hallway, desperate to hold on to what was now slipping through their fingers. The heaviness that hung in the air between them said it all.

Kathy clung to Jesse as memories flashed through her mind of the life they had shared together. They had been partners in life, parenting, and ministry for three solid decades. Jesse had been at her side through everything. What would she do without him?

This couldn't be happening.

After what seemed like forever, they reached the front door of the hospital and stepped outside. The parking lot was still full of parked cars, people were still coming and going, and the sun was still shining. Everything appeared to be just as they'd left it before their appointment, but nothing would ever be the same again. What were they supposed to do next?

As Kathy stepped off the sidewalk, her grief broke free again. She grabbed hold of Jesse, and he turned to her right as she fell into his arms.

"What did the doctor say?" Kathy asked through convulsive sobs. "Did he say *fatal*? Did he say you're *dying*? What is happening? Did he say three to five years? How are we going to tell the girls?"

Jesse held his wife tighter. "I want to tell the girls myself," he answered calmly.

Kathy searched her husband's face, wondering how he always managed to stay so calm.

"I can't think straight," she said, attempting to dry her eyes. But the tears continued to flow as they held tightly to one another.

Suddenly, responsibility interrupted their new reality.

"Oh no! Emily's track meet!" Kathy exclaimed. "If I'm late, she'll know that something is wrong."

After deliberating, Jesse decided to attend the track meet rather than go to work. He handed his wife his pair of sunglasses to keep her face from giving away what she wasn't yet ready to talk about, and they both headed to the track meet in their separate vehicles.

As she followed Jesse's car, Kathy's thoughts and questions kept crashing into one another, making her head spin.

How would this affect the girls' faith? Would Jesse get to see his grandchildren grow up? Would he make it to Emily's high school graduation, which was still five years from now? Who would walk Emily down the aisle? How would she live without her husband? What would their church do without its pastor? Would God heal Jesse?

There were no answers, only an increasing number of questions. But there was one thing she knew without a doubt: the path ahead would be difficult and painful.

But for now, she had to press on. Together they would cheer Emily on at her first-ever junior high track meet. Her excitement had been palpable at breakfast that morning.

This news would have to wait. Her sunglasses could keep her grief hidden at least for the next few hours. And she would avoid anyone she knew so the news didn't make its way out prematurely.

This afternoon, she and Jesse would enjoy something they had always loved—watching their daughter compete, together.

# 49

*May 5, 2008*

# FLICKERS OF HOPE

*Praise the Lord, my soul, and forget not all his benefits—who forgives all your
sins and heals all your diseases, who redeems your life from the pit and crowns you
with love and compassion...*

—Psalm 103:2–4

As Jesse sat in the bleachers at the junior high track meet, watching as Emily's coach prepared her for her event, God did the same for Jesse—preparing him for the impossibly hard road ahead... speaking, promising, and assuring him of what was true. Conversations Jesse had had with his Heavenly Father surfaced in his mind, but it wasn't like watching an old rerun. It was more like watching a fire ignite and burn with increasing intensity.

Over the years, Jesse had started many fires on family camping trips. The match's tiny flame would light the kindling and eventually ignite into a full-blown fire—as long as it had fuel to burn. Now the Holy Spirit was igniting the truth Jesse had faithfully read, believed, and studied over many years. Each verse, each word, each message had been another log on the Holy Spirit's fire.

Jesse had committed Psalm 103:1–5 to memory while driving with a Scripture memory CD playing. He thought back on the words now:

Praise the Lord, my soul; all my inmost being, praise his holy name.
Praise the Lord, my soul, and forget not all his benefits—who forgives
all your sins and heals all your diseases, who redeems your life from

the pit and crowns you with love and compassion, who satisfies your desires with good things so that your youth is renewed like the eagle's.

He would bless his Lord with everything that was within him, including this disease. God had the ability to heal him.

*Let the redeemed of the Lord tell their story—those he redeemed from the hand of the foe, those he gathered from the lands, from east and west, from north and south.*
—Psalm 107:2–3

Jesse remembered how God had redeemed him from the hand of the evil one. God had brought him to a country filled with opportunity, gave him a new, eternal, and abundant life, delivered him from depression, and given him a purpose that was worth pursuing. Because of Jesus, no matter when Jesse died, he would live.

*We demolish arguments and every pretension that sets itself up against the knowledge of God, and we take captive every thought to make it obedient to Christ.*
—2 Corinthians 10:5

Doubt, fear, and confusion weren't absent within him, but Jesse handed them over to Jesus, who held them captive where they wouldn't be allowed to rule. Jesus Christ, his living hope, would anchor him through this surprise storm.

This fresh fire was igniting something he desperately needed: hope.

*Yes,* he thought, *I will have hope in God.*

Now he had to figure out how to tell his girls. This would no doubt be the most difficult part. As their father, it was his God-given responsibility to provide for and protect them. Yet he had to tell them that he wouldn't be around to do that anymore.

Much like the night he'd been prompted by the Holy Spirit to pray for his girls' protection on the night of their accident, he prayed fervently. They would need God's protection from fear, doubt, despair, and discouragement.

God could be trusted to take care of his family, even when Jesse couldn't. He had never been a man of many words, but now he needed to find some.

# 50

*May 5, 2008*

# OKAY

*"Because he loves me," says the Lord, "I will rescue him; I will protect him, for he acknowledges my name."*

—Psalm 91:14

"*P*ray for your girls' protection."

That had been the prayer the Holy Spirit prompted him to pray all those years ago. His daughters' survival that night, when he couldn't be there, was undeniable proof of what he needed to believe right now: God could be trusted to take care of his girls, even when he couldn't.

Perhaps especially when he couldn't.

He had been dreading this since receiving the diagnosis. While the news would be devastating for all of his daughters. The older three were married and more mature in their faith. Emily was only twelve. He and Kathy weren't done raising her. It would likely be more than three to five years until he gave her away to a husband's care and protection. Would he be around for that?

Since Christina only lived five minutes away, Jesse drove over early that day to deliver the news in person. He sat in his daughter's living room and delivered the news to Christina and son-in-law Frankie.

"I have amyotrophic lateral sclerosis, also known as A–L–S." He punctuated each letter.

There were many tears… and more questions than answers. When he left his grieving daughter, Frankie was there to comfort her. She would be okay.

Next he called Angela.

"How are they going to fix it?" his firstborn asked. "What's the cure?"

He tried to help her understand what he himself was still processing: he had three to five years to live. Though Jesse didn't understand much about the disease, he knew what the doctor had said. This wasn't like one of the many vehicles that had gone through his garage over the years; he had been able to fix every problem any vehicle had thrown his way, but he couldn't fix this.

Angela's husband Jordan wasn't home, but she packed her two small kids into the car and drove in shock and sadness to the farmyard to tell her husband the devastating news and take comfort in his arms. She would also be okay.

Next he made the phone call to me. I assured him that Mike was home. More tears. More shock. More questions. But he knew I would be okay.

Jesse took a deep breath. This next one would be the most difficult.

"H–Em..." Jesse called out. The subtle slowing of his tongue seemed to further accentuate his accent. "Come and sit down."

Emily was his baby. When his older daughters had been babies, life was different. He had been running from God. He and Kathy had always wanted another child after the first three, but the timing had never seemed right. Seminary had needed all their attention, as had starting a new church.

A year after he'd graduated from seminary, Emily had arrived. There were ten years between Emily and myself, and thirteen between Emily and the twins. Eager, ambitious, and full of joy, she had completed their family and lit up their world. Jesse had always been so proud of all his girls, but Emily occupied the softest place in his heart.

Upon hearing his voice, Emily immediately bounded down the stairs, still on cloud nine from her earlier victories at the track meet.

Jesse smiled. She loved being with her friends, competing, and the overall atmosphere of her first junior high track meet. Emily was always so full of life, so full of joy. And today the track meet seemed to have left her with an extra dose of excitement.

"H–Em," Jesse began carefully as she sat down. "H–I need to tell you something."

Jesse watched helplessly as the news of the diagnosis settled over his youngest daughter's face. The life and joy slowly drained out of her.

Emily's eyes darted back and forth between her solemn father and sobbing mother. She was quiet, so much like him. She processed things internally.

"I... I... I... am going to my room," Emily managed.

She stood up, needing to get away. She wanted to hit rewind and go back to a few minutes ago when her world had still been in one piece. She had to get to her room. What had she just heard? Her dad was dying?

Jesse followed her up the stairs, wanting nothing more than to make it all go away.

Emily paused and turned around. "I just want to be alone," she said quietly.

His eyes said it all—he didn't want her to be alone, not ever. He wanted to make sure she was okay. But she wasn't okay. Her dad was dying.

Then he said the words he would continue to speak to her on repeat, and full of faith, over the next fifteen months: "Em, you and Mom are going to be okay."

Emily had always trusted her dad; he'd never given her reason not to. If he said they were going to be okay, they would be, even if nothing about this situation felt okay. They had each other. She could take his word for it.

With that, she turned, finished her ascent up the stairs, and closed the door to her room, wishing she could also close the door to the hurt that was overtaking her heart.

# 51

*May 6, 2008*

# THE PROMISE

*I will say of the Lord, "He is my refuge and my fortress, my God, in whom I trust."*

—Psalm 91:2

"You do your part. I will do mine."

The promise filled Jesse with hope.

It had been two days since the diagnosis. In the wake of the life-changing news, Jesse had done the only thing he knew how to do, the same thing he had done in every season of his life no matter the challenging circumstances life threw his way. He kept going.

Upon hearing the news, both Angela and I had wanted to immediately drop everything and come to Calgary, but Jesse assured us it wasn't necessary. We could wait until the weekend when we were already planning to come for a family friend's wedding.

Jesse was scheduled to attend the annual Outreach Canada retreat in Bellingham, Washington, so he did. He boarded the plane Tuesday morning and planned to be back in Calgary with plenty of time to spare before the wedding on Saturday.

His family decided not to share the news of the diagnosis publicly until after the wedding, not wanting to dampen anyone's spirits. Every time he delivered the news of the diagnosis, it felt a little more real.

The most recent example was telling his older brother Bert, who picked him up at the airport in Vancouver.

"I'm sick," Jesse said evenly in their native tongue of Pampango. "Have you heard of Lou Gehrig?"

"I've heard the name... that baseball player from the twenties and thirties?" Bert asked as he drove Jesse to his in-laws' home in Richmond.

"The real name of Lou Gehrig's disease is ALS, amyotrophic lateral sclerosis," Jesse continued. "It's not a painful disease. The doctor said I have three to five years to live."

Bert looked at Jesse in disbelief, unable to believe his younger brother was dying. Jesse wasn't supposed to die before him.

Jesse delivered the news to all of his siblings, one by one, mostly over the phone. Like him, none of them had heard of ALS. Everyone wanted to know the same things—how had he gotten it and what was the cure? ALS was particularly rare among Filipinos. Hardly anyone knew what Jesse was talking about. He was still trying to understand it himself.

Jesse carried on, borrowing his in-laws' car to drive himself from Richmond to Bellingham. There he remained quiet, acting normally, not saying anything to the other Outreach Canada staff members. It wasn't necessary to worry anyone or draw attention to himself.

But eventually he could no longer keep it in. He told Gerry, the director of Outreach Canada, unable to mask his concern, yet feeling positive that he was going to somehow be okay.

Gerry responded full of compassion and gave him permission to do what he most needed. "Jesse, go spend time with your family."

Jesse called his younger brother Lope in Seattle and asked him to come pick him up.

The diagnosis was about to feel more real.

———

"C'mon, man," his brother Lope said, looking back over his shoulder at him. Jesse was lagging fifteen feet behind him as they walked across his niece's university campus in Bellingham.

Jesse had always stayed closely connected with Lope. They had a bond that time and distance couldn't weaken. They often made the effort to spend time together, even outside of Morales family gatherings. And of course troubleshooting the latest car problem always gave the mechanic brothers a reason to pick up the phone and call.

Lope looked at Jesse, eyes wide. The mixture of confusion and bewilderment on Lope's face said he couldn't believe his brother was dying.

Jesse was always one to run to help someone in need. And now he couldn't keep up while walking?

Jesse willed his legs to move faster, but they wouldn't listen. It was already happening; the disease was slowing him down.

He felt tired and relieved when they finally made it back to Lope's Thunderbird. Lope turned on a Kapampangan[6] album full of the latest songs as they made their way back to Seattle. Jesse smiled. He hadn't heard music like this since immigrating. The music triggered many old memories as he and his brother reminisced about their days in the Philippines.

Some memories brought easy laughter. They recalled Jesse's tough guy persona when he'd acted as Lope's protector. Jesse had known how to handle his younger brother, tricking him into cleaning his fully restored 1956 Mercury Monterey in exchange for the promise of driving it.

Despite Jesse's playful antics, he had always been gentle and easy on his little brother.

They laughed remembering the brand-new watch Lope had gotten from their mother when Jesse had been preparing to immigrate. Jesse had convinced Lope to give it to him, promising to replace it when he arrived.

Not only did Jesse not replace it, but when Lope arrived in Canada a few years later, asking for it back, Jesse laughed sheepishly. When Lope pressed him on its whereabouts, Jesse confessed that he had lost it in a bar fight.

They laughed recalling the days when the three brothers, including Bert, had all lived together in Vancouver, allowing ample opportunity for them to continuously take each other's money in chess. The wager, even if small, always made the win sweeter.

When the conversation turned to their work in the shop and the subject of their dad, Jesse's expression changed. The light laughter they'd shared only moments earlier vanished.

"After all these years," Jesse said quietly, "I still don't understand why he treated me the way he did."

---

6    This is the term for people native to the province of Pampanga in the Philippines.

Lope glanced at him, clearly surprised. It made sense. Because Jesse had never mentioned their father's treatment of him, Lope had assumed that Jesse had left it behind when he'd left the Philippines.

They were both quiet, the silence of this unanswered question sitting heavily between them.

Then another question brought them back to reality.

"When was the first time you experienced symptoms?" Lope asked.

"I got into the car one day and put the keys in," Jesse said. "I couldn't turn the ignition. Another time, I was holding a grocery bag, and it just dropped to the floor. At the time, I didn't think they were connected, but now, looking back..."

He trailed off, the neurologist's words drifting back into his mind: *"You have several classic symptoms."*

The slowness in his tongue the day he'd struggled to finish sharing his testimony at the men's Bible study. The weakness in his finger. The twitching in his muscles. The loss of grip in his hands.

There had been a reason for all of it. A terrible one.

Jesse had to be strong for his family, but in the safety of his brother's presence he allowed all his concerns to spill out, one after the other. He had thought he had more time. What about Kathy? What about his girls? He wouldn't be there for them or with them. He wouldn't get to meet all his grandchildren. How was he going to survive as he slowly and surely lost his abilities and independence?

Some moments he felt completely healthy and normal, and other moments he couldn't will his legs to move or his tongue to speak clearly. He had to keep living as long as God allowed him, even in the face of dying, but how?

Less than two months earlier, Jesse and Emily had visited Seattle to watch an NBA game. During that trip, Jesse had told Lope that even though he was sixty, he still felt young and strong. Now, only six weeks later, Jesse was staring at the homestretch of his life.

How was that even possible? Everything had changed so quickly without warning.

The heaviness he felt was interrupted by hope as Jesse remembered the promise God had spoken to him while he was still in Bellingham: *"You do your part. I will do mine."*

Whatever Jesse's part was, he would find a way to do it. And God would be faithful to do His.

# 52

# GUARANTEED

*He will wipe every tear from their eyes. There will be no more death or mourning or crying or pain, for the old order of things has passed away.*

—Revelation 21:4

"God will heal your dad," Liz said confidently.

I was all ears. This promise sparked hope in a time that was characterized by heaviness. I felt hope rise inside me.

Liz had journeyed with her dad through his ten-year battle with Parkinson's disease and could relate to the loss of a parent at the hand of a neurological disease. She knew the pain of a daughter losing her dad. Her husband Paul had worked as a registered nurse and once provided private care for an ALS patient.

Jesse had made friends with Paul the same way he'd made most of his friends—through a chance encounter and strong personal connection.

After beginning his work in corporate chaplaincy, Jesse had been invited to a Christian businessmen's Bible study full of entrepreneurs. They had welcomed him, affirming the shared faith and risk that church-planting and entrepreneurship both required.

When Jesse was getting acquainted with his new colleagues, he sat next to a man named Paul, who introduced himself as a professional musician.

Later that day, Jesse had visited Kathy at her office in Cochrane and informed her, "I met this guy named Paul who says he's a professional musician. He sings country music. I think I'm going to ask him to be the new worship leader at our church plant!"

"What's his last name?" a nearby officemate inquired, perking up at Jesse's description.

"I'm not sure," Jesse shrugged. "He just said his name was Paul."

The women stole glances at one another. How many professional musicians named Paul could there be in Calgary? With a quick online search, they pulled up Paul Brandt's website.

"Is this the guy?" one of them asked.

"That's him," Jesse exclaimed, legitimately surprised. "You've heard of him?"

They all laughed, thinking Jesse must be joking. After all, what self-respecting Calgarian hadn't heard of Paul Brandt?

"Is he any good?" Jesse asked the starstruck women.

The next week, when Jesse returned to that Bible study, he casually said to Paul, "You'll never believe it. My wife has actually heard of you!"

Because of his experience in healthcare, Paul had an intimate and experiential knowledge of the cruel nature of the disease and how it impacted the patient and their family. Paul and Liz wanted to give my sisters and me space to process the diagnosis.

The hope I felt rising in me for healing didn't depart. I leaned in close to hear what Liz had to say, wanting to know more about this guaranteed healing. God would *for sure* heal my dad?

"It's just a matter of whether it's on this side of heaven or the other," Liz finished.

The truth Liz shared that day shifted the way I understood healing. We hoped and prayed healing would come on this side of heaven, but we didn't yet know. God was faithful and He had all of eternity to fulfill His promises.

But either way, my dad would be healed of ALS. The day with no more tears, suffering, or pain would come. Guaranteed.

# 53

*May 2008*

# START

*Come and hear, all you who fear God; let me tell you what he has done for me.*
—Psalm 66:16

We couldn't be there for everyday life, but we did take every opportunity to spend time with my dad, travelling home most weekends. The most recent of which had been a weekend trip to Canmore with my parents and Emily, which felt like a brief respite from the staggering new reality. There, my mom had expressed how much of a relief it was to have a break from the house phone. As word spread, the phone rang off the hook with people calling to express their care, concern, and desire to hear the latest news.

As much as this made my mom feel cared for, constantly retelling the story of the diagnosis and prognosis was emotionally exhausting and time-consuming.

In my most recent semester at university, we had been introduced to a new communications tool: a blog.

"I'll start a blog about Dad's progress and then you don't have to keep updating people over the phone," I offered my mom.

I sat down at my computer, opened Blogger, and typed in a few possibilities for the title. Jesse's Journey was taken, but www.jessemoralesjourney.blogspot.com was available. I claimed the domain and my fingers flew across the keyboard.

*June 11, 2008*
# WALK WITH US

Since my dad's diagnosis on May 5, 2008, our phone has been ringing off the hook with supportive and loving people wanting to know how he is doing. I thought an online blog to keep people updated on his status would be more efficient and a bit easier on my mom, dad, and Emily!

For those of you just tuning in, my dad, Jesse Morales, was diagnosed with ALS, commonly known as Lou Gehrig's disease. He first started noticing a loss of strength in his hands last January. After several visits to the family doctor, a neurologist, and an ALS specialist, we found the reason for it. We were told that the average lifespan after diagnosis is three to five years. Naturally, we were shocked and saddened by this news, but in the midst of this tragedy God has still shown Himself faithful.

When my dad first shared the news with me, he said, "Steph, get into the Word!" He shared with me a passage out of Luke 18, the parable of the persistent widow. Here is an excerpt from it: *"Then Jesus told his disciples a parable to show them that they should always pray and not give up… And will not God bring about justice for his chosen ones, who cry out to him day and night? Will he keep putting them off? I tell you, he will see that they get justice, and quickly"* (Luke 18:1, 7).

I find that we seem to seek God more desperately immediately following a crisis. As time passes, we tend to adjust and accept the reality of situations. I pray that this is not my attitude and that I will continue to ask for healing until the day I see it.

I hope that you will join my family in lifting my dad up to the Lord in prayer every time you think of him!

I hit post before beginning the second update:

*June 11, 2008*
# JESSE'S GIRLS RUN FOR ALS

As many of you know, Christina, Emily, and I started the team Jesse's Girls to participate in Betty's Run for ALS. As the word spread, we had many people sign up to walk/run with us and to contribute to our fundraising goal of $10,000.

We ended up with over sixty people participating with us and raising over $13,000 as a team! Special thanks to the Three Sisters and the Beaulieu family for your added fundraising efforts!

My dad was one of several people with ALS who participated in the walk. He was so strong and I was so proud of him! There was quite a cheer and a few tears when he came across the finish line. Around fifty other friends and family participated in the walk with him. I along with ten others braved the eight-kilometre run and were encouraged and cheered on by our fellow walkers.

Our team, the sea of lime green, was easy to spot thanks to Don Taniguchi. His firm, LTNS Accounting, sponsored team T-shirts for the events. You could spot anyone from a mile away!

It was a great day! We look forward to raising more money next year and having more people come out and participate with us! Thank you to everyone who was a part of it!

# 54

*June 2008*

# HEALING HOPE

*Therefore confess your sins to each other and pray for each other so that you may be healed. The prayer of a righteous person is powerful and effective.*

—James 5:16

"**I** believe that the body has the power to heal itself," my dad said to Dr. White, the ALS specialist, with humble confidence. The bold statement came from his belief in God's healing power. Nothing was impossible for God. The same power that had raised Jesus from the dead lived inside of him. Therefore, God could heal naturally, with medicine, with a miracle, or in the healing waters in eternity.

Either way, my dad would live.

He came across a book about a patient who was "winning" against ALS. The book wasn't favoured by the health community, as it gave ALS patients hope based on a testimony that wasn't supported by research. My dad asked me to read it and glean anything that might help him to "do his part." He was prepared to fight with everything he had.

In the past, Dr. White had issued gentle but firm warnings about this kind of hope: "You will have many opportunities to spend money on remedies, and you are welcome to do so. But know that research doesn't support any of these. There is no cure for ALS."

I sat next to my dad and waited for his response to my dad's most recent hope-filled statement.

"Allow me to give you a rather crude example," the doctor said. "If you cut off your arm in an accident, your body will not grow another one. ALS is like that."

His tone wasn't heartless, but it was no-nonsense, dashing our hopes of "winning" against the disease in the way this book had suggested was possible.

We both stared at the neurologist, the gravity of his example slowly sinking in. Yes, the body could heal naturally from other ailments, such as a cold or a cut, but it was becoming increasingly and painfully obvious that ALS was different.

Dr. White went on to explain how the motor neurons in my dad's body were being cut off from life. The motor neurons weren't going to heal themselves naturally. There was no medicine. The dead motor neurons wouldn't regrow.

It would take an earthly miracle or an eternal promise.

Dr. White was consistently compassionate but firm in communicating, as often as was necessary, that the research showed there was no cure.

Still, the sparks of hope mixed with shock, sadness, and grief wouldn't die easily. My dad dug even more deeply into the Word than normal, listening for the Holy Spirit's voice and trying to discern what God had promised to do.

God had said, *"You do your part. I will do mine."*

Each time I visited home, my dad had a new encouragement to share with me from the Word of God. He continually urged me to read it for myself.

"Steph, King Hezekiah was on his deathbed. He cried out to God to extend his life and God healed him," he shared.

Science wasn't on our side, but that wasn't where we placed our hope. God could still intervene. A miracle was not out of God's reach.

Healing could still come. Healing would come.

What was the part my dad was to do? It was the same thing that had been his part for the past twenty-two years: have present and active faith. It was to trust the timing and plan of God. It was to continue to seek first the kingdom and His righteousness, trusting that God would take care of everything else. This included all the things that didn't make sense—all the needs that didn't seem to have ends that would meet, all the uncertainties and unknowns. God would sustain him and those he loved even in the face of death by a thousand losses.

As we waited to see just how God's plan would unfold, there was always great hope in that promise: *"You do your part. I will do mine."*

# 55

*June 2008*

## COME HERE

*One generation commends your works to another; they tell of your mighty acts.*
—Psalm 145:4

"Steph," my dad called later that day from the garage.

Growing up, if your name was hollered from the garage, it meant you were to stop what you are doing and go help. Unless you didn't answer, in which case Dad would move on to another daughter. If I didn't want to be interrupted, I would simply ignore the call, pretending I hadn't heard. Then he'd go through the list: "Steph? Angela? Christina?" And then finally: "Emily?" Our youngest sister was available and eager and often ended up being the helping hand he needed.

I didn't ignore his invitation this time. I wouldn't miss any chance to be with, talk to, and learn from my dad. So when I heard my name, I didn't hesitate. He was still able to get into his coveralls in the garage but needed someone else to be his hands.

My dad was installing new spark plugs in my car. He had laboured to this point but couldn't grip the socket wrench tight enough to secure the new spark plugs.

He handed me the socket wrench.

Avid listening was not my strong suit, but in this season I was tuned in—both to God and to my dad. We leaned over the hood together and he pointed out the area we were working on. He explained the motion with words and demonstrated with his hands how to tighten it. He then described the click I was listening for to ensure that the spark plug was secure.

I heard the wrench twisting, but no click.

He tried again, his expression telling me that it pained him not to be able to do this job that would have normally taken him only minutes. It was becoming more and more apparent that do-it-yourself was no longer the name of his game.

A man who had spent his whole life serving others was entering a season of total dependency, one that didn't come naturally to him. He would need to be served. He would need to simply receive.

Eventually those spark plugs did click, but not as a result of his own two hands.

The passing of the baton had begun.

———————

"Steph, come here," my dad called during another weekend that my husband and I spent with my parents in Calgary.

I came downstairs to find him standing in the kitchen. It wasn't uncommon for him to cook up a storm. If it was hunting season, it was wild game. But on any given day, there were a few of his favourite dishes. Kapampangans have always been known for their great cooking and my dad was no exception.

I raised my eyebrows inquisitively, seeing no initial reason for his calling out to me.

He gestured for me to pull a kitchen chair right into the small galley kitchen so he could sit, giving rest to his easily fatigued muscles.

"I need to teach you some Filipino recipes," he said.

His tone told me this wasn't one of his jokes.

My expression must have relayed my confusion. My dad had taught me how to wash dishes, how to wash a car while spending the least amount of money on the timer, how to do a left-handed layup, and how to cook rice by touching the top of the uncooked rice with my fingertip and using the first crease in my finger as the fill line.

I had enjoyed eating his cooking over the years, but it wasn't something I had ever expressed interest in learning. And he had never tried to teach it.

"I realize I've never passed these recipes on to you," he said.

*Really? Right now?*

But I kept my thoughts to myself. Apparently today was as good a day as any.

He didn't tell me what we were making, only that we were cooking. From his chair, sitting upright, his arms beginning to hang limp and loosely on his lap, he gave me one instruction at a time. Add this. Saute that. Chop this. Stir that. Bring it here so I can try it.

What on earth were we making? But I didn't dare halt the process in order to ask the expert if he knew what he was doing. For the life of me, I couldn't think what dish would contain both tomatoes and soy sauce. Would anyone want to eat it?

But my job remained the same: follow his instructions.

This step-by-step instruction went on for the better part of an hour before I finally began to recognize what I was cooking—caldereta, one of my all-time favourite dishes.

He seemed satisfied with the outcome. He had passed on a recipe.

The next generation wouldn't only be eating my mom's lasagna; I was learning to respond to my dad's call, trust his words, and carry out his instructions—a pattern that would be much-needed in the days to come. Because when you trust someone, you don't need to understand. You can simply obey.

# 56

*July 2008*

# THE PHILIPPINES

*A cheerful heart is good medicine, but a crushed spirit dries up the bones.*
—Proverbs 17:22

"I was so tired of my dad's abuse that I decided to run away," my dad explained. I don't recall the first time I learned that my grandfather hadn't treated my dad well, only that once I was a young adult I became vaguely aware of it. He didn't hesitate to share any part of his story if it would be a source of encouragement to a weary heart and point someone to Jesus.

But it wasn't an everyday topic of conversation around our home or something my dad had ever directly brought up in conversation with me.

I listened intently to him speak, just as I did to all his stories during this season of our lives. Yet no matter how hard he tried, he couldn't get the words out.

Along with the voluntary muscle loss that accompanied ALS came a strange symptom: either uncontrollable laughter or uncontrollable tears. Thankfully, for my dad, it was uncontrollable laughter. He already laughed harder at his own jokes than anyone else, and now he physically could not stop laughing.

We were in the Philippines, a once-in-a-lifetime family trip, and it had brought back a flood of memories for him. We soaked in the stories that were being stirred up.

On this particular day, we sat in the hotel room at The Manor at Camp John Hay in Baguio, waiting in anticipation for the punchline of his story. It contained the reason he had ultimately decided to return home to his abusive father rather than stick with his plan to run away.

After many minutes of uncontrollable laughter, and his captive audience growing impatient, I passed him my laptop.

"Just type the story, Dad."

Watching my dad tell a story he thought was hilarious was its own bit of comedy, even if the actual story wasn't. He sat at the computer for several minutes, alternating between throwing his head back in uncontrollable leg-slapping laughter and collecting himself only long enough to type a few letters at a time.

And to think, we had almost missed the opportunity to walk down memory lane in such a literal way.

Initially, he had politely declined his friend Jack's offer following the news of the diagnosis. The offer? A trip for you and your family anywhere in the world.

Through his work at Outreach Canada, Jesse had worked for Jack Van Deventer as a chaplain at his flooring company. He also considered the man to be a friend.

It was a more generous gift than he knew how to comfortably receive. Our family—two parents, four daughters, three sons-in-law, and two grandkids—were eleven people in total. We had only ever been all together on an airplane once, and that trip had also been a gift from generous, kingdom-minded people.

Getting to the Philippines, of all places, wasn't easily affordable—part of the reason that we hadn't fulfilled the dream of going back together.

Thankfully, Jack hadn't let him off the hook so easily.

"I can't do anything about this disease, Jesse," he had said. "But I can do this. Let me do this. You've always talked about wanting to take your girls to see where you grew up. Why don't you do that?"

My parents had been deliberating about accepting this generous offer in the neurologist's office when my mom mentioned they were considering taking a short vacation at Christmastime.

The neurologist interjected. "I wouldn't wait that long," he said knowingly.

My mom was taken aback. He wouldn't wait *that* long? Christmas was only six months away.

Dr. White, again compassionate and firm, seemed confident in his recommendation. The initial prognosis had been accompanied by a life expectancy of three to five years. But my dad's indicators were showing a more rapid prognosis. If we waited until Christmas, it might prove too difficult to go—or even impossible.

It wasn't only about how much time my dad had, but his mobility and physical independence during the time remaining.

Without knowing it, they had already bid farewell at that point to many of his fine motor skills. My parents often didn't know an experience was the last until it had already passed. Tying his shoes was now impossible, so he had rubber laces. As already mentioned, he could no longer grip a socket wrench. His food had to be cut up, as even large-handled cutlery was difficult to use. The strength in his legs held up most days, but he fatigued more easily. There was no telling what he would and wouldn't be able to do by Christmas.

Though facing so much loss, the trip was something he would be able to do—at least for now.

Reluctantly, my dad accepted his friend's offer and we finally left on the trip my dad had always dreamed of taking, although under much different circumstances than he had ever imagined.

The first week was spent at the old Clark Air Force Base near my dad's hometown in Dau, Mabalacat where we saw the house he had grown up in, as well as his high school, Holy Angel University. He told stories of refolding the newspapers he'd already sold to the army officers and reselling them to double his profits. He showed us the fields where he had eaten stolen sugarcane.

For the second week, we visited Puerto del Sol in Bolinao, Pangasinan. Afterward Angela and her family, and Christina and her husband, returned home. My parents, Emily, Mike, and I spent the extra week in Baguio where Mike had been born and spent his early years before coming to Canada in 1990. Mike hadn't been back home since first immigrating.

Here we were, sitting in the hotel, stuck in the middle of my dad's story, waiting to hear why he had decided to return home and subject himself to his father's mistreatment.

He continued typing the story a few letters at a time, breaking for more uncontrollable laughter. Finally, after twenty minutes of this comedy, he gestured to me to come and read the punchline: *"The pain of hunger in my tummy was worse than the pain of my dad's abuse so I went home."*

We all stared in disbelief. Were we supposed to laugh or cry? He had gone home because he was hungry. For a man who had always been a bottomless pit, hunger was serious business.

Perhaps this was related to the part God had promised to do—to keep the man who'd suffered from depression only a few years earlier healthy with regular doses of the best kind of medicine: laughter.

It felt a little like witnessing a small miracle.

# 57

*August 2008*

# THE FASTER LANE

*Therefore we do not lose heart. Though outwardly we are wasting away, yet inwardly we are being renewed day by day. For our light and momentary troubles are achieving for us an eternal glory that far outweighs them all.*

—2 Corinthians 4:16–17

Every update brought a mixed bag of loss and hope. Writing was a helpful tool for processing the bad news. It was painfully evident that the initial estimate of three to five years had been too optimistic.

I sat down to type a blog entry about the new reality. It felt like the gas pedal being slammed down in a season when we were trying to hit the brakes.

*August 18, 2008*

## BACK FROM THE PHILIPPINES!

Thanks for your prayers over the last few months. We've had some blessings in the midst of this struggle. One of my dad's bosses from Corporate Chaplaincy sent our whole family on a vacation to the Philippines. We also had a generous donation from our church family at the Bridge to help pay for it. We went from July 18–August 10. It was a lifelong dream of my dad's to show us where he grew up and it finally came true. He was very excited during our time there and looked very alive showing us down memory lane!

Unfortunately the disease is progressing, and faster than the doctors initially thought. He went for his third assessment last Wednesday at the ALS Clinic. They initially thought his breathing had gone from 100% (last June) to 54%, but after a reassessment they figured that it was at 70%. The doctor said that once breathing drops to 50%, no one has ever lived more than nine to twelve months. A "normal" rate of progression should have left him at 85% by now, so we know it's progressing faster. He's also lost almost all the strength and mobility in his arms and hands. He struggled with walking and balance a couple of times on the trip but now stairs and longer journeys are tough.

When we returned from the Philippines, he decided that he would not be returning to work. He has been struggling a lot with walking and talking and he does not feel that he can serve the people effectively anymore. Please pray for him. My dad has always been very active physically and busy serving people. It will be extremely hard for him to be at home and lose mobility. His love language is acts of service so he is used to doing things for everyone else!

Please pray that God continues to provide for my parents at this time. He has been so faithful in the past. My mom is still completely trusting in him for the future. Please also pray for my mom and Emily. The two of them will be his primary caregivers. Pray that God would give them strength and daily renewal.

Please pray for the rest of the family. It's hard being away, especially for Ang, as she lives twelve hours north. It's hard being here for us too. I start school in a couple of weeks and all I want to do is be at home!

Thanks for your continued prayers, encouragement, and understanding during this time!

# 58

## GOOD MEDICINE

*Our mouths were filled with laughter, our tongues with songs of joy. Then it was said among the nations, "The Lord has done great things for them."*
—Psalm 126:2

F aith and family were still alive and well despite my dad's continual decrease in function. When family gathered, a good dose of fun always seemed to be waiting in the wings. A recent visit from my dad's family was no exception.

*September 2008*
## GOTTA GIVE HIM PRAISE

My dad saw a respirologist today who confirmed that his lung capacity has not declined since August. Each new day is a gift, and every day that the symptoms don't worsen, we celebrate!

This past month, three of his sisters made the long drive up even though they only had a one-day turnaround. Among the many highlights of that short visit was when one of my aunts was stir-frying Dad's healthy breakfast cereal, thinking it was brown rice. She added the usual onions, soy sauce, etc. to oatmeal! The best part was that she ate it! Bless her heart for not wanting to waste food! It was fun to find so much joy in the little things.

Afterward, Uncle Lope and his family drove up. He made my dad laugh hysterically on more than one occasion. Although uncontrollable laughter is a symptom of ALS, we had unanimously decided that was, at least, our favourite symptom! Praise God for laughter.

We're on a hard road. But as a godly woman once told me, "You have to revel in those little moments of happiness that God brings your way. Otherwise we're doomed to being a victim of circumstances."

# 59

*September 2008*

# WITHOUT WORDS

*However, I consider my life worth nothing to me; my only aim is to finish the race and complete the task the Lord Jesus has given me—the task of testifying to the good news of God's grace.*

—Acts 20:24

Jesse waited in the front row like he had so many other Sundays in the past decades. Though he was no stranger to sweaty palms and perspiration forming around his temples, this was different. In all his years of pastoring, he'd often worried about having something to say during his sermon preparation time, but never once had he worried whether he would be physically able to speak at all.

Angela had asked him to share a few words at the baby dedication at their church for little Ethan and Maia. Jesse had made the special trip up to Worsley for the occasion. With his physical condition declining so rapidly, he hadn't known if he would be able to make the trip again.

The light in Jesse's car had always signalled him when it needed fuel. The light would indicate that the tank was running low, but the display would also tell him exactly how many kilometres he had before completing running out.

ALS wasn't so considerate. Sometimes his legs would give out without warning, or his tongue would stop working. Up until this point, it had always started working again, but Jesse never knew if it would or wouldn't. Things that were once so simple suddenly felt like Russian roulette. Would his tongue work? Sometimes it did. Other times it felt stuck in his mouth… heavy, unable to form words.

The anxiety he felt over this uncertainty only seemed to worsen the outcome.

His fears had come to pass this past summer at the annual church convention on Prince Edward Island he attended with Kathy, Emily, and myself. Gerry Taillon, his friend, co-pastor, and the national leader of their church convention, had asked him to share his journey at one of the evening services.

Jesse had stood on stage next to Kathy, struggling to find words. He'd tried swallowing, hoping it might reset his tongue and make it work... but still nothing. Hundreds of people stared back at him from the audience.

Gerry had seemed to sense his difficulty, and kindly and patiently explained to the audience what was happening, asking for their understanding.

It had been so difficult to get words out that day. Between his weeping wife and his paralyzed tongue, they had still managed to share a bit of their journey.

Later on, when we were alone, he expressed his frustration with not being able to say what he had really wanted to.

"What did you want to say?" I asked, pulling out my camera. "Why don't you just say it now?

With no audience and no anxiety, the words came easily.

"If you were to live with the perspective that today could be your last day on earth, what would you do to make a difference in the kingdom of God? In the people you interact with and in your church?"

That was it. Those few words were the essence of what he had wanted to say. It wasn't the same now, without hundreds of people listening, but at least he'd gotten the chance to say it.

This was all Jesse wanted—everyday people just like him to live their lives with eternal purpose, perspective, and passion. So much of this life was temporary. He wanted to invest in what would outlast him. And he desperately wanted to urge people to make their lives count for eternal purposes.

But getting out a few simple words wasn't so simple anymore. To him and his family, his speech was slower than usual and sounded slurred, almost as if his accent was thickening. At least we could still understand him.

So he had come to the baby dedication, sitting in the front row with a small crowd behind him, hoping he would be able to find the words.

He stood up in front of the small congregation and opened his mouth to speak.

Nothing came out.

He tried swallowing.

Nothing.

He tried to laugh it off.

Nothing. He couldn't will his tongue to work.

Anything that required the willful movement of muscles was on the chopping block, including his ability to walk and talk, the two things he needed most to serve as a chaplain and pastor. The strength in his arms was almost completely gone—and according to the neurologist, it was a matter of time before his legs followed suit.

As he stood on the stage, wordless, his mind was intact. But no matter how much his brain shouted at his body, it wouldn't cooperate. It was like being trapped in a room where no one could hear him.

Angela had prepared the pastor for what could happen when Jesse got up to try and speak. Recognizing Jesse's helplessness, the pastor stepped forward to serve as Jesse's voice. Jesse tried whispering his words so the pastor could amplify them, but even then it was difficult to be understood.

For a while, the two of them fumbled through the words that had been on Jesse's heart. Then he finally sat down, feeling embarrassed and slightly defeated. How would he continue to spread the message of Jesus if he couldn't speak?

# 60

# SURPRISED BY JOY

*…weeping may stay for the night, but rejoicing comes in the morning.*

—Psalm 30:5

"Steph! I found a way to hold Maia!"

With no more strength or grip in his hands or arms, a simple act that had once brought Jesse incredible joy, holding his grandchildren and playing with them, had seemed like a thing of the past.

Yet my dad's excitement and enthusiasm from the other end of the phone were palpable. And contagious. In a season of so much bad news, any sliver of good news brought an injection of fresh hope.

"Angela put her in the Jolly Jumper," he reported. "I sat on the floor and played with her and was able to hold her!"

*Thank God for whoever invented the Jolly Jumper,* I thought to myself.

"Dad, that's amazing! I'm so happy for you."

"It was funny," he went on. "It was like Ethan was taking care of me."

He relayed a story of how on the last night of his visit to Worsley, two-year-old Ethan had asked Angela, "Mama, 'nuggle Papa?" Even in his declining state, Papa hadn't been able to refuse a bedtime snuggle. It didn't matter how difficult the formerly simple act of climbing into bed felt, he wouldn't miss the opportunity.

As he'd attempted to ease himself down into the 'nuggle position, he'd hit his head on the headboard. He didn't have the same muscle control as he once had.

Ethan's big brown eyes had been filled with concern.

"Okay Papa?" With that, his two-year-old grandson leaned in, kissing him softly on the forehead with the tenderest care and said, "All better Papa."

As they snuggled together, Ethan proceeded to softly run his little hands up and down Papa's arms, just as he had seen his mom doing all week. Arm massages had become a regular part of the routine in order to try and stimulate blood flow to ease the discomfort of muscle atrophy.

ALS could take many things, but it couldn't touch the most important ones—his faith and his family. Jesse had settled into the role of receiving care, even from his grandson.

I hung up the phone feeling lighter. So many days in the past months had felt so heavy, but there were also pockets of joy like this one. Today we could celebrate the surprise gifts to be found through a Jolly Jumper and a tender-hearted two-year-old.

# 61

*October 2008*

# LAMENT

*A prayer of an afflicted person who has grown weak and pours out a lament before the Lord. Hear my prayer, Lord; let my cry for help come to you.*

—Psalm 102:1

Kathy leapt up from the bed, startled. She had heard the strangest sound, one she had never heard before. It had sounded like a dying animal moaning.

Jesse?

She had just helped him to the bathroom. Had he fallen? She carefully opened the door to their ensuite, unsure of what she might find.

When Jesse saw her, his eyes clearly said what his mouth couldn't: *Get out. I want to be alone.*

She closed the door quietly, with no strength to fight the tears that surfaced as Jesse wailed.

For the past five months, her husband had faced one loss after another: the strength to walk, talk, work on cars, move independently, shoot hoops in the driveway with his daughter, hold her close… and this was only the beginning.

Through it all, Jesse had remained strong, unmoved in his conviction that he was to do his part and God would do His. He was confident that God could perform a miracle. Surely, they had both reasoned, a miracle healing would bring God the most glory. Kathy needed her husband. Their girls needed their father. Their church needed their pastor.

Of course, it was still possible. God could do anything.

Regardless of what the future held, the past months had been filled with loss. And Jesse's grief and sorrow demanded to be felt.

He needed to lament.

Kathy waited quietly as time passed, helpless to do anything except ask God to meet her husband in his grief and comfort him.

Once it was quiet, she returned to help him out of the bathroom.

The angst in his eyes was gone. The wailing in his mouth was quiet. The moment of grief had passed. In its place was sadness, yet also peace.

Jesse would still do his part, even if God's might look different from what he had originally hoped for.

# 62

*November 2008*

# RUNNING

*Therefore, since we are surrounded by such a great cloud of witnesses, let us throw off everything that hinders and the sin that so easily entangles. And let us run with perseverance the race marked out for us...*

—Hebrews 12:1

They weren't working. Why wouldn't his legs just work? Jesse shuffled slowly, with only his son-in-law to keep him from collapsing onto the floor.

"H–i awnt to ruhhn," Jesse mumbled.

His words and desires were so clear in his mind. His mind was telling his muscles to move. Why wouldn't his body cooperate? His mind still said he could do simple things like utter words, take steps, or get up and run. But his body wouldn't respond.

Today Jesse wanted no more of this. He wanted to rebel.

For the most part, despite his physical decline, Jesse was still in good spirits. God was continually lifting him out of the pit and setting his feet and hope back on the rock of Jesus Christ.

God was doing his part and Jesse was still doing his, trusting. Nothing, not even ALS, could take away his hope in Christ.

Having conversations with visiting friends and family was a highlight of his days, despite how difficult communication had become. The continual loss of muscle movement in his mouth made speech difficult. Patience, repetition, and laughter helped him navigate all the miscommunication.

Along with speaking, eating had become increasingly difficult and fatiguing. Jesse was down twelve pounds since the diagnosis, but thankfully he'd gained 1.2 pounds in the past week. At the beginning, getting a feeding tube installed in his body had felt like pouring water on his faith. He hadn't been able to imagine exercising faith that God would heal him while simultaneously planning for his decline. The two seemed incompatible.

Jesse had gone back and forth but ultimately decided against a feeding tube. If God chose not to heal him on this side of heaven, he would have a healthy body waiting for him on the other side. It didn't make sense to him to prolong the suffering for himself or his family.

But at this moment, Jesse wanted to defy his body. He wanted to run.

"What?" Mike asked, confused, trying to understand while neglecting to steady his father-in-law. Mike thought he was simply helping with a slow and easy transfer from one room to another. It was like steadying a toddler learning to walk, only a larger one who wouldn't bounce back up a few seconds after falling.

Jesse could no longer walk around the house without assistance, whether it be in the form of a shoulder to lean on or a hand to steady him. For longer outings, such as Emily's basketball games he refused to miss, they packed the wheelchair just in case. Jesse would have much rather walked, even if it was a slow shuffle, than be pushed around.

He fell more often now, a constant sobering reminder of what he could and couldn't do.

One night, he awoke in his bed convinced that it wasn't necessary to wake Kathy for the simple activity of walking to the bathroom. She was exhausted and needed to sleep. He could manage.

He took one step, and then another, determined to succeed in the short trek. Only a few more steps. He inched himself along the dresser, using it for support.

He let go, took another step, and before he knew it he found himself in a confusing, painful pile on the floor. He moaned in pain.

"Are you okay? What happened?" Kathy asked, jolted out of her sleep by the sound of his body hitting the ground. She was still half-asleep, trying to make sense of her husband crumpled on the floor in front of her.

Jesse laid there silent, the realization of what had happened settling over him like a suffocating blanket he couldn't throw off. Determination was no longer enough.

But today, shuffling through the house, helped along by his son-in-law, it didn't matter that he might end up in a pile on the floor. All Jesse wanted was to stretch his legs and run, to move himself from one location to another like he'd used to without giving a second thought to the risks.

He would never again take such a thing for granted if God restored his ability on this side of heaven.

It seemed like just yesterday when he'd asked his daughters if he could join them on their run at the very last minute, when they were ready to head out the door. Their yes was accompanied with an eyeroll. Probably because he had made them wait while he put on his socks, carefully wiping the lint from between every toe.

And then, though he would never admit it, he only made it to the mailbox at the end of the street. But he didn't care. It was five more minutes of running together than he would've done on his own before his body demanded a break.

"You go on, I'll catch up," he'd said as soon as he reached the mailbox less than a kilometre from the house.

"Sure you will," they had replied, knowing that he would never catch them. They could always go farther and faster than he could.

What he wouldn't now give to run to the mailbox, his greatest concern being the feeling of being short of breath.

"H–I... w–ant... to... run!" he said slowly to Mike. Slower, louder, and more emphatically, trying to annunciate the syllables as much as his tongue would allow.

"You want to run?" Mike asked, confused.

Jesse always joked that it was easier to ask for forgiveness than permission, so he didn't bother asking. He clumsily attempted to sprint towards the front door, Mike his only source of balance.

His attempt to rebel against the disease that was slowly stealing his independence caused a ripple of laughter that soon spread to each family member, watching in wide-eyed disbelief.

He could no longer run. He could barely walk with assistance. He needed help with the simplest of everyday tasks. But today he tried anyway—and laughed about it, giving everyone a brief dose of good medicine for their heavy hearts.

Now that his running days were over—not to mention his day of eating independently—Jesse had only one goal, one that Paul had so succinctly summarized in Acts 20:24: *"However, I consider my life worth nothing to me; my only aim is to finish the race and complete the task the Lord Jesus has given me—the task of testifying to the good news of God's grace."*

The finish line didn't seem as far away as it once did. Jesse didn't know how long he had left, but he had full confidence that his daughters could go faster and farther with Jesus than he ever could.

# 63

*December 2008*

## ON THE INSIDE

*But the Lord said to Samuel, "Do not consider his appearance or his height, for I have rejected him. The Lord does not look at the things people look at. People look at the outward appearance, but the Lord looks at the heart."*

—1 Samuel 16:7

"**W**as he in a car accident?" the stranger asked me, gesturing towards my dad.

I tried to ignore the question, but I could always feel the curious glances people cast in our direction when we were out in public at Emily's basketball games.

A mixed bag of emotions stirred inside me. My dad was a curious site—bound to a wheelchair, sporting the homemade neck brace that gave his head the support his neck muscles could no longer provide. He couldn't speak audibly and a letterboard rested on his lap.

If a stranger recognized him from Emily's previous basketball season, they wouldn't know what had happened to him. They wouldn't know what I knew—that despite his appearance, my dad was exactly the same person he had always been.

He was still stubborn and particular. When I had tried to clean out his second ear using the same end of the Q-tip I'd used on the first ear, he'd jerked away in protest. One day when a caregiver tried to enter the house, he objected. After a few minutes of not understanding what he was panicking about, I told him to spell it out. His answer: "S–H–O–E–S." I burst out laughing before asking the woman to take off her shoes.

Despite the fact that he could barely speak, outdoor shoes inside the house were still blasphemous.

He was still helpful, asking us to put things away and lighten the load for my mom. He still assumed the role of coach, spelling out feedback on the letterboard for Emily. For example: "S–H–O–O–T–M–O–R–E." He was still caring. He asked visitors how they were, intuitive about how they were feeling. He still had biblical advice for any problem, opinions on every basketball game, and encouragement for people who came to see him.

On this particular day, I understood the stranger's confusion. Only a few months earlier, I'd had no idea what ALS was. The extent of my knowledge of this cruel disease was the sign that hung annually off a bridge on one of Calgary's main roads that read "Betty's Run for ALS." I would silently wonder who Al was and why Betty was running for him... I didn't give it a second thought.

That is, until the next year when I saw the same sign and knew exactly what it meant.

So I couldn't fault anyone for not knowing. Yet part of me felt defensive, wanting to shout, "He's more than what you can see. He's not slow, he's sick. He is my dad. You don't know him."

I didn't want him to be misunderstood.

My emotions waged war, fighting for the most prominent place in my heart—grief and gratitude, despair and hope, sadness and joy, anger and acceptance. Eventually I would learn that the human heart could handle the tension of holding both. But in that season, I didn't give darker emotions too much air, for fear that they might overwhelm me.

On this day, I didn't shout. Instead I smiled at the stranger.

"No, he wasn't in a car accident," I explained. "He has ALS, Lou Gehrig's disease."

I'm not sure if my dad overheard the conversation. If he did, he was unmoved by it. He showed no concern for the glances of onlookers, needing no one to come to his defence. He seemed unconcerned with being misunderstood, satisfied with doing something he had loved for decades: intently watching and intentionally coaching his daughter.

He looked over at me, gestured towards Emily, and spelled "S–H–O–O–T."

With many emotions swirling in my soul, this was the only thing I needed to shout about. I laughed and hollered, "Em, *shoot* the ball!"

My dad smiled. In that moment, it was all he needed.

# 64

*December 6, 2008*

# HIGH AND LOW

*The King will reply, "Truly I tell you, whatever you did for one of the least of these brothers and sisters of mine, you did for me."*

—Matthew 25:40

"I just feel like I'm a burden to everyone," my dad whispered, unable to stop the tears from forming in his eyes as he slumped down onto the closed toilet seat.

I tried to choke back my own tears, unsure of what would happen if we both opened the floodgates. My feeble attempts weren't enough; the tears found their way out.

My dad, my hero, a man I had thought was made of steel yet with the softest heart of anyone I knew, felt absolutely helpless. I could relate to the helplessness as I stood there unable to pep talk my way out of the sadness overtaking us.

I stood holding his toothbrush. He sat, arms collapsed on his lap, his head hanging.

Quiet tears said what neither of us could: it wasn't supposed to be this way.

Mike and I were home visiting for another weekend and had just returned from taking my dad to a house party to watch Manny Pacquiao defeat Oscar Dela Hoya in a boxing match. After some convincing, my dad had reluctantly agreed to go, concerned that his presence might put a damper on the party.

But since I had inherited his stubbornness, I'd refused to take no for an answer. At the party he had appeared to be having the time of his life, intently watching the fight alongside his old friends from the FilCan days. As I watched his face light up and communicate with those who kept coming over to have conversations, he just seemed so... Dad.

And now here he was, only hours later, feeling like a burden to those he most loved. He had devoted his whole life to serving others—whether it was fixing cars, sharing Jesus, or doing the dishes. The man never stood still.

And now it was all he could do.

"Dad, you are not a burden," I said quietly but firmly, careful to make eye contact so he couldn't dismiss my words. "You've spent your life serving us. It's an honour for us to finally be able to serve you."

Our tears finally quieted. I finished brushing his teeth as he sat, still looking defeated with no other choice but to receive help. Little did he know that someone else could fix my car, other believers could share the gospel, anyone else in the world could do the dishes, but no one else in the world could ever be my dad.

And if he was never able to lift another finger, being my dad was more than enough.

# 65

# CAN'T STOP HIM

*Therefore go and make disciples of all nations, baptizing them in the name of the Father and of the Son and of the Holy Spirit, and teaching them to obey every-thing I have commanded you. And surely I am with you always, to the very end of the age.*

—Matthew 28:19–20

"Nothing can stop you, huh?" I said to my dad, smiling as he recounted the story of how he had shared Jesus with his newest caregiver earlier that week.

He smiled his trademark smile and laughed as if he knew it was true. Nothing could ever stop him from telling people about Jesus, even the fact that he was barely able to speak.

With mumbled words and the letterboard, my dad had told his new caregiver Sonia about how to have peace with God and eternal life through a relationship with Jesus Christ. She had joyfully received Jesus by grace through faith on Monday, December 15, 2008.

"I've heard so much about you," I said to Sonia, extending my hand. "It's so good to meet you!"

"Your daddy's my hero," she gushed in her thick Spanish accent. "Because of him, I know Jesus!"

"He's mine too!" I agreed with a smile.

"I request to care por him five days a week because I am so bless by caring por him," she said as she bid farewell for the day and headed out the door.

I stood marvelling at the goodness of God and the blessing Sonia had been to our family. Finding a caregiver who was a good fit had been a huge help to my mom. My dad had always been independent and particular about his way of doing things—bathing babies, washing dishes, cleaning the house, and taking care of himself—and the disease hadn't seemed to change this. He still liked things done a certain way, making him a grateful yet still somewhat picky patient.

So having a caregiver who shared the load with my mom, instead of adding to it, was a gift.

That week, my mom often found my dad and Sonia at the table doing a Bible study together even after her caregiving shift had ended. Even in the homestretch of his time on earth, God still had a purpose. His race wasn't finished; his calling was not yet fulfilled. There were still disciples to make, still people who were ready to receive Jesus.

My dad wasn't finished testifying to the gospel of Jesus that had so radically changed his life. Even here in this place of suffering, Jesus was still saving and changing lives.

# 66

*Monday, December 29, 2008*

# BIRTHDAY BLESSINGS

*For I am already being poured out like a drink offering, and the time for my departure is near.*

—2 Timothy 4:6

What do you give a dying man for his final birthday?

December 25 afforded the opportunity to celebrate three birthdays along with all the Christmas festivities. In the past, my dad had been delighted by the simplest gifts—a new frying pan to perfectly cook his moose bistek recipe (a Filipino favourite), or perhaps a new pair of socks or pants.

But now all these gifts seemed useless. At the rate the disease was progressing, it was more and more evident that this was very likely the last Christmas and birthday combination we would celebrate with him. It would be the last time we took the annual birthday photo with Angela and Christina sitting on his lap, his smiling face poking out from between them. It would be the last time he fell asleep mid-present opening because he hadn't yet had his coffee.

It had to be a true celebration.

An idea began to form in my mind, but I knew it was going to take more than just me to pull it off. I sat in front of my computer, the place I'd recently learned to process so many of my feelings, and began typing the email that would invite many to participate in this final celebration. I could hardly wait to give him this gift.

My mom peeled back the wrapping paper Christmas morning since my dad's hands no longer listened to the instructions from his brain to move. I watched his face as the realization of what he was staring at settled over him.

Mom was already a puddle of tears and Dad was misty-eyed. He had no words—literally. He couldn't speak. But even if he'd been physically able, he likely still would've been speechless. He knew who he had been and what Jesus had saved him from. He was utterly convinced God deserved all the credit for the transformation in his life and the way he was able to live. He was never interested in sharing any of God's glory. Instead he deflected the credit to the One who deserved it. He was far more comfortable behind the scenes than standing in the spotlight.

But that Christmas and birthday morning, his misty eyes said what he couldn't say—that he was overwhelmed in the best way, his humble heart learning to receive.

Staring back at us from the front cover was a picture of my dad's happy and healthy face complete with his broad smile, eyes lit up, taken only a year and a half earlier.

The title "A Celebration of a Faithful Servant" stretched across the top. I invited family and friends to write about him in one of three ways: a favourite memory, a funny story, or how God has impacted their lives through him. The responses ranged from his influence as a basketball coach to a shepherd, a mechanic, a raft captain, an evangelist, a father figure, a pastor, and a man with a great sense of humour.

As I flipped through the forty-some odd letters held together by coil, some words came to mind that my dad had recently shared with me: "Kingdom work is about quality, not quantity" and "The key to making an impact in the kingdom is to practice the presence of God." My dad much preferred one-on-one conversation in a quiet corner than speaking to the masses from a stage.

But as I flipped through the many pages, it was evident that in pursuit of making quality disciples he had also quietly and effectively touched a large number of lives.

I suspected that the book only represented a fraction of the lives that had been impacted by his simple desire to follow Jesus. He had influenced men and women alike, family and friends, young and old. Almost all the letters echoed the same few points: he had taken the time to care for and invest in the lives of others.

If this was the last birthday I would ever celebrate with him, I was grateful it was spent truly acknowledging and celebrating who he was.

I chose one to read aloud, from a former basketball player my dad had coached.

I met Mr. Morales when I was in the tenth grade. I was a skinny punk who cared for nothing in life except sports. Mr. Morales was the most soft-spoken and encouraging coach I'd ever met.

We used to have early morning practices, after-school meetings, and games. I don't remember how I played, if we won or lost or what drills we did in practice, but I remember Mr. Morales taking us aside before everything and leading us in God's word. There wasn't practice unless we had time with the Lord first.

I know God used my coach's love for us to tug at my heart. Jesse Morales would lead in prayer before and after games. I couldn't believe how serious this man was about his faith. I could see the love for Christ in his family, in his love for basketball and his time with us. I remember thinking, 'I'd like to know God like that.'

It was on a night at my house in the middle of my Grade Ten basketball season that I gave my life to Christ.

Mr. Morales, thank you for taking one-on-one time with me to show me what a man of godly character and love looks like. Thank you for sharing your love of basketball with me while I wouldn't listen to anything else. You've had a big impact in my life although you probably didn't know it. I'm honoured to finally tell you that.

Everyone was quiet, enjoying the gift and simultaneously taking in the heaviness of it being one of many lasts.

The greatest gift we were all learning to savour was the one of simple presence. We were sitting around the table. We were together. Today, we had time. We had this Christmas. We still had each other.

And we would take in each and every moment we were offered, tears and joy alike.

Christmas morning presented the first of two opportunities we were given to pause and celebrate God's faithfulness in and through his life. The first church he'd started, FilCan (now known as The Bridge International Church), had invited him to A Tribute to Pastor Jesse for his birthday the following Sunday.

We settled into our chairs. It didn't look like it was going to be a quick affair. There was a long line-up of people who wanted to share about how he had impacted their lives.

A long-time member of FilCan, Eileen, kicked things off with many laughs.

"Pastor always call me H–Eileen, wit da H at da front," she said. "He always say, H–Eileen, how's your walk with God?"

She went on to share about the six or seven friends and members of her family whom PJ, her nickname for Pastor Jesse, led to the Lord and baptized, including her husband's brother-in-law who passed away from ALS in 1997. PJ had performed the funeral.

"Though you can no longer say the words from your mouth, we can still hear the words coming from your heart," Eileen managed through tears. "Though your feet are weak, your faith is still strong."

Next up were two brothers, David and Dan, who had grown up in that first church. They shared about the many Sunday afternoons the youth group had spent at the Morales house. They noted how Pastor Jesse had always taken time to invest in young people. On a lighter note, they remembered the moonwalk he had done at Family Camp a few years ago. David pointed out that he had built a church that was an authentic family with a true feeling of belonging and fellowship.

Many others shared about how he had picked them up for Bible study or was there to walk with them through life's storms. We mostly laughed, but we also cried a little. Though he probably would've been more comfortable crawling under a chair, he sat and listened, having to humbly receive the encouragement from an imperfect life well-lived. I sat next to my dad feeling so proud to be his daughter.

Lastly, it was my turn. I closed the time of sharing with a scripture that was ringing so true for me in my dad's final season of life:

*Therefore we do not lose heart. Though outwardly we are wasting away, yet inwardly we are being renewed day by day. For our light and momentary troubles are achieving for us an eternal glory that far outweighs them all. So we fix our*

*eyes not on what is seen, but on what is unseen, since what is seen is temporary,*
*but what is unseen is eternal.*

—2 Corinthians 4:16–18

In the face of watching my dad physically waste away, we were given an invitation to fix our eyes on the unseen. In light of eternity, there was more to this ugly disease than just gut-wrenching difficulty. Compared to the eternal glory that would one day outweigh the trouble, the suffering was light and momentary.

My dad was healing, but by all earthly measures it looked like it would be fully realized in heaven. Fixing our eyes on Jesus was the way to access this invitation, this eternal perspective—a gift I hadn't anticipated this difficult season of suffering would bring. And while we waited, fixing our eyes on Jesus anchored our hearts to the hope only found in Him.

As one friend wrote in the birthday book, "No matter the outcome, you have already won. And most of all, Jesus has won eternal life for you."

As it turned out, there were gifts to be given and received in this season. Just not the kind money could buy.

# 67

*December 2008*

## SHOWING UP

*For I am poor and needy, and my heart is wounded within me.*
—Psalm 109:22

"You're going," Kathy said adamantly. She rarely if ever played the mom card with her husband, but she knew Jesse needed this.

Jack, Jesse's former chaplaincy boss and friend at TriJay Flooring, had invited him to the annual Christmas party, assuring him that his presence was welcome despite his hesitancy.

Resigning from his chaplaincy work the previous summer had been an incredibly difficult but necessary step. Jesse loved the people he had served. He loved bringing them coffee and donuts, laughing with them, listening to their stories, and sharing truth when they were open to it. He loved giving Jesus away to other people.

The first three months following the diagnosis had been filled with hope for an earthly miracle—physical healing from ALS. Surely God's promise—*"I will do my part"*—meant that a miracle was in order.

God was able. Jesse believed He would be willing. But after a few months, it was clear that his declining condition was making his work more of a challenge than an encouragement. Stepping away from it was crushing, but he could no longer live like the disease wasn't a reality.

Kathy knew that he would enjoy his time at the party if he would just be willing to show up. Plus, his friend and fellow chaplain was already there to pick him up.

But Jesse didn't see it that way.

He shook his head no, his face determined to go a few more rounds with her in refusal. He didn't want to be a damper on the party. He was aware that people sometimes felt uncomfortable with his new condition or struggled to know how to respond. Strangers often looked at him with pity, their eyes wondering if he had been a car accident victim or was physically or mentally disabled. People who hadn't seen him since he was healthy often did a double-take and it wasn't uncommon for a person's eyes to fill with tears.

It didn't matter that Jesse's mind was intact; his body was what people saw first. Could he go to a place he used to serve by walking and talking, now bound to a wheelchair for mobility and a letterboard to communicate?

Despite his protests, it looked like his wife was going to have her way. Kathy promised that he only had to stay for one hour. Jesse reluctantly cooperated with the help required to transfer him from the house to the vehicle and off he went to the party with his friend around 11:00 a.m.

———

Kathy glanced up at the clock when she heard the car outside. It wasn't noon but 4:30 p.m. Jesse was sporting his trademark smile as his friend went on to report how he had pushed Jesse around the party in his wheelchair with his letterboard on his lap.

Jesse had been too busy being a chaplain to return home after an hour. Laughing, talking, praying, ministering, and simply being with the people he loved had breathed fresh life into his heavy heart.

He hoped his smile communicated to his wife what he couldn't with words—"Thank you for making me go." If he was still alive, God still had a purpose for him. He could still serve. He could still love. It would simply look different.

# 68

*January 2009*

# GOODBYE

*Brothers and sisters, we do not want you to be uninformed about those who sleep in death, so that you do not grieve like the rest of mankind, who have no hope.*
—1 Thessalonians 4:13

B rian's son Lucas had always been my dad's little buddy, and it was time to say goodbye. The tears welled up in the boy's eyes and broke through all the adult pretence of keeping it together. This was a sad moment and the tears needed out. The weight of saying goodbye seemed to press on his heart and spill out, giving the rest of us permission to do the same.

Brian and his family had driven from Tennessee to visit my dad and our family while on our final family vacation in Florida. Life was lighter when he and my dad were together. Burdens were divided. Joy was multiplied. Laughter was had. And this time was no exception as Brian strolled down memory lane.

"One time we stayed at this cabin in Mount Eagle, Tennessee," he told us, his southern accent giving him away. "It was me, Jesse, Mike, and Judd. There were four beds all in one cabin and the shower was in the corner and it only had a curtain. There wasn't any privacy. Jesse was over there in the shower, so we went outside to give him some space—but we opened the window curtains first. Mike had gotten every one of Jesse's clothes and his towel. The only thing he could grab was the shower curtain. It was the only thing he could grab. We were all out in the field watching him try to move around, like a snake sliding out of that shower onto the ground. He finally got to the bedspread and came out the door. He had just one word: 'Mike!'"

We all roared with laughter as Brian told of how the four of them had rolled on the floor laughing so hard while Jesse got his clothes back on.

But then we came to the most painful part of the visit: goodbye.

For these friends, saying goodbye normally just meant "See you later." Over the years, they had become like family and enjoyed at least annual visits.

But time wasn't on our side anymore. Given the distance between Alberta and Tennessee, this was very possibly the earthly goodbye for my dad and the dear Harrell family. There would likely be no next annual visit.

Lucas's tight hug said that he was struggling to figure out how to say goodbye, something we are *all* struggling to do. Though unable to reach his limp arms around to reciprocate, my dad spelled out some final words of encouragement to Lucas and he nodded to receive them.

Thanks to Jesus, this painful goodbye wasn't permanent. It was still only a "See you soon." Instead of next year, though, that next meeting would take place on the other side of heaven—with no more tears, pain, sickness, or fear.

# 69

*January 10, 2009*
# PREPARING

*Do not let your hearts be troubled. You believe in God; believe also in me. My Father's house has many rooms; if that were not so, would I have told you that I am going there to prepare a place for you?*

—John 14:1–2

"*Do not let your hearts be troubled.*" Jesse breathed in the promise of God, like fresh air to his tired lungs. Jesus had given this promise to His disciples when they were troubled about His impending departure, and now Jesus was reminding Jesse of it.

He was grateful. Without the promises of God, there was plenty to feel troubled about.

Jesse could no longer sit at the dining room table each morning like he had for most mornings of his life with his cup of hot coffee and open Bible. His fingers and hands would no longer cooperate to turn the pages. Thankfully, his friend Paul had lent him an iPod complete with the audio Bible. He could still get into the Word. He needed to be reminded of the promises of God as desperately as he needed his next breath.

Now he could close his eyes, lay back in the recliner, listen to the Word of God, and pray.

In the fall, I had done a research project at university to try to determine whether exercise had any impact on the prognosis of ALS. Each weekend when I was home, my dad asked me for a report on what I had learned. Had I discovered anything hopeful? Were there any new findings? Anything to thwart the prognosis?

The answer was the same week after week. Physical activity, a feeding tube, and one drug could potentially impact one's length of life, but there was absolutely nothing to improve the quality of life for someone living with, and dying from, ALS.

With each passing day, Jesse's voluntary muscle system worked less and less. There was nothing in the research to stop his muscles from wasting away, nothing that would make his muscles work the way they were supposed to, nothing to decrease the difficulty he had swallowing or the panic he felt when he was choking.

All his food now had to be pureed, with the exception of scrambled eggs and arrozcaldo. His friend Dom saw to it that Jesse had a regular supply of this Filipino comfort food—rice and chicken porridge flavoured with ginger and fish sauce. It tasted like home and it was easy to swallow.

But Jesse still had the promises of God.

ALS could take many things, but not his faith. And not his family. His mind drifted back to John 14 and Jesus's promise. For the past month, he had been thinking more and more about what it would be like to meet Jesus face to face.

*You believe in God; believe also in me. My Father's house has many rooms; if that were not so, would I have told you that I am going there to prepare a place for you? And if I go and prepare a place for you, I will come back and take you to be with me that you also may be where I am. You know the way to the place where I am going.*

—John 14:1–4

Jesse closed his eyes, wondering what his place would look like. The weaker he felt, the closer that day felt.

Jesus had prepared a place for him; Jesse wanted to be prepared for the end of his time on earth. He didn't want any interventions that would prolong his suffering.

He motioned for Kathy to come and bring the letter board.

"F–U–N–E–R–A–L," he spelled out to Kathy.

"You want to talk about your funeral?" she asked.

He nodded slowly before gathering the strength to spell out the details for Kathy—the people he wanted to be part of the service, and most importantly to ensure the most important message of all was preached.

"M–A–K–E–S–U–R–E–T–H–E–G–O–S–P–E–L–I–S–P–R–E–A–C–H–E–D," he spelled to his wife.

Even after he was gone, Jesse wanted to make sure people heard more about Jesus than they did about him.

He wanted to be prepared.

# 70

## IT

*The Lord is my strength and my shield; my heart trusts in him, and he helps me.*
*My heart leaps for joy, and with my song I praise him.*

—Psalm 28:7

"This could be it," I said softly to Christina.

We had driven mostly in silence following my parents in the ambulance towards Peter Lougheed Centre, where Dad had been admitted. It had been less than a year since the diagnosis and, according to the doctor's original prognosis, far too soon to be "it."

But it was obvious that my dad was deteriorating rapidly.

Though small in stature, standing about 5'6 and weighing in at no more than one hundred fifty pounds at his heaviest, he'd always stood tall, perhaps because he was often actually on his tippytoes. To me, he always seemed solid and strong, sort of like Mr. Miyagi.

However, atrophy was taking its toll. His once-muscular forearms, strong from turning wrenches, now hung limp. His once-strong legs, which used to get him up and down the basketball court or chase grandkids, were noticeably thinner, barely able to carry him around the house without falling. He looked skinny, his once-healthy cheeks increasingly gaunt, and with each passing day he looked more and more like a man who was dying, except for his trademark smile that still found a way to light up his eyes and always handsome face.

He was battling a cough now, and it was winning. Each cough felt like a convulsion, with no muscles to keep them in check.

The cough had kept him up all night and we were all afraid it might get worse.

The team had informed us that pneumonia was often the early end of an ALS patient's life, marking the point when their lungs had weakened and their body could no longer fight. I had no idea how much fight my dad had left in him, only that he looked weaker by the day.

Christina gripped the steering wheel and stared straight ahead, continuing to drive as the hospital came into view. Heavy silence hung between us.

*I'm not ready to lose my dad,* I cried silently from my heart. *Not yet, God.*

There was no ideal time for death, but I felt certain this was not it.

The answer was swift, sure, and gentle. It was never the answer I wanted, but always the invitation God offered: *"Will you trust me?"*

*Yes, I trust You.*

We parked and made our way into the emergency room, not knowing what sort of news awaited us.

Once we located Dad's room, I was relieved to see him on a triage bed, smiling and laughing with one of the ER nurses. I hadn't realized I'd been holding my breath until I breathed a sigh of deep relief.

When we'd loaded him into the ambulance back at home, it had felt like we should say our goodbyes. But at this moment, he looked like a man who had just been given a little more time. The doctors had given him codeine for the pain and discomfort and put him on antibiotics to attack the pneumonia before it got the better of him.

No one knew how much time we had left, but at least tonight wasn't going to be "it." My dad was coming home. For now.

# 71

*Spring 2009*

## EMPTY

*From the ends of the earth I call to you, I call as my heart grows faint; lead me to the rock that is higher than I.*

—Psalm 61:2

E xhausted, Kathy bolted up in bed feeling like she had only been sleeping a matter of minutes.

*Ding.*

The bell. Jesse needed something.

The bell rested close to Jesse's new hospital bed, stationed right next to the one they had once shared. The simplest of gifts, like rolling over and being embraced by him, were now a thing of the past.

At a friend's recent fortieth wedding anniversary celebration, Christina had performed her and Jesse's wedding song, "Can't Help Falling in Love," at their friend's request. Jesse had motioned for help getting out of his wheelchair to dance with her. Mixed emotions had welled up in Kathy as she held up the arms that had once held her.

Like most things these days, the losses came without warning, and without a chance to say goodbye—like speeding past the turn you were supposed to take and not knowing until you were looking at it in the rearview mirror, helpless to rewind time.

Jesse could no longer reciprocate physical touch. She couldn't remember the last time he had been able to embrace and comfort her.

She was just so tired. The short stretches of broken sleep through the night weren't enough to renew her strength and physically restore her. Care was needed around the clock, and even with help, it was taking its toll.

Their friend Paul checked on her regularly, helping her organize the overwhelming amount of information and caregivers that seemed to come through their now revolving door. His past work with an ALS patient seemed to give him an inside understanding of the toll caregiving took on the family, particularly on the spouse.

It was Paul who fundraised among Jesse's business Bible study friends to provide a night-time caregiver to ease her load. Thankfully, they now had three caregivers who were compassionate, patient, and had a sense of humour.

Kathy just needed sleep.

She tried to be strong for her daughters as they grieved the slow loss of their dad while she grieved and processed the loss of her husband, friend, and lover. Everything left her physically, emotionally, and mentally exhausted.

The disease was taking so much, so quickly.

In the middle of the night, Jesse often struggled to get comfortable. If he had an itch that couldn't be ignored, he needed it scratched. If he moved at all, he often needed help getting more comfortable. She had no gas left in her tank, only she had to keep going.

*Ding.*

She stumbled out of bed, trying to find her way to her husband. She quickly tried to adjust his pillow, scratch his head, and get him comfortable before falling back into bed, drifting back into much-needed sleep.

*Ding.*

What now? With the tiny bit of strength she had left, she climbed back out of bed just long enough to help her husband before climbing back in, desperate for the restoration only sleep could provide.

*Ding.*

Without realizing what was happening, Kathy jumped out of bed, every emotion spilling out of her mouth. But it didn't come out as sadness or exhaustion but yelling and screaming. She couldn't stop herself. She was so tired. So spent. So empty. And it all spilled out as anger. It wasn't supposed to be this way.

"I can't do this anymore!" Kathy screamed.

Realization washed over her as Jesse's helpless expression broke through her fit of rage and she immediately regretted her words.

Kathy collapsed on the floor, her remaining bit of energy coming out as convulsive tears. Feelings of guilt flooded all the empty places exhaustion had left.

How could she have done that? Jesse needed her. In sickness and health... that had been her vow.

She was just so tired. More tears. From the floor she looked up, unsure what she would see.

With wide eyes, Jesse looked at her helplessly.

After almost three decades of being married to this humble man, she could read his mind. His eyes said what his mouth could not: *I understand. It's okay. You shouldn't have to do this. I'm supposed to be taking care of you. It wasn't supposed to be this way. I'm so sorry.*

Kathy lay on the floor in an exhausted heap until all her tears were cried.

"I'm sorry," she whispered. "I'm sorry... I'm sorry. This is not your fault. I'm just so tired."

———

Jesse watched as sleep came over his wife. Kathy had done so much for him. She was everything.

It was Kathy who had prayed for him and loved him before he became a Christian. It was her love and kindness that had softened his heart towards Jesus. And as she'd grown in her faith, her love for him had only grown deeper.

Now she did everything for him, even the simplest things.

She had loved him in health and now she was loving him in sickness. She had been with him through all the trials and challenges, always ready to help him. She was his greatest resource.

It pained him to not be able to hold her close, comfort her in sadness, and be with her in her pain. He wanted to tell her he loved her, and just how grateful he was.

But he couldn't speak or move his arms. He recalled the words of Philippians:

*Do not be anxious about anything, but in every situation, by prayer and petition, with thanksgiving, present your requests to God. And the peace of God, which transcends all understanding, will guard your hearts and your minds in Christ Jesus.*

—Philippians 4:6–7

Jesse wasn't helpless or hopeless. There was still something he could do; he prayed for his wife. He pleaded with God to comfort and strengthen her. He prayed for God to provide for her needs. He trusted God to take care of Kathy in a way that only He could.

As Jesse drifted off to sleep, peace overtook his mind. God had always taken care of Kathy, and He could continue to do so, especially when Jesse couldn't.[7]

---

7   Although this section is speculative, since my dad wasn't able to share many of his thoughts and experiences during this time of his life, it accurately portrays the love he had for his wife and his understanding of the truth.

# 72

*March 25, 2009*

# I JUST WANT TO DIE

*For to me, to live is Christ and to die is gain.*

—Philippians 1:21

Jesse sat in his usual spot at the kitchen table, feeling trapped in his body. How many times had he sat at this very table to eat something he had just cooked with his own hands, or to talk with friends or family? How often had he moved the chairs around to recreate a basketball play from one of his daughter's games the night before while they ate breakfast?

The simple act of standing up and sitting down was one he hadn't ever given a second thought to. If he was thirsty, he'd get up and fill a glass of water. If he had an itch, he'd scratch it. He'd turn the pages of his Bible and record his thoughts in his journal. After hunting season, he'd cook up his famous bistek with fresh moose meat from that year's hunt. He'd throw on a pot of rice or brew a pot of coffee. He'd chop vegetables, add seasoning, and scrub the dishes without giving any of it a second thought.

Now he stared at his limp arm, willing it to move. It refused. His eyes confirmed that his hands were still attached to his arms, and his arms to his body, but that felt like the only proof they belonged to him at all. They no longer listened.

If someone held the weight of his hand, only then could he awkwardly move his hand around the letterboard to spell words. It was the only way to communicate, and it was tiresome.

The beginning of the journey had been so full of hope: *"You do your part. I will do my part."* That had been what God said, wasn't it?

Yes, Jesse was sure of it. God had said He would do His part. Jesse had prayed, believed, and begged God to have mercy and let him live. Jesse had read and reread the story about King Hezekiah in the Bible, a man who had cried out to God on his deathbed and God had extended his life. He believed that God could do the same for him.

He had read and reread the parable of the persistent widow and believed the lesson of praying and not giving up. He was doing his part.

Yet with each passing day, he had become more and more like a helpless child, utterly dependent on everyone around him.

From his seat at the kitchen table today, he could see his grandchildren, who had just arrived with their mom Angela for a visit, playing. How thrilled Jesse had been just a short three years earlier when he'd finally got his boy—"Ethan my boy," as he'd fondly called him. Jesse had taken every opportunity to snuggle him as a baby and play with him on the floor. Ethan had spent a few hours with Papa as a little apprentice in Papa's garage. Jesse's annual hunting trip up north to Angela's had allowed them to spend special time together.

He'd had all kinds of plans for his Ethan. They'd been going to fix cars together. He would have taught him to play basketball.

But not anymore.

Now three-year-old Ethan was certainly more independent than he was. And one-year-old Maia was gaining the independence Jesse was losing. As he had been taking his last steps, she had been taking her first. As she had been learning to feed herself, Jesse had needed to be fed. And as she had verbalized her first words, Jesse had spoken some of his last.

For a brief moment, his heart swelled with joy as he watched them play, but sadness and defeat were close behind as he remembered that he couldn't join them on the floor, or take them in his arms. He couldn't do any of the things he loved. He was no longer the healthy papa he had been only a year ago when he'd snuggled baby Maia for the first time, gently kissing her head when she was cuddled up against him… when he'd played cars on the floor of their farmhouse with Ethan.

Now he couldn't even hold a cup, let alone his grandchildren. His heart ached to remember the day shortly after the diagnosis when he had taken two-year-old Ethan to the grocery store. It had been a special time, just like he'd done with his daughters when they were little. Ethan had started to run ahead in the parking lot, easily loosening his hand from Jesse's weakening grip. Jesse had panicked and called out to Ethan, willing him to stop.

Thankfully, Ethan had been fine, but Jesse wouldn't ever forget that feeling of realizing he could no longer keep those he loved safe.

There had been other days like this. That fall, when travelling with Angela to her home for the grandkids' dedication, she had asked him to hold baby Maia while she took Ethan to the bathroom at a gas station. He had agreed. His body had been feeling well so far that day.

Then, suddenly, he had felt his arm muscles give way and his eight-month-old granddaughter slip. He'd tried to yell for help to the cashier, but without words the cashier had no idea what was going on.

Thankfully, Angela had come out of the bathroom just in time to rescue Maia before his strength failed completely.

He'd felt embarrassed, afraid, and angry at himself. It was yet another loss.

Sure, there were good times. He had been able to hold Maia as she happily jumped in her Jolly Jumper. At that point he'd been able to lay on the floor while Ethan played around him. But now it felt like too much.

Before Christmas, he had found himself wondering what it might be like to meet Jesus. He thought of it often now.

Some days were filled with hope, and on others his helplessness gave way to hopelessness.

Jesse saw the toll that the disease took on his family. Without being able to speak, he had a lot of time to observe and listen. He knew Kathy was exhausted. Emily often disappeared to her room. Christina came every Friday to spend time with him, feed him breakfast, and take care of him. Angela would come down to help take care of him for a few days. I visited every weekend.

All Jesse could think about was what a burden he was to his family. If he could have thrown his hands up in surrender, he would've, but even that was out of reach. His hands barely moved.

Angela's helpless gaze met his agitated stare. She couldn't interpret his moans and attempted gestures to communicate the discontent and discomfort he needed relief from. His frustration was mounting and he couldn't hide it.

She sighed. "Dad, I don't know what you need! I'm sorry!"

His determination to get her to understand abandoned him. Instead he nodded towards the letterboard.

Angela lifted his limp hands and placed them underneath the letterboard. As she watched her dad slowly move his hand from letter to letter, she said them aloud to make sure she was hearing correctly.

"I–J–U–S–T–W–A–N–T... I just want..." she began, following his motions. "T–O–D–I–E... to die?! Dad, no!" She gasped, but he wasn't finished. "I–T–W–O–U–L–D–B–E... it would be..." Tears flooded her eyes. "E–A–S–I–E–R–F–O–R–A–L–L–O–F–Y–O–U."

Jesse finished without shedding a tear, plagued with frustration and defeat.

This didn't stop Angela's tears from flowing.

*How could he say that?* she wondered frantically, desperate to convince him of the truth.

"I–F–E–E–L–L–I–K–E–A–B–U–R–D–E–N–T–O–E–V–E–R–Y–O–N–E," he continued on the letterboard.

"No!" Angela said adamantly, emotion overtaking her. "You are *not* a burden to everyone! You don't want to die! You can't die! We like taking care of you."

She moved towards him, taking his limp upper body in her arms, willing him to believe her.

"You matter," she sobbed. "You are still so valuable to us."

Jesse had held his daughter many times over the years when she needed comforting. That was the way it was supposed to be. For all the times he had held his daughter when she cried, he still couldn't believe how much their roles had reversed. It wasn't right. He was responsible to take care of his family, not the other way around.

He was convinced of what Paul had written to the Philippians: *"For to me, to live is Christ and to die is gain"* (Philippians 1:21). And right now, it felt like there was much more to gain if he could die sooner rather than later.

# 73

*April 8, 2009*

# SUPERNATURAL STRENGTH

*The Lord is my rock, my fortress and my deliverer; my God is my rock, in whom
I take refuge, my shield and the horn of my salvation, my stronghold.*

—Psalm 18:2

My mind spun as I processed the news my mom had shared over our latest
phone call. The pace at which sand was slipping through the hourglass was
far too rapid.

Less than a year had elapsed since my dad's diagnosis. It had been less than a
year since the neurologist had given my dad three to five years to live. Though it
was far less time than we wanted, two years would've allowed him to be present
for Emily's Grade Nine graduation. Two years would've allowed him to be at
my university graduation. Five years would have allowed him to be present for
Emily's high school graduation and her postsecondary basketball opportunities.
Five years would've allowed him a chance to be present for the birth of more
grandchildren. Five years would've allowed him the opportunity to celebrate
three decades of marriage to my mom.

But instead, only eleven months later, the prognosis was alarming. We didn't
have years; we only had months.

I was not alone in my processing. I tearfully brought the latest news to the
women I met with for weekly Bible study. As the news landed, their eyes were
filled with tears, hugs were offered, and sorrow was divided.

This same group had been present with me days after receiving the diagnosis. Week after week, they had shown up to meet together. They had cried with me and prayed, listened and talked, anticipated and met some of my tangible needs.

The biggest gift of all is that they were simply present in a painful season. Because of that, we experienced deeper authenticity and closeness than the average friendship.

After the gathering was finished, one friend lingered behind.

Exhausted, I sank into the carpet of my living room floor as more tears found their way out. She knelt next to me. We exchanged no words; we simply shared tears.

Finally, she broke the silence.

"God, we aren't asking You for an easy time," she whispered. "We're asking for You to do whatever it takes to make us more like You."

We said goodbye and I sat down to update the blog. Each time I thought, spoke, or typed the words "three to six months," more tears came.

*April 8, 2009*
## NOT SO GOOD NEWS

We had been anticipating Dad's appointment at the ALS Clinic today for the last few weeks. It has been evident as time passes that the disease progresses at an even more alarming rate than before. Angela and her family were visiting for the last two weeks and she noticed just over the course of her visit, many rapid changes.

Today at the clinic they assessed his breathing and it is at 51% (down from 59% in January). Gravely, the average lifespan from this point on is three to six months. The doctors say that sometimes they can outlive this timeline, but it's hard to say for sure. The disease can change very quickly as we've learned in the recent past.

There are hardly any words right now. Though I had anticipated something like this, there is still no way to prepare yourself for the news. There are many things to lift up in prayer right now—end of life decisions, how to spend our time and our family.

I have a special burden for Emily as she tries to make sense of this situation. Pray for her, that God would protect her during this time like He can and continue to draw her close to Himself.

Pray for my mom, Kathy. She needs a supernatural strength right now. She is tired and weary, but I'm sure she's still finding rest in the Lord.

We don't know, but God does.

I clicked post and lay awake in bed, tears still streaming, wondering how I was going to make it—not just through the next three to six months and beyond, but through the next day. I was in the middle of my teaching practicum, and in a few hours a classroom full of teenagers would demand my attention.

As I drifted off to sleep, I whispered the words that had become my lifeline: "I trust You."

When I woke up the next morning, my mind immediately replayed the previous day's news. My body wanted to rebel after only getting a few hours of sleep and disappear under the covers, but life wouldn't wait. I still had to get up and go teach.

My surprisingly dry eyes were accompanied by unexplainable strength. As we drove out to the small town outside the city where the school was located, I relayed the latest news to my carpool mate. My eyes remained dry.

She stared wide-eyed, curious about my unexplainable calm.

"I don't think I would be able to function!" she said. "God knew exactly what you needed this morning to get through the day. He's giving you the strength to make it."

Feeling equally surprised, I told her the truth: I hadn't been functioning when I'd gone to sleep the previous night for a few hours. There was nothing I could take credit for except admitting my own inadequacy to find comfort or strength from within.

In my sorrow was His strength. In my pain was His presence. And it wouldn't be the last time.

# 74

*April 11, 2009*

# DEAR DAD

*Hold firmly to the word of life; then, on the day of Christ's return, I will be proud that I did not run the race in vain and that my work was not useless. But I will rejoice even if I lose my life, pouring it out like a liquid offering to God, just like your faithful service is an offering to God. And I want all of you to share that joy. Yes, you should rejoice, and I will share your joy.*
—Philippians 2:16–18, NLT

Angela could hardly put into words what it was like to see her dad so defeated. Ever since returning home after her two-week visit, she had felt a sense of urgency to encourage her dad. She had seen him decline physically more and more and he needed fresh hope.

Her dad simply had to know how important he was, not only to her but to the entire family.

With the letterboard, he had been able to tell all his caregivers about how to have a relationship with God through Jesus. All three of them—Sonia, Nella, and Abbi—had prayed to receive Jesus as their Lord and Saviour. Clearly, God wasn't finished with him yet, but he needed to be encouraged so he didn't lose sight of the truth.

The ALS Society had loaned him a DynaVox computer that he could control with a laser sticker from his forehead. This gave him the independence to check his email, so Angela emailed him as often as she could.

Today in particular Angela felt a sense of urgency to share a verse God had given her the previous night. The news that he only had three to six months to live had been a hard day for everyone in the family. It was the fourth quarter and the clock was running down. There were no timeouts left.

Would her dad be encouraged or discouraged by the news? Angela didn't know anymore. It didn't feel like enough time. It never did. But for a man suffering and struggling, she didn't know. Maybe it felt like eternity.

Her fingers flew across the keyboard as she typed.

Hi Dad,

I was reading in Philippians last night and here is a verse for you: *"Hold firmly to the word of life; then, on the day of Christ's return, I will be proud that I did not run the race in vain and that my work was not useless. But I will rejoice even if I lose my life, pouring it out like a liquid offering to God, just like your faithful service is an offering to God. And I want all of you to share that joy. Yes, you should rejoice, and I will share your joy"* (Philippians 2:16–18, NLT).

I hope you remember, Dad, that your life and your work continues to be used by God. You are still useful to this world and especially to our family. I am so grateful for how you have impacted my life and continue with your unwavering faith! You have always been and still are my hero!

You could be listed in Hebrews 11!

Have a great rest of the weekend with everyone there. I wish we were there too, but I'm glad my kids aren't getting you sick. I love you and have a wonderful Easter!

PAPA STAY STRONG!

Love Ang (Jordan, Ethan, and Maia)

It was hard being so far away. She visited as often as she could, but like everyone else, Angela wished there was more she could do.

The thousand miles between them felt like a million. Every day she wanted to get in the car and drive home to be with her dad. Time was not on their side.

But she couldn't.

So instead she clicked send and prayed that somehow God would give him the faith to believe that what had always been true was still just as true today.

And then she waited.

# 75

*Spring 2009*

# FRIDAY MORNING

*Wait for the Lord; be strong and take heart and wait for the Lord.*
—Psalm 27:14

"I just don't understand," Christina cried. She couldn't keep her unanswered questions to herself. "Why is this happening to our family?"

She pushed her dad along the sidewalk in his wheelchair, careful to avoid the lingering piles of melting snow from the spring thaw. It had been their Friday morning routine since the fall, when weather permitted.

After the diagnosis last spring, she had planned to drop out of university to help take care of her dad, but he had given her a very adamant no. She would do no such thing.

Thankfully, her schedule contained this open block, which had become her special time with her dad. On Friday mornings, she fed him his favourite—eggs with salsa. Chewing and swallowing was slow and laboursome for him these days. This gave her plenty of time to fill him in on her life.

She and her husband Frankie hadn't planned on having kids this soon, but after the diagnosis they had moved up their timeline in the hopes that at least one of their children could meet their Papa.

It didn't make any sense. Her mom and twin sister had had no difficulty or delay conceiving. She should've been able to get pregnant by now.

"Why are things not going as planned?" she lamented. "Why is it taking so long?"

She was interrupted by her dad's moans. He was trying to get her attention. She paused and walked around to face him in front of the wheelchair. He was signalling to the letterboard.

She removed his hands and the letterboard from under the blanket meant to keep him warm on this chilly spring day. He gestured for her to listen.

"W–H–Y–A–R–E–Y–O–U–B–E–I–N–G–S–O–I–M–P–A–T–I–E–N–T," he spelled.

"Why am I being so impatient?" Christina asked. "Because it's taking forever! I wanted my child to get to meet you!"

Her dad smiled, his famous smile still recognizable on his increasingly bony but still handsome face.

"B–E–P–A–T–I–E–N–T," he spelled, his smile still intact.

"Dad, did God tell you something? Do you know for sure that Frankie and I are going to have kids?"

She searched his face for a clue. Did he know something she didn't? Had God given him a promise?

All she could see was his smile—and his eyes, which reiterated the same message he had just spelled to her: just be patient.

Jesse continued smiling as his daughter resumed pushing him. He remembered the email Angela had sent him. Yes, he still had a purpose. He still needed to intercede for his family. They still needed to know that they could trust God—and he could help them with that.

Jesse talked to God a lot these days. He had a lot of time to pray for his girls.

He wanted his girls to know that he loved them. He believed in them. He knew they would succeed. They brought him so much joy. He was confident in them.

Most of all, he wanted their faith to be strengthened. He wanted them to love, follow, and serve Jesus and teach their kids to do the same.

He also had a lot of time to pray for his grandchildren. He knew he would have more than two. All of his girls loved children as much as he did, and he prayed that his daughters and sons-in-law would be godly parents who would train up their children in the way they should go.

God wasn't finished with him yet. Jesse wouldn't throw in the towel. He would keep believing and keep praying, lifting up his family before the Father until his last breath.

# 76

# THE REPLY

*Therefore encourage one another and build each other up, just as in fact you are doing.*

—1 Thessalonians 5:11

It had been over a week since Angela had sent her dad that verse. She had been checking her email regularly hoping to see a reply, but nothing so far.

Today, her inbox said otherwise. There was one unread message from Jesse Morales.

Angela steadied her breath and hoped to God that it contained good news. She scanned the email and pieced it together. The DynaVox often cut and pasted his words out of order when he transferred them to his email. She smiled as she realized what the message said.

Hello Angela,
I want you to know that the passage you gave me inspired me to keep on living out my purpose. I still feel blessed to have four girls who show and demonstrate their love for God.

God knows I love little kids so He gave us two at this point in time. My only regret is I cannot hold Ethan and Maia and play with them. This is it for now.
Give Ethan and Maia kisses for me.

And then a few hours later, she got the rest. His new DynaVox computer was controlled by a laser dot on his forehead. He could communicate one painstaking letter at a time. Any accidental lingering on a letter or button could unintentionally delete entire thoughts and prematurely send emails.

Hi ang,

the First mail was v the page while I was transferring my notes from one program to another. I am hoping to master (it) e before it is too late. (emailing and moving things over)

    I Just hope you will understand what I wrote.

    Love dad

    this machinery disorganized. The cursor was jumping all over. this machine is malfunctioning again i hope they will fix this time dad

# 77

*Tuesday, May 26, 2009*

## ONE MORE

*Now I want you to know, brothers and sisters, that what has happened to me has actually served to advance the gospel.*

—Philippians 1:12

"**G**reat story!" Jane called out as she poked her head out of the bathroom where she'd been cleaning. While telling a visiting friend the story of how Jesse had shared the gospel with his palliative care nurse, Carol, Kathy hadn't realized that she had an audience.

"Have you been listening?" Kathy asked, surprised.

Jane was further proof of God's care in the midst of the most trying season of the family's lives. Jesse's discovery group of Christian businessmen, the same group where he had met Paul, had rallied around so many of their needs—renovating their main floor bathroom to add a wheelchair-accessible shower, providing much-needed respite in the form of a night shift homecare worker a few times a week, and now they'd hired Jane to help Kathy with the housework she couldn't seem to get to in the midst of Jesse's high level of care.

Jane's eyes filled with tears as she whispered her answer, "I've been listening since the first day I came."

Kathy was amazed at the activity of God, even in this season when they were confined to their home. It was as if God Himself had personally ushered people through their door who had an open heart.

Jane's heart, much like Jesse's caregivers—Sonia, Nella, and Abbi—was ready to respond to God. She gladly prayed and confessed that she believed Jesus had come down to the earth to die on the cross for her sins, and then rise again to give her eternal life.

Despite the heaviness she felt, Kathy smiled at the miracles of salvation taking place around them.

Yes, from her perspective it would've brought God glory if He had miraculously healed Jesse of ALS. But God was still healing people of their sin, despite the fact that Jesse couldn't speak at all. He couldn't chaplain or pastor in the same capacity as before, yet God was still using him.

Jesse fatigued easily, and it seemed like with each passing day eating and swallowing became increasingly difficult. He wasn't able to have long conversations, even with the letterboard, as his energy ran out long before his desire to communicate. He was more and more unstable on his feet, even with much assistance when transferring from one location to another.

But somehow he still found a way to share Jesus, the thing he hadn't stopped doing since that February day in 1986. Not even this ugly disease could stop him from telling people about the One who had so profoundly changed his life. Jesus had saved Jesse, and because of that, even in the face of death, there was still hope and the promise of life. And occasionally, there was still a twinkle in his eye.

# 78

# STAND

*Be devoted to one another in love. Honor one another above yourselves.*

—Romans 12:10

Christina glanced up at her parents to acknowledge their presence. She had known they were planning to come to her graduation, but she'd had her doubts. given her dad's current state As she paraded down the aisle with the rest of her class, she saw her family up at the top level of the gymnasium. She had an entire cheering squad—her parents, sisters, aunt and uncle, grandparents, and husband.

When the master of ceremonies asked friends and family to stand in honour of the graduates, Christina felt a pang of sadness, yet she was filled with appreciation and gratitude. Her dad could barely stay awake while sitting; there was no way he would be able to stand.

But when she glanced up, he was standing.

She blinked, confused, feeling shocked. Tears overwhelmed her. Even from all the way down on the gym floor, she could see her dad's face. He looked so proud of her.

She didn't know that only moments earlier he had managed to squeeze out the word "Up," prompting Kathy to immediately help him to his feet to honour his daughter. Kathy held his failing body on one side and his brother Lope on the other.

Christina couldn't remember the last time she had seen him stand, but she was sure she would never forget this one for as long as she lived.

Tears flooded her eyes and blurred her vision for the remainder of the ceremony.

To know her dad was proud of her was everything—and to know that he would spend every last bit of energy he could muster, even in his dying days, to show up and stand up for her meant more than she could put into words.

He was tired, weary and ready to go home to heaven and be healed in the presence of Jesus. But today he was here, holding on, and still standing.

# 79

## CHANGING TIMES

*In all this you greatly rejoice, though now for a little while you may have had to suffer grief in all kinds of trials. These have come so that the proven genuineness of your faith—of greater worth than gold, which perishes even though refined by fire—may result in praise, glory and honor when Jesus Christ is revealed.*

—1 Peter 1:6–7

S omething had changed. Jesse could feel it in his body, and he had a sneaking suspicion that he was in his final days.

Now more than ever, Jesse wanted to pray a blessing over each of his daughters. Using the letterboard and leg motions, he requested that all his girls gather round.

He often remembered the first words that had travelled through his mind when the neurologist initially told him about the three letters that would forever change his life: "I'm going to see my Lord sooner than I thought." It was a strange feeling to know he was so close to that day.

It had been three and a half months since the doctor had given him three to six months to live. Now it was just a waiting game. How much longer? Only God knew.

He thought of heaven often now and wondered what it would be like to finally see Jesus face to face, to hear Him audibly call his name. That moment would make everything worth it—all the suffering, all the trying times, and all the times when life just wasn't working.

His affliction didn't feel light and momentary, but the Bible said that it was exactly that compared to the surpassing glory that would be revealed.

He was so tired, his body literally wasting away, and he could hardly wait for his new body. No more pain. No more suffering.

Healing and wholeness were close. Jesse could sense it.

It seemed almost impossible to believe that a year earlier he had been walking and talking in the Philippines, reliving stories as he passed them on to his family. The days had been long, but the year short.

Now the finish line was in sight. He was waiting to die, which also meant he was waiting to live.

What would it be like to die? What would it be like to see everything he had trusted in faith since that February day in 1986?

With his girls gathered around him, Jesse took his time, not wanting to rush these moments. They would never hear or know the words being uttered from his heart, but he knew they would live out what he was asking God for. How much of his life had he spent hurrying from one place to the next? Now all he wanted to do was slow down time.

Each of his girls meant something different to him. He could remember snuggling and kissing them as babies and watching their personalities develop as they grew up. Each was uniquely gifted, and each had blessed him. His girls were everything to him.

Jesse had always been a man of prayer, but this past year he had had more time than ever to pray. On this day he focused all his energy on asking God for His will in their lives.

He continually spelled out to them on the letterboard: "L–I–V–E–F–O–R– J–E–S–U–S–Y–O–U–W–I–L–L–H–A–V–E–N–O–R–E–G–R–E–T–S."

It was all he wanted—for his girls to live for Jesus. He prayed often that seeing him suffer wouldn't discourage their faith in Jesus.

Jesse had communicated earlier with Kathy that he wanted his daughters to pray for a peaceful transition for him from this life to the next. He'd endured so many choking episodes and had no desire to experience a traumatizing exit from this life for him or his family.

His girls prayed with all their hearts that the transition would be peaceful.

Next, Christina and Angela sang a song Christina had been writing for the funeral. Jesse already had no words, but hearing this expression of his daughter's heart left him choking on emotion:

## Changing Times

When I was young, people would ask, "What do you want to be?"
How could I choose, with so many paths; they all appealed to me.
But I made up my mind; it soon became clear this is what I want to be.

I want to be wise, but not too proud to show my weakness.
I want to be strong, but not ashamed to ever cry.
I want to have faith that never wavers in the storm.
I want to be light in this dark world, and love with all I am.
Dad, I want to be just like you.

I could've learned to use my hands, to fix a car or truck,
Or gone to school to teach and preach or coached teams and tested my
luck,
But seeing your professions, now here is my confession: this is what I
want to be.

I want to be wise, but not too proud to show my weakness.
I want to be strong, but not ashamed to ever cry.
I want to have faith that never wavers in the storm.
I want to be light in this dark world, and love with all I am.
Dad, I want to be just like you.

You were always my hero; when I was sad, you knew what to say.
You could fix anything that came your way.
Now that I'm all grown up, I still take comfort in your love.
You lived and showed me that this life's more than the world can offer
me.

So I want to be wise, but not too proud to show my weakness.
I want to be strong, but not ashamed to ever cry.
I want to have faith that never wavers in the storm.
I want to be light in this dark world, and love with all I am.
Dad, I want to be just like you.

His girls were so much better with words than he was.

Then Emily and I sang a song that turned our tears into laughter. This truly was the best aspect of life, surrounded by his family and carried by faith.

Emily sat down and I remained standing.

"I started writing this poem last December," I began, my misty eyes meeting his. "I figured it was time to finish it. I hope you like it. It's called 'You're Still My Dad.'"

You're still my dad
Though your speech has gotten slow
You still have so much wisdom
That I need to help me grow

You're still my dad
Though your feet don't move as fast
Your faithful steps have guided many
In the present and the past

You're still my dad
Though you no longer talk a lot
I can guess what you are thinking
When the twinkle in your eye lights up

You're still my dad
You are not the burden that you feel
I have prayed that in your heart
You would truly know that's real

You will always be my dad
Even when you are no longer here
The impact you will have
Will forever be so near

You will always be my dad
When many years have come to pass
I only hope to be the faithful servant
That you were until your last

Jesse's girls—his girls, his greatest gifts—were still giving him priceless gifts money could not buy in these final days.

# 80

# PREACH ALWAYS, WORDS OPTIONAL

*Now this is eternal life: that they know you, the only true God, and Jesus Christ, whom you have sent.*

—John 17:3

*W*hy am I still here Lord?

It had been over a week since Jesse first felt like something had shifted within his body. He just knew it was the beginning of the end. He'd never felt so weak and tired, and he wanted God to take him home. He wished he had more time with his family, but now that he was this close to the end it felt like sooner would be better than later.

He closed his eyes, wishing he could shift his weight around to get comfortable. Almost every muscle hung limp. His body was covered in sores from sitting in the same position, since he split his time between the small-wheeled chair and the recliner. He could never get comfortable on the hospital bed.

The healthcare workers didn't know why he had gotten sick. Vomiting was traumatizing, considering his lack of muscle strength, and while sick he had continuously and silently cried out to God, asking Him to please just take him.

He closed his eyes and sighed. *How much longer, Lord?*

He could faintly hear the sound of voices. Kathy was greeting Carol, the palliative nurse, at the door. She had visited him intermittently in the last few months.

He willed himself to wake up, even though all he wanted to do was fall asleep and wake up in the presence of Jesus.

But he was still here, so it wasn't his time yet.

"Hi Jesse!" Carol greeted him.

He gave her a head nod.

As Carol began her routine check of his vital signs, Jesse felt the familiar prompting of the Holy Spirit, something he often felt when God wanted Him to share the good news about Jesus.

*"Tell her about Me again."*

Jesse was always more interested in talking about salvation than his symptoms. He didn't have much energy, so he chose his words wisely: "T–E–L–L–M–E–A–B–O–U–T–Y–O–U–R–F–A–I–T–H," he spelled.

"I've gone to church my whole life," Carol answered. "But I have my doubts about God. Even still, I believe in Him."

Jesse's reply on the letterboard was straightforward: there was no time to waste.

"E–V–E–N–T–H–E–D–E–M–O–N–S–B–E–L–I–E–V–E," he spelled, quoting Scripture.

She seemed only slightly taken aback by his boldness. "What must I do to assure my salvation?"

Kathy must've heard all the spelling from the basement where she was folding laundry because she suddenly appeared, able to fill the words he didn't have the strength to spell.

With Kathy's help, he told Carol that Jesus was knocking at the door of her heart and all she had to do was open it and accept Him in. Together, they led Carol in a simple prayer to acknowledge her need for Jesus to forgive and save her, and to invite Him to take up residence in her heart.

As she was leaving that day, Carol said to Kathy, "Jesse is the talk of the healthcare circle. There's something so different and peaceful about him."

Jesse smiled. Jesus was the difference. Jesus was his peace. Giving Jesus away always had a way of pouring life back into him.

Despite Jesse's weakening pulse, shallower breathing, and ongoing sleepiness, he suddenly felt very full of life. Something about spreading the good news gave him energy. God was still faithful and His power was still made perfect in weakness. Jesse was living proof.

# 81

*Monday, August 3, 2009*

# ONLY THE TRUTH

*So I will always remind you of these things, even though you know them and are firmly established in the truth you now have.*

—2 Peter 1:12

"W-H-A-T-A-R-E-Y-O-U-W-R-I-T-I-N-G-O-N-T-H-I-S-B-L-O-G?" Jesse spelled on the letterboard.

Many of his visitors had mentioned the blog to him, and it hadn't occurred to me that he didn't know what a blog was. Around the time of his diagnosis, he had been excited to receive his first few text messages. Besides using the DynaVox and listening to the Bible on the iPod, the latest technology wasn't part of his life.

Of course he didn't know what a blog was.

I smiled. "I'm just keeping people up to date on you and what God is doing. And whatever else comes to mind at the time."

"N-O-O-N-L-Y-W-R-I-T-E-T-H-E-T-R-U-T-H," he spelled as he shook his head. "O-N-L-Y-T-H-E-T-R-U-T-H-C-A-N-C-H-A-N-G-E-P-E-O-P-L-E."

"Okay, Dad," I told him. "I'll only write the truth."

# 82

# THE ENERGIZER BUNNY

*I am torn between the two: I desire to depart and be with Christ, which is better by far.*

—Philippians 2:23

"Papa, do you love me?" Ethan asked him.

Jesse wanted nothing more than to cuddle his three-year-old grandson and play with him on the floor. Instead he raised his right leg, the last of his voluntary muscles that would ever so slightly cooperate with what his mind willed it to do.

"He said yes!" Ethan shrieked excitedly.

Spelling on the letterboard had become too taxing. Now his family had to ask questions and Jesse would simply raise his right knee for yes, and his left knee for no. It was all he could manage.

One-year-old Maia wandered up to him and began softly rubbing his hands, imitating the hand massages she had seen many other family members offering.

"Of–oo!" she said. (Love you!)

He was tired again. It seemed like he could only stay awake for a few minutes at a time before being overcome with fatigue. Kathy had stopped the flow of visitor traffic into their home, wanting to reserve what little energy he had for his family.

As he drifted back to sleep, he heard Maia say, "Sshh… Papa." She knew he needed quiet in order to rest. But he would take the sounds of the grandkids and his daughters over the silence any day of the week.

The feeling of not being able to breathe was distressing, and the healthcare workers had given him a new drug to help him sleep and relax.

He prayed it wouldn't be too much longer. He was so ready to be healed.

"Is that what you're thinking, Dad?" Ang asked as we all watched an old movie on TV titled *Heaven Can Wait*. "That heaven can still wait?"

He shook his head.

"You're probably thinking heaven can come anytime now?" I offered.

He nodded.

Jesse was clinging to the Apostle Paul's words which he knew so well:

*For to me, to live is Christ and to die is gain. If I am to go on living in the body, this will mean fruitful labor for me. Yet what shall I choose? I do not know! I am torn between the two: I desire to depart and be with Christ, which is better by far; but it is more necessary for you that I remain in the body. Convinced of this, I know that I will remain, and I will continue with all of you for your progress and joy in the faith, so that through my being with you again your boasting in Christ Jesus will abound on account of me.*

—Philippians 1:21–26

To depart and be with Christ would be far better. It felt necessary to remain for his family's sake, but Jesse knew they would be taken care of. His faith gave him full assurance.

He just had to hold on to faith and wait.

# 83

*Friday, August 7, 2009*

# TRANSFORMATION

*Therefore, if anyone is in Christ, the new creation has come: The old has gone, the new is here!*

—2 Corinthians 5:17

My eyes skimmed the blog's comment section. The closer we seemed to get to the end, the more I had been updating it—and the more people had been interacting. A longer chunk of words caught my eye:

Transformation. Two Greek words combined to create this word, metamorphosis, and it describes the transformation process of a larva becoming a caterpillar and ending into a beautiful butterfly.

I knew Jesse before he surrendered his life to Christ in Richmond, B.C. in the mid-1980s. Kathy prayed consistently, expectantly, patiently for his conversion for four years before he finally did. And what a joy it was to see the transformation the Spirit of God brought to him. From one who ignored Jesus into a man who fell in love with Him. Jesse just could not stop talking about Jesus.

Before his conversion, he and Kathy once attended the Bible study I led in Richmond, and he slept through it.

After his conversion, he immediately shared his faith, getting to work early Friday morning for Bible study with whoever wanted to come and listen. No, it was not merely that Christ was in his life; no, it was not that Christ was part of his life; but yes, Christ was his life!

Knowing Jesse, he would now probably want us to talk more about his Christ than about him. The Christ that Jesse loved and served is One whose arms are open to embrace the repentant sinner, with the words "Welcome home, dear one. I've been waiting for you. What took you so long?" These same loving arms will welcome Jesse with the commendation: "Well done, good and faithful servant." Having experienced it firsthand, Jesse always sought to connect people with the transforming power of Jesus Christ.

This is Jesse's challenge to me. What about you?


I laughed and cried. It was almost word for word what my dad had instructed for his funeral: "Don't talk about me; talk about Jesus."

I often forgot that my dad had lived an entire life without Jesus before me. I had been almost four months old when he got saved, so my only memories of him were as a follower of Christ, eager to share the transforming power of Jesus Christ with anyone who would listen.

Hope filled my heart once again. God had done so much in his life. Surely, He wouldn't stop now.

# 84

*August 17, 2009*

# SAY GOODBYE

*I have fought the good fight, I have finished the race, I have kept the faith.*
—2 Timothy 4:7

*Who's at the door?* Kathy wondered as the bell echoed through the quiet house. She wasn't expecting anyone on this Monday morning. The last nurse who'd visited on Saturday had said that Jesse was stable, so all the girls had gone their separate ways for a few days—Emily to NBC Camp, myself back to Lethbridge, and Christina and Angela back to Christina's house.

Kathy opened the front door to see a long-haired woman dressed in scrubs.

"I'm here to cover today," the woman said.

Kathy frowned in confusion. "We weren't expecting anyone."

"Ohh? Let me call my supervisor and double-check. Do you mind if I step inside?"

Kathy opened the door all the way and gestured for her to come in. They both stood there, waiting for confirmation, but there was no answer from the supervisor.

"Well, since I'm here, can I meet Jesse?" she asked.

There was no harm in it. Plus, Jesse had been too tired to move from the bathroom back to the chair. Kathy gestured towards the bathroom and introduced her to Jesse before heading to the next room to prepare the suction equipment for their morning routine.

Kathy's ears and heart soon perked up at the beautiful sound coming from the bathroom. The nurse was speaking Scripture and singing over Jesse. This mystery nurse must know God.

The nurse helped move Jesse back to the chair to begin the daily routine of suctioning out his mouth. Since he was no longer able to swallow, his mouth and throat needed to be cleared out regularly to reduce the risk of choking.

But the suction wasn't working and Kathy needed a longer hose. The team had told her to call if the six-inch one stopped working sufficiently.

"I'm going to call the respiratory team," Kathy told the nurse, who was sitting by Jesse's side. "I need a longer hose."

Kathy's dialling was quickly interrupted by the nurse, who sat next to Jesse, studying his face.

"Um, I work in palliative care and I sit with a lot of people who are at the end," the nurse said. "Jesse doesn't need a longer suction. He's dying."

Kathy stared at the new nurse. She must be mistaken. "No, he couldn't be. The nurse on Saturday said he was stable. He can't be dying now. The girls are all gone. We thought we had more time."

"You don't have much time," the nurse said softly.

Kathy glanced down at Jesse. How had she not seen it? Of course he was dying. His colour was grey. His breathing was shallow. His pulse was weakening. He could hardly keep his eyes open.

She grabbed the phone, and with trembling fingers began to dial.

———————

I stared at my empty fridge. It had been so long since I'd spent any length of time at my own house. 1:19 p.m. I should probably eat something.

My thoughts were interrupted by the phone ringing.

"Hello?"

"Say goodbye," my mom cried. "This is it. He's dying right now. Say goodbye, quick. I need to call your sisters!"

My mind raced. Nothing could've prepared me for this moment.

"Dad, I love you," I choked. "You were the best dad. Goodbye."

No words seemed like enough. But just like that, the moment was gone.

I sat there, stunned. It was happening.

Despite having known this moment was coming for the last fifteen months and seven days, I felt so unprepared. I wasn't ready. I never would be.

I picked up the phone to call Mike. Before I knew it, we were back on the road to say our last goodbye.

———

Angela couldn't shake the unsettling feeling that overcame her that day. She had stopped in at her parents' house earlier that morning for a quick visit with Ethan and Maia. Her dad had looked so close to death, like a man who was barely hanging on.

She had wanted nothing more than to stay and hold on with him, but he'd wanted to rest as he could barely keep his eyes open.

Instead, she decided to run a few errands for her mom. Angela had just gotten Ethan a burger and fries when her phone rang.

She drew a quick breath. It was her mom. Was this it?

"We don't have much time," her mom cried. "Tell Dad whatever you want to tell him."

"You were the best dad ever," Angela said softly into the phone, a burger in one hand and tears pouring from her eyes. "I love you so much."

She raced back to drop the kids off at Frankie's and Christina's, where her husband Jordan was waiting, before hurrying in a teary blur back to her parents' house.

———

Christina glanced at her cell phone and sucked in a sharp breath. Was this the phone call? The last few weeks had been full of so many this-could-be-it moments.

"Hello?"

She could tell from her mom's voice that this was it. "Say goodbye," her mom cried.

Christina was already in her car. Maybe she could still make it back to say goodbye in person. She was only ten minutes away from her parents' house.

"Dad, I love you," she said. "Thanks for being a great dad. Goodbye."

Her heart thudded and the tears streamed as she drove up Sarcee Trail. This was the end.

After everything they had been through, this was it—the end of their time together on earth. Kathy held Jesse's hand as each breath became slower than the time before. He looked like death—his skin tinged with grey, his head and arms hanging heavily in front of him just as they had for months.

All of a sudden, Jesse lifted his head. His eyes locked on the upper corner of their family room. His tired eyes were bright and filled with life.

He turned his head to look at his wife, who had loved him so faithfully and he smiled at her. The biggest smile Kathy had seen erupted on his face.

Jesse looked back to the corner of the room.

And just like that, he was gone.

Jesse was finally healed of ALS. He was whole. He was with his saviour Jesus—and for the first time, they were meeting face to face.

# 85

*August 17, 2009*

# TIME TO GO

*There is a time for everything, and a season for every activity under the heavens…*
—Ecclesiastes 3:1

Emily's heart sank deep as she saw her brothers-in-law, Frankie and Jordan, enter the gymnasium with the camp director. Her eyes filled with instant tears.

Her dad had insisted she still go to the weeklong basketball camp an hour away from home. The past three weeks had been full of moments that felt like they could be his last. He hadn't wanted the family to be waiting around.

"You have to keep living your lives," he'd been telling the girls since the diagnosis.

Her dad had wanted her to go have fun.

If anything happened while she was away, they wouldn't call. Someone would simply come pick her up. That was the plan.

She had been at camp less than a day—and now, Frankie and Jordan were here.

It could only mean one thing.

Her dad was gone.

It was time to go.

Nine years later, on August 5, 2018, Emily waited in the wings, her floor-length veil cascading over the long, loose waves of hair that framed her beaming face.

An excited entourage of ringbearers and flower girls stood nearby. The boys shifted in their loafers, trying to balance the "Here Comes Your Bride" sign in their small hands, their bowties and combovers still intact. The girls clutched their baskets of petals, ready to adorn the aisle and unable to hide their smiles or contain their giggles.

Emily's sisters attempted to keep them still and quiet with one hand while balancing their bridesmaid bouquets in their other. There were eight of them under the age of eight: Jessalyn and Josh (Christina and Frankie's children), Leila, Bella, and Arianna (Angela and Jordan's three youngest daughters), and Sophie, Jonah, and Elijah (mine and Mike's children).

Ethan stood with the other usher, standing on either side of the double doors, waiting for the signal. Maia stood among the entourage, needing no threats or bribes to cooperate in her role as junior bridesmaid.

For Emily, the years since her dad had passed away had been full of much wrestling, wondering, and waiting. Would God take care of her as He had promised? Would she really be okay as her dad had said she would? Could she trust God the way her dad had?

Almost a year ago to the day, Emily had stood in nearly the same spot, in the same gym, at the same basketball camp she had attended on the day Jordan and Frankie had walked through the door. Only this time the August day hadn't signalled an end, but a beginning: it was the first time she laid eyes on Mike Greeno. Immediately she'd had a sneaking suspicion it might be the start of something new—her very own redemption story.

This wedding day was an opportunity to celebrate God's faithfulness. He had beautifully woven her and Mike's stories together. God would always take care of her. He would see to it that she was okay. And He most certainly could be trusted.

The man waiting for her at the end of the aisle was proof of that.

Emily linked arms with her mom, whose strength, resilience, and beauty was perfectly summarized by her simple yet elegant, floor-length dark grey gown.

It was time to go.

# 86

*August 24, 2009*

## SEE YOU SOON

*For we walk by faith, not by sight.*

—2 Corinthians 5:7

I stood behind the black curtain next to my dad's casket. Of all the times I had said goodbye in the last fifteen months, this would be the last one. This was really it, at least for now. I only had a few more moments before they would close the casket and wheel his old body into his celebration of life.

For the rest of my time on earth, I would only see his face in pictures and maybe in dreams. I would only hear his voice in my own memory.

It was the last time I would stare at his face, even though it didn't look like him. All the makeup in the world couldn't make death look like life.

It was the last time I would hold his once callused and strong hands. It was the last time I would feel the comfort of being in his physical presence.

It wasn't supposed to be this way.

We were not created for goodbyes like this, but here we were. The tension between this earthly life and the promises of eternal life with God through Jesus felt especially thick at this moment. The pain, sorrow, suffering, and disappointment were heavy, and so was the hope of a day with no more tears, pain, suffering, or fear.

This is the place of faith—the in-between.

I wanted to freeze time and linger here a little longer. I wanted to ask my dad more questions. I wanted him to walk Emily down the aisle. I wanted him to play with his future grandchildren and teach my sons how to fix cars and fear the Lord. I wanted him to grow old with my mom.

But there wasn't time. The clock had run out.

I didn't want to say goodbye. I didn't want this to be the end.

Thankfully it wasn't. I would see him again in heaven thanks to faith in Jesus, just not for a little while.

I whispered my last words and took my place in the long processional line as they closed the casket and wheeled him into place.

It was my turn to walk by faith.

*Spring 2005*

# EPILOGUE

*If you declare with your mouth, "Jesus is Lord," and believe in your heart that God raised him from the dead, you will be saved.*

—Romans 10:9

I sat in the front row listening intently as my dad said with sincerity, conviction, and confidence, "Following God has been the greatest adventure of my life." As his words drifted into my ears and settled in my heart, I thought to myself, *I want that same kind of adventure.*

The very word adventure intrigued me, perhaps because my life had felt fairly ordinary, with no significant life-altering events, positive or negative. The possibility of some excitement, remarkability, and unpredictability felt welcome.

Perhaps this adventure, this life of faith, is intriguing to you too. God has one for you and it begins when you say yes to Jesus. How does one begin?

One of my daughter's favourite camp activities is the zipline. Last fall, I got up on the platform thinking, *How hard can this be? If my daughter can do it, so can I.*

I knew the harness would hold me. I knew the rope was secure.

So I stood on the platform, staring down at the ground, which looked a million miles away, and knew that it wasn't enough to know the harness and rope would hold; I needed to transfer my weight. It wouldn't happen until the moment I placed my faith in the harness, the moment I took my weight off my own two feet and let the rope take me.

The first time you say yes to placing your faith in Jesus is a lot like that. In that moment, you take the weight of your salvation off yourself and entrust your life to Jesus. This isn't about the kind of church you go to; this is about whether your faith and salvation rest on Jesus Christ alone. He came to this earth to live a perfect life, die on the cross, and be resurrected on the third day so you and I could be forgiven and have eternal life.

The adventure of the zipline was thrilling but short-lived. The adventure of living with Jesus will last much longer. It starts now and continues on for eternity.

If you want to say yes to Jesus today, it would be my great pleasure to lead you in this prayer:

Lord Jesus, I know I am a sinner. I need a Saviour. I believe You lived the perfect life I couldn't, and died the death so I wouldn't, and rose from the grave victorious. I put my life in Your hands and ask You to come into my life and be my Lord and Saviour. I receive your forgiveness and this gift of salvation by faith. I receive Your Holy Spirit, who will empower me to live the life You have invited me to. In Jesus's name, amen.

If you have given your life to Jesus, you have a brand-new identity. You now belong to God. You are seen, known, chosen, and loved. You have a new name, a new eternal home, and a new purpose. The Bible says that you have been transferred from the domain of darkness into the kingdom of light. This is who you are now.

Find yourself a Bible and take those words in like food and water. The Bible is your playbook for life. It will tell you all about who God is, who you are, and the life you've been invited to live.

Find a family of God, also known as a church, that will help you grow in your faith and know what your next yes is with Jesus.

God writes the best stories and unfolds them as you continually say yes to Him. Don't settle for just one yes. There's always a next one. Your very own anything-but-ordinary life of bold faith, steadfast love, and unwavering hope awaits.

Keep saying yes.

"Live for Jesus. You'll have no regrets."

—Jesse Morales

# ACKNOWLEDGEMENTS

They say it takes a village to raise a child; it also takes an army to birth a book. I'm grateful for each and every person who made this book possible.

To Connie Taillon, my dear friend and mentor, I can still hear Gerry's words to me at the viewing service: "Connie likes your writing. And she's picky!" Thank you for encouraging me as I discovered my writing voice in my earliest blogging days. You've answered my questions, shared your wisdom, poured hot tea, and caught my tears too many times to count. The book and I both needed you desperately. Thank you for breaking your rules, sharing honest feedback, and asking the hard questions. It is a true joy to be your little buddy.

To Megan McDougall, before I ever had an inkling about blogs or book writing, you were the very first one, all those years ago at RDC, to plant the seed that one day I should write a book.

To those who graciously endured the earliest version of the book. Jennie Thompson and Carolyn Reinholz, thank you for the hours you spent editing. Karen Willoughby, thank you for your straight shooting and asking the hard questions that brought much-needed clarity. John Hasegawa, Mike Bischke, and Dustin Williams, thanks for testing the water and being my first male audience.

To Bonnie Pue, thank you for calling to tell me about the Braun Book Awards contest you'd caught wind of and that I should enter it. And thank you for calling me again to tell me the deadline had been extended and there was indeed more time and still hope!

To Ariana Forsman, Marina Reis, and the team at Word Alive Press, thank you for choosing *Anything But Ordinary*. Thank you for being committed to the very best version of this story and making it possible for this message to get into more hands and hearts. Evan Braun, thank you for showing me which darlings to murder and which ones to keep. Your editing expertise was an answer to prayer. Thank you for your honesty, patience, and flexibility, especially in the fourth quarter.

To all the interviewees without whom I could not have written this book, thank you for your friendship with my dad. Thank you for getting behind this book and generously sharing the pieces of his story that each of you held: Herb Reesor, Ron Hogue, Richard Navarro, Richard Cheng, John Judd, Rey David, Jack Jakovac, Petar Rakic, Fred Olarte, Bob Shelton, Auntie Barb, Dan Lodovica, Sig Shuster, Kevin Trick, Brian Harrell, Jim Messner, Greg Villabroza, Jack Van Deventer, Bruce Mitchell, Richard Osiowy, Gerry Kraft, Omar Rodriguez, Kurt Nissen, Bong Castillo, Paul Brandt, Hamish Buntain, Barb Messner and Nathan Vedoya.

To all the Morales siblings—Bert, Cleo, Rose, Remie, Beth, and Lope—thank you for your sharp memories, holding nothing back, your unique perspectives, and blessing me to tell some of the untold story. "Tup Guy" is forever grateful.

To the Pinkie Swear Running Club, thank you for cheering me on when no one else was watching, your always timely encouragement, praying through the birth pains, and giving me grace and space to sow in tears from the grief that writing this stirred up when we first met face to face.

To my Wild Women, it's a privilege to live our stories together. Thank you for celebrating the wins and praying for me through every obstacle. Thank you for saving me a seat.

To the Prayer Warriors, thank you for reading the email updates with continual requests. Thank you for praying for me through every single assignment the Lord gives to me, including this book. Heaven only knows the mountains that have moved because of your faithful prayers in and out of season.

## Acknowledgements

To Dorothy and Richard, thank you for your endless love for us and the kids, and your willingness to step in and grandparent whenever needed. Thank you for all the extra time you spent. You are the best and most generous in-laws a girl could ask for.

To my sisters—Angela Rossworm, Christina O'Brien, and Emily Greeno—thank you for your willingness to relive pain and allowing me to share your vulnerable moments. Thank you for reading your parts and checking them for authenticity.

To my Mama, Kathy Morales, without you and your faith not only would there be no book, there would be no story. The legacy started with you. We are all different because you had faith in the living room. Thank you for living this story so beautifully. You are the true pioneer of faith that works when life doesn't. Thank you for answering a million questions and picking up the phone when I had just one more. Thank you for allowing me to write anything and everything that would bring God glory. The ways you invested in me and this book are too many to count. My house is cleaner for it! I still want to be like you when I grow up.

To Mike, how do you love me, let me count the ways… Thank you for blessing me to lock myself in my office and write, or schedule another phone interview during the craziest season of pandemic homeschooling and parental leave. Thank you for the countless times you cleaned up the kitchen, put the kids to bed, or took on whatever you could from my load in addition to yours so I could write and rewrite. Thank you for always serving and protecting us. Sophie, Jonah, Eli, and Evie, I love you all so much. Thanks for all the extra ways you helped your mama out over the past couple of years.

Finally, to God my Father, thank You for keeping every one of Your promises. You have been so faithful. Our family would be in a ditch somewhere if not for Your great mercy. Thank You, Jesus, for not wasting the pain.

# ABOUT THE AUTHOR

Stephanie Morales-Beaulieu is a lover of God's Word and shares that passion online, from the stage, in her living room, and anywhere else God opens the door.

Through losing her dad and learning how to hold onto God's promises came a passion to make the transforming power of the Word accessible to those new to it, overwhelmed by it, or longing to be changed by it.

She is the creator of Bite-Size Bible Study® and has authored *A Roadmap to Trials (Journey through James)*, *Walk in Love (Ephesians)*, and most recently *The Flourishing Life (The Parable of the Sower)*. She is a born communicator with contagious love and enthusiasm for Jesus.

As a wife to Mike and mom of four littles, she shares from her wealth of relatable stories that will inspire you to see everyday life through the lens of truth. She is authentic, funny, and you will wish she lived next door.

To learn more about Stephanie, visit https://www.everydaytruth.ca/